ARIEL LIKE A HARPY

Shelley, Mary and *Frankenstein*

by

CHRISTOPHER SMALL

LONDON
VICTOR GOLLANCZ LTD.
1972

© CHRISTOPHER SMALL 1972

ISBN 0 575 01393 1

MADE AND PRINTED IN GREAT BRITAIN BY
THE GARDEN CITY PRESS LIMITED
LETCHWORTH, HERTFORDSHIRE
SG6 1JS

To K.M.A.

Thought can with difficulty visit the intricate and winding chambers which it inhabits. It is like a river whose rapid and perpetual stream flows outwards—like one in dread who speeds through the recesses of some haunted pile and dares not look behind.

P. B. Shelley: *Speculations on Metaphysics*, 1812-15

... above all, let me fearlessly descend into the remotest caverns of my mind, carry the torch of self-knowledge into its deepest recesses...

Mary Shelley: *Journal*, entry for 25 February, 1822

Nothing is more strange to man than his own image.

Karel Capek: *R.U.R.*, translated by P. Selver, 1923

ACKNOWLEDGEMENTS

This is not a work of scholarship, but I have had the help of various scholars, which I gratefully acknowledge. I owe special thanks to Professor M. K. Joseph, of Auckland University, whose admirable edition of *Frankenstein* (1969) was the stimulus to the whole inquiry, and who gave me further help in tracing the publishing history of the novel; to Professor I. F. Clarke, of Strathclyde University, to whose unrivalled knowledge of science fiction I am indebted for many suggestions; to Mr John Miller, of Glasgow University, who pointed out the Promethean references in the early works of Karl Marx; and to Mr Black, FLA, the City Librarian of Glasgow.

C.S.

CONTENTS

11

ONE

INTRODUCTORY : METAPHOR AND MYTH

MARY SHELLEY'S NOVEL *Frankenstein* occupies a singular place in literary history. It was written in an age which relished prodigies and extravagances of fiction, and should by the second decade of the nineteenth century have been pretty well inured to them; nevertheless it produced shock and bewilderment, and has continued to have these effects in some degree ever since. It was written in the fashion of the time, and using its materials, and can be set in retrospect into a general literary-historical scheme. Nevertheless, again, it remains impossible to categorise satisfactorily, except in terms of its own numerous descendants; the book itself is startlingly new to every fresh generation of readers—although in another way, shortly to be touched on, familiar to them before they begin to read.

When it first appeared its newness may fairly be called staggering. It was not a novelty of form or style, but almost wholly of content; there was something *monstrous* about its central idea that produced the typical reactions of people confronted with a *lusus naturae*, a breach in the accepted order of things. No pun is intended in so describing it, and yet it cannot be avoided; that the story of *Frankenstein*, about a monster, is itself monstrous, is entirely characteristic of its special position when new and of its subsequent role in popular fancy. It was, so to speak, a living pun from the beginning : that is to say, an abstract idea, expressible in verbal form, which, incarnate through a work of art, commented and continues to comment and reflect upon itself. It is as word made flesh in such a sense that it is the subject of this inquiry.

The authorship of *Frankenstein*—the age, personality, and circumstances of the writer—has a direct bearing on the question. But the story from the start has had an independent existence, in a sense stronger than may be applied to many books. That a work of such power and originality should have been produced by a girl of less than twenty is astonishing, and has been found so ever since Mary Shelley was identified as the author. But it did not, of course, have any part in the effect of its first, anonymous appearance, nor has it played much part in popular knowledge of the tale since. *Frankenstein* has been read—and heard of, in more or less garbled form, vastly beyond the number of actual readers—by multitudes who have little or no idea who Mary Shelley was: even during her lifetime and subsequent career as a writer her reputation, so far as the public was concerned, rested upon her first nameless debut, as "the author of *Frankenstein*".

The later novels so subscribed have long been forgotten by the generality of readers, but *Frankenstein* lives on, in popular imagination, detached from its origins, as part of the folk-lore of modern man. Part of the business of understanding folk-lore, however, consists in examining origins, which in this case, both personal and circumstantial, are well documented. The book therefore offers a rare opportunity to investigate the way that an individual work can merge into general consciousness: how a personal act of imagination may become myth. The following study is an attempt to relate the two, especially to trace backward the growth of a metaphor of almost universal application in relation to its occurrence and use—sudden, strange, and violent—in an individual mind.

Mythology is metaphorical thinking in which the metaphor assumes independent and continuing existence. Metaphor itself, the representation of something or things as something else, is usually thought of as a product of individual fancy or conceit, and the part only from many of which a larger whole, myth or work of art, is constructed. But a metaphor, stronger than simile—which sets like by like, leaving both unchanged—is itself a work of art, sharing the quality of using emotional rather than "objective" associations, and the ability, in showing things disguised as other things, to borrow from both sides to make a third, independent and new. Thus a winged man is not "like" anything in nature, but as metaphor conveys powerful and manifold meanings. It is consequently described as symbolic; yet if symbol be reckoned the sign for an idea or ideas, readily recognisable by those who have learnt the code, and unchanging, metaphor seems the better term. For metaphor can develop and change, and it is just in the process of such development that it becomes myth.

We do not then speak of it as invention because, rightly, we assume its relation not to individual fancy but to general facts of human thought; nevertheless, metaphors are invented. The absolute point of origin of a myth—the historical point at which, taking the same example, the idea of a man with wings could be called metaphor and not yet myth—is not more easy to determine, perhaps, than that of any other form of life : it is never possible to go "back to the beginning" in an individual mind because every such beginning has others behind it. But there are times—and those particularly, for obvious reasons, of turmoil and change in men's ways of thinking about the world —when the development of metaphor and its assumption of the qualities of myth are processes rapid enough to be observed; when a metaphorical expression of the simplest kind, such as "man makes himself" can be seen working in an individual mind, and taking shape, both in relation to its ancestry and in the special circumstances of these times, at once in the isolation of a single case and with mythological power.

At these times, one may say, a metaphor turns up new or significantly modified, a sport or mutation in this analogue of organic evolution. Like such it may die out quickly or it may permanently influence the development of myth, and through it the growth from individual genesis to generalised existence can be studied and, perhaps, partially understood. Such a natural history of metaphor is exemplified in *Frankenstein*.

The spread of the "Frankenstein myth" cannot be measured, as has been said, by any count of readers alone, even if they could be reckoned. To some extent indeed it might be argued that the myth has had most hold where the book hasn't been read. Nevertheless its publishing history is worth briefly rehearsing as showing how constantly the canonical form, so to speak, has been kept in being. *Frankenstein* was first published in 1818, with a further, unaltered edition in 1823; a revised edition, with Mary Shelley's name attached for the first time, and with her own introduction, came out in the series of "Standard Novels" in 1831, reprinted in 1839 and 1849. Six subsequent editions are listed in the British Museum Catalogue between 1851, the year of Mary Shelley's death, and the present, with reprints in most cases.[1] Other cheap editions have regularly appeared which do not figure in the Catalogue, and paperbacks have lately added to their number. At least seven further editions have been published in America between 1845 and 1949. Translations have appeared in many European and, recently, Oriental languages.

The story has also been disseminated by other means than print. Within five years of its original appearance as a book, *Frankenstein* was put on the London stage with great success, in melodrama versions by at least two different authors. In the summer and autumn of 1823 it was the talk of the town, with *Presumption, or, The Fate of Frankenstein,* by Richard Brinsley Peake (chiefly a writer of farce) at the English Opera House, reappearing as *Frankenstein, or, The Danger of Presumption,* at the Royalty, and in a quite different version as *Frankenstein, or, The Demon of Switzerland,* by another hack writer, H. M. Milner, at the Coburg. Mary Shelley, who had just returned to England, noted its "prodigious success as a drama"[2] and herself went to see the show, apparently the first of these versions; she remarked her own amusement at the way the horrific mechanics of her plot were rendered as stage effects, and also with satisfaction that it "appeared to excite a breathless eagerness in the audience". It was enough, as she said, to make her or her story "famous" in a way which the novel for all its immediate impact had not; and a further seal of fame was soon provided by the appearance of a parody. *Frank in Steam, or, The Modern Promise to Pay* was the title of a burlesque in London the following year, its precise nature unfortunately unrecorded; one would dearly like to know what comment on the story, and also presumably on the new steam age, lay behind this elaborate pun. Other *Frankenstein* burlesques occur in London stage records in 1849 (by W. and R. Brough) and towards the end of the century, in 1887, by "Richard Henry" (Richard Butler and H. Chance Newton).

Frankenstein's brief but effective career on the stage has been repeated, of course, on a greatly magnified scale, on the screen : it is above all as a film, and a film of a particular kind, the twentieth century equivalent of nineteenth century melodrama, that the story, in increasingly mangled form, has become known to masses of people. Its progress may be traced from 1931, when the original *Frankenstein* film was made in Hollywood, incorporating elements from the Yiddish tale of *The Golem*. In this first screen version the actor Boris Karloff played the Monster and fixed on the public mind not only an appearance that obscured all his other roles but a permanent image (which is in fact a copyright one) of a man-made being, a mixture of machinery and flesh and blood. That Boris Karloff's Monster bore little relation to the Monster of the text —certainly not in the letter, though it did honour the spirit in some important ways—can be seen as an instance of the way metaphor growing into myth may be lastingly modified through another work of art.

The great success of this film produced a whole series of sequels, including *Bride of Frankenstein* (1935), *Son of Frankenstein* (1939), *Ghost of Frankenstein* (1941), *Frankenstein Meets the Wolf Man* (1943), and *House of Frankenstein* (1945). The progressive transformation, not to say travesty of the original material may be judged merely from the titles. More recently British studios have taken over from Hollywood with a remake of the first screenplay as *The Curse of Frankenstein* (Hammer Studios, 1956) and a number of sequels, including *Frankenstein Created Woman* (1966), *Frankenstein Must Be Destroyed* (1968), and, the latest to date, *The Horror of Frankenstein* (1970), which returns in great part to the original story and, notably, to the period of the early nineteenth century. It is worth remembering that most of the *Frankenstein* films have presented the tale as contemporary, or in some cases projected into the future; one may speculate whether, now it has reached the stage of being a period piece, the story may not have come to the final phase of its film career, but it seems unlikely.

The tendency to gross extravagance in elaborating the fantasy may be seen in such recent American films, exploiting the name of Frankenstein and little else, as *I Was a Teenage Frankenstein* (1957), and *Frankenstein and the Space Monsters* (1965); in 1966 there was a Japanese film called *Frankenstein Conquers the World*, presumably carrying matters to a logical conclusion. Parody or burlesque, already noted as having over-taken the stage *Frankenstein*, has clearly been an element in many of these stereotyped "horror films"; in at least one instance, *Abbott and Costello Meet Frankenstein* (Hollywood, 1949), the entire thing became knockabout. And the Monster is apt to turn up in many comic situations, for example as a recognisable *Frankenstein* derivative in the American TV comedy series *The Munsters*.

A further point of resemblance between the early stage adaptation and *Frankenstein*'s current life on the screen has been the interchangeability of Frankenstein himself and the Monster. In the production seen by Mary Shelley the latter was played ("extremely well", she said) by T. Cooke, who is also recorded elsewhere as having played Frankenstein: the same transposition was made by Boris Karloff who, as the first and best-known of screen Monsters, transferred in a later production, *Frankenstein 1970* (1958) to Frankenstein himself. The popular confusion between the Monster and his maker, which has produced "creating a Frankenstein" as a proverbial expression, is notorious, and its significance will be examined later; it is convenient to note here, however, that simply as a matter of casting, both in the theatre and the cinema, they have been regarded as alternative roles.

Through such means as these "horror" films the myth has been simultaneously universalised and degraded. It is not easy to separate one part of the process from the other, since the qualities in the story itself which enable it to speak so power-fully to the modern condition of man are just those qualities which lend themselves to the crudest and most mechanical treatment. Just as the book could be described, with no facetious intention, as "monstrous", so the progress of the story on the screen shows it becoming par excellence a *mechanical myth*. The term is not a mere play on words but describes both subject and its form, as a species of manufactured sensation, verging on burlesque, which is at the same time a comment upon such manufacture.

It can be argued that such an element was always present in the story, being even on its first appearance one of the causes of its characteristic double effect, exciting simultaneous repulsion and attraction. The first readers of *Frankenstein* felt that they were being *got at* in a way both frightening and unfair, since the story was almost by definition "unnatural", but at the same time it was exactly the point of the story, showing the results of going beyond or parodying nature, that held their attention. It is worth having a look at some of the original reviews which followed first publication in 1818 and which, though varying widely in emphasis and tone, produced very much the same reasons for approval and disapproval.

The reception given by the *Edinburgh Magazine* was typical, both in recognition of the novel's affinities with the work of William Godwin—jumping to the conclusion that its author was not his daughter but his notorious son-in-law, Percy Bysshe Shelley—and in the evident mixture of shock and unwilling admiration :

Here is one of the productions of the modern school in its highest style of caricature and exaggeration. It is formed in the Godwinian manner and has all the faults, but likewise the beauties of that model. In dark and gloomy views of nature and man, bordering too closely on impiety, in the most outrageous improbability, in sacrificing everything to effect, it even goes beyond its great prototype; but in return it possesses a similar power of fascination, something of the same mastery in harsh and savage delineation of passion, relieved in like manner by the gentler features of domestic and simple feeling. There never was a wilder story imagined; yet, like most of the fictions of this age, it has an air of reality attached to it, by being connected with the favourite projects and passions of the times. The real events of the world have, in our day, too, been of so wondrous and gigantic a kind, the shiftings of the scenes in our stupendous drama have been so rapid and various, that Shakespeare himself, in his wildest flights, has been completely distanced by the eccentricities of actual existence.

It is one of those works, however, which, when we have read, we do not well see why it should have been written; for a *jeu d'esprit* it is somewhat too long, grave, and laborious, and some of our highest and most reverential feelings receive a shock from the conception on which it turns, so as to produce a painful and bewildered state of mind while we peruse it. . . .[3]

Another example may be given, from *Blackwood's,* in which a series of "Remarks on *Frankenstein*" (later identified as by Sir Walter Scott) expressed something like enthusiasm for the book but also bewilderment. The assumption again was that the author was Shelley:

This is a novel, or more properly a romantic fiction [the review began] of a nature so peculiar, that we ought to describe the species before attempting any account of the individual production. [There followed a long disquisition upon "the marvellous" in fiction, with the observation that its "more philosophical and refined use" was "to open new trains and channels of thought, by placing men in supposed situations of an extraordinary character". A summary of the plot was provided. with the concluding comment that in it] the author seems to us to disclose uncommon powers of poetic imagination. The feeling with which we perused the unexpected and fearful, yet, allowing the possibility of the event, very natural conclusion of Frankenstein's experiment, shook a little even our firm nerves. . . .[4]

The *Gentlemen's Magazine* more briefly (as well as providing an admirably succinct statement of the plot: "In the pride of Science, the Hero of the Tale presumes to take upon himself the structure of a human being; in which, though in some degree he is supposed to have succeeded, he forfeits every comfort of life, and finally even life itself") expressed in its gentlemanly way much the same double opinion:

This Tale is evidently the production of no ordinary Writer;

and, though we are shocked at the idea of the event on which the fiction is founded, many parts of it are strikingly good, and the description of scenery is excellent.[5]

The fullest and most revealing discussion was in the *Quarterly,* at the height of its tyrannical authority, which devoted a lengthy piece to *Frankenstein* most curiously exhibiting at once its inveterate enmity towards "the Godwinian school" and particularly Shelley himself—assumed, again, to be the author—and the fact that the reviewer had been painfully gripped by the book. The *Quarterly* was at that time in the full atrabilious flow of its feud with Shelley and all his works and associates; the immediately preceding issue had contained a gratuitous attack on him in the course of reviewing Leigh Hunt's poem *Foliage*[6]; it was ready with the same righteous indignation to deal with *Frankenstein* three months later.

The review was in many respects shrewd. The singling out, for instance, of Frankenstein's necrophilia—that "in examining the causes of *life,* he informs us, antithetically, that he had recourse to *death*"—and the observation of the Monster that "his education has given him so good a taste as to detest himself; he has also the good sense to detest his creator for imposing upon him such a horrible burden as conscious existence"—strike one now, despite the sneering tone, as highly perceptive, more perhaps than the writer realised.

The general tenor of the review, however, was outrage. It admitted "passages that appal the mind and make the flesh creep" and allowed that if it was like " 'a tale Told by an idiot, full of sound and fury, Signifying nothing' "—the *Quarterly,* like *Blackwood's* was reminded of *Macbeth*—"still there is something tremendous in the unmeaning hollowness of its sound, and the vague obscurity of its images". But this was as much as it would grant :

Our taste and our judgment alike revolt at this kind of writing, and the greater the ability with which it is executed the worse it is—it inculcates no lesson of conduct, manners, or morality; it cannot mend, and will not even amuse its readers, unless their taste have been deplorably vitiated, it fatigues the

feelings without interesting the understanding; it gratuitously
harasses the heart, and only adds to the store, already too
great, of painful sensation. The author has powers, both of
conception and language, which employed in a happier direction might perhaps (we speak dubiously) give him a name
among those whose writings amuse or amend their fellow-
creatures; but we take the liberty of assuring him, and hope
that he may be in a temper to listen to us, that the style which
he has adopted in the present publication merely tends to
defeat his own purpose, if he really had any other object in
view than that of leaving the reader, after a struggle between
laughter and loathing, in doubt whether the head or the heart
of the author be the most diseased.[7]

The furious cry of rage and pain of a settled mind disturbed
has not perhaps a better example. It must be remembered, of
course, in considering this bitterly prejudiced attack, that the
Quarterly, faced with such a work "piously dedicated to Mr
Godwin and . . . written in the spirit of his school", felt itself
embattled on behalf of the establishment with all the forces of
disruption : not altogether without reason. It is not to the
purpose here to give any general survey of the social and
political background : but it may be instructive, and a convenient way of reminding ourselves of this background, to
glance at some of the other topics dealt with in these journals
at the time, subjects which their readers might be expected to
be thinking about.

Technical innovation and "the March of the Mind" are
much to the fore—Blackwood's, for instance, supplies in the
same issue notes on a Self-Registering Hygrometer, remarks on
the histories of the Kraken and the Great Sea Serpent, and a
description of a moveable axle for carriages—and the Quarterly
gives, alongside the Frankenstein review, something like a summary of the current preoccupations of the lettered upper classes.
There are accounts of geographical exploration and discovery,
including the recent Russian voyages in the Arctic and British
expeditions in the Far East and the Congo; articles on "The
Origin and State of the Indian Army" and "Ancient and
Modern Greenland" ("the ice offers many strange phenomena,

which deserve to be investigated by a philosophical observer");
and, as a principal contribution, a full-dress attack on the
Poor Laws as imposing an intolerable tax-burden on landed
property and corrupting the lower classes.

This piece of political journalism is so striking an illustration
of certain prevailing attitudes among the ruling classes of
Britain at the time that it is worth summarising. The Poor Laws
were denounced as iniquitous not because they oppressed the
poor but because their administration demanded money from
the rich; and because their application, however niggardly,
was on the basis of need rather than "merit" and on "that
popular maxim of justice", which the *Quarterly* considered
dangerous, that every man should be judged innocent till
proved guilty. The writer went on from there :

> This degree of liberality is honourable to the society which
> ventures thus to prefer the immediate interest of the supposed
> offender to its own. . . . But here liberality should stop : if it
> be extended to a general principle that every man is *meritorious*
> till he is proved otherwise, this is to mingle right and wrong
> with an unsparing hand—it is to render good conduct and good
> character of no available value, and thereby as far as possible
> to annihilate both. . . .

Relief, the writer recommended, should be given on the
basis of merit rather than poverty : and those of the poor who
could not show that they were deserving must, by the best
utilitarian law, starve. The article assumed that such measures
were likely to lead to an increase in crime (apart from and
added to the crime of poverty) and to a greater pressure on
already grossly overcrowded prisons; but that might be alle-
viated by the use of harsher measures than mere imprisonment :
fetters and "low diet" were suggested.

What has this to do with *Frankenstein*? It is a background
that must be taken into account in considering the virulent
hostility of the *Quarterly* towards "the Godwinian school",
which in the writings of William Godwin and others took a
very different view of man's obligations to his fellows. The
Quarterly was speaking here for one of the extremes into which

Britain in these years appeared increasingly to be divided, and in an atmosphere and situation which, if not actually revolutionary, was certainly feared to be by many, Waterloo but three years behind, "Peterloo" a year ahead. In the fear and hatred of the poor which the writer reveals—the industrial and agricultural proletariat, increasing daily in numbers, destitution, and desperation—the *Quarterly* article shows rather well why the story of *Frankenstein* in particular should make respectable persons uneasy. Property, comfort, reason, taste, political order and religious orthodoxy were all called in question : and though such questioning was not new in itself, and *Frankenstein* only a single late item in the powerful forces of romantic subversion, it may not be fanciful to find in it something peculiarly repugnant to those who already saw all their certainties assailed and the world changing at an appalling rate before their eyes.

The opinions embodied in the book were familiar enough by 1818, though not less detested on that account; but the story itself was not only new but took newness as its subject. Novelty in the most hair-raising form, the irruption of newly-created and destructive agencies, supplied the substance of the plot; that these were shown to be fearful was no recommendation, but merely increased such readers' existing fears. For *Frankenstein* and works like it are not read, any more than they are written, as deliberate allegories whose moral may be approved or disapproved, but as events in themselves, and it was from the book as an event, a summing-up of the actual processes and forces of disturbance and change, that those frightened by change in general involuntarily recoiled. Such a reaction was, one may say, instinctive, and reasons were found for it later, or remained unspoken. The feelings, without the reasons, of those who took the book in such a way were emphatically stated by Mrs Piozzi, writing in 1820—in her eightieth year, and within a few months of her death—to Fanny D'Arblay. She had been reading "the wild and hideous tale of Frankenstein", and exclaimed, "How changed is the taste of verse, prose, and painting since *le bon vieux temps*. Nothing attracts us but what terrifies us and is within—if within—a hair's breadth of positive disgust".

The book was disgusting and terrifying, but Hester Piozzi read it. It has continued, with these qualifications, to be read ever since: its popularity something different on the one hand from that of a respectable novel of character and incident, and on the other from the briefer careers of most of the abundant tales of terror of the period. It has led, for 150 years, a kind of underground existence, never accorded the consideration due to a reputable work of literature and predestined, it would appear, to land up with *Dracula* and the mechanical ephemerae of space fiction with an "H" certificate on the screen or on the paperback bookstalls. To these certainly it bears a relation, both directly ancestral and collateral, which in itself is of interest. A book may always gain by being looked at down the perspective of its descendants.

But *Frankenstein's* descendants are not merely literary, nor is it most interesting if regarded simply as an odd landmark in literary history—unless such history is allowed wider terms of reference than it is usually given. In that case, if literary history embraces not only the thoughts and acts of those who write books and of those who read them, but the thinking and acting of which books are no more than the visible point, the position of *Frankenstein* is indeed singular, its significance more than that of being (to quote one modern comment) "a 'period piece', of not very good date: historically interesting, but not one of the living novels of the world".[8]

The same writer, Mrs Glynn Grylls, biographer of Mary Shelley, also notes the interest of *Frankenstein* as a *"tour-de-force"*, written when Mary was only nineteen; and it is at this point, not pursued further by Mrs Grylls, that the book begins to reveal its most remarkable qualities. Not of course in the mere age and sex of the author (*Blackwood's*, when it learnt some years later who she was, fell over backwards like a floundering Samuel Johnson, exclaiming, "For a man it was excellent, but for a woman it was wonderful"[9]) but in her personal character and circumstances. It is through Mary Shelley's personal life and against its background that her *"tour-de-force"* begins to emerge as the truly astonishing work that it is; and it is when some of its personal connections are assembled and studied that its impersonal life as a work of art can be more fully understood.

If such an approach to any piece of writing offends against the rules of pure literary criticism I must plead guilty, but then (to make a personal statement of my own) I do not believe there is any such thing as purely literary criticism or, a sufficient reason why there cannot be anything of the kind, any such thing as pure literature. Writing is a part and product of life in general, it influences life and is influenced by it, both on the individual and the social scale; if indeed we could conceive of writing that was not "part of life" it would most certainly not be worth writing about. A piece of writing, like any other work of art, is produced by its maker and thereafter assumes, it is said, independent existence; it no longer has anything to do with its author or, if it has, is like a mask which conceals his actual face. His actual voice—begging the question of what that may be—is not heard, his personal life "disappears".

Nevertheless we know that, if invisible, he has been there, as the necessary mediator between his "own" experience—all of the knowledge available, all the multifarious forms of influence brought to bear upon him—and what he transmits to us as his work. He is the lens which, collecting rays of light through a wide angle, projects the image of which they are the components upon us, the retina : one doesn't "see" the lens, but one couldn't see without it. So much is obvious, but its implications in study of the artistic or creative process are commonly ignored : because the process is mysterious there is a general agreement to speak as though it did not take place. We study sources and derivations, the materials of an individual act of artistic making; we study the work itself. But the transformation and transmission of the one into and through the other appear out of the reach of study. Only the unsophisticated trouble themselves about it : How does he do it? is a naive question which, indeed, the artist of whom it is asked hears with impatience, since he doesn't know the answer

26

himself. But it is a real question in the sense that it asks about something that really takes place, if impossible to describe; and there are certain cases in which not only many of the components of a work of art can be identified (as J. L. Lowes in *The Road to Xanadu* discovered the sources of Coleridge's poetry, to take a model example), but their combination can be elucidated, in some degree, in personal terms.

The actual linking of the "hooks and eyes", as Coleridge called it, is bound to be indescribable; but something can be surmised about the approaches to the act, the internal economy as well as the external materials of the work. And where such guesses can be made they will, though only guesses, suggest conclusions about the nature of art and what is called the artistic imagination not new, but still surprising. The works of the imagination emerge in metaphor, which may become myth; at the point of their emergence, and with knowledge of what they emerge from, it may be possible to see connections between them; the effect of the impersonal or general upon the personal, the personal transforming itself in turn into the general.

An opportunity for such observations is presented by *Frankenstein*; and indeed the novel seems to clamour for them. As some of the early comments upon it show, it was precisely the naive question, How was it done? that was provoked by its first appearance. The mingled feelings of shock, admiration, and curiosity are summed up in the "review" written by Shelley himself in 1817, before its first publication. The novel is, he wrote:

> One of the most original and complete productions of the day. We debate with ourselves in wonder as we read it what could have been the series of thoughts—what could have been the peculiar experiences that awakened them—which conduced in the author's mind to the astonishing combination of motives and incidents and the startling catastrophe which compose this tale.

What follows is an attempt to answer these questions. Clearly it cannot be more than very partially successful; indeed if

Shelley himself could not answer them—and there is no reason to believe they were asked by him disingenuously—who else can hope to do so? The immediate circumstances he knew, and the "series of thoughts" he if anyone should have been able to surmise. There are particular reasons, however, why, except in a superficial way, Shelley couldn't answer his own questions. The reasons why it was difficult or impossible for him to do so are themselves, it will be seen, part of the answer; and in looking at what he couldn't see and trying to understand at the same time why he couldn't see it, time and distance may be a positive advantage.

That "we can think of nothing which we have not perceived" was a favourite maxim (borrowed from Hume and Berkeley) in Shelley's metaphysical speculations. It is a two-edged one, as he was well aware himself. On the one hand it restricts the creative activity of mind to "combination" only— "the most astonishing combinations of poetry, the subtlest deductions of logic and mathematics, are no other than combinations which the intellect makes of sensations according to its own laws". On the other, it asserts a "comprehensive and synthetical view" of mind which allows it the same supremacy in "the catalogue of existence" as downright solipsism : "A catalogue of all the thoughts of the mind and of all their possible modifications is a cyclopaedic history of the Universe."[10] Such an approach to epistemology is no longer in favour, but it is an important key to Shelleyan thought that we shall have recourse to later; and in the meantime it may be taken as a useful tool for the task in hand.

If the range of perception be allowed to include—as Shelley in his speculations insisted that it should—the internal perception of thoughts and emotions, then Mary Shelley, in producing *Frankenstein*, may be said to have "thought of nothing which she had not perceived"; and what she perceived, both externally and internally, is to a considerable extent available to study. To examine the "peculiar experiences" that awakened her thoughts, and to guess at some of the components of the thoughts themselves, are the first objects of this inquiry. They can be arranged under three heads. First, there are the actual circumstances of the author at the time, well known and attested. Secondly, the direct influences, both literary and personal, that may be inferred from the book itself and from what is known of Mary Shelley's reading, of her character, and the character of those intimately associated with her. Thirdly, there are the more remote or indirect forces brought to bear upon the book, social and historical, including its own distant effects.

This last is paradoxical, and may be thought plain nonsense. The confusion in imaginative literature between cause and effect, and the question whether they can or should be absolutely distinguished will be subjects of discussion in the final section. *Frankenstein* is obviously and notoriously a "prophetic" book, but it is by no means clear what that implies. What is meant by prophecy in literature and what it indicates about the uses of the imagination in general, these investigations may I hope a little illuminate.

TWO

BIRTH OF THE STORY

TO OUTLINE FIRST events and people in Mary Shelley's life up to her twentieth year, when she wrote *Frankenstein*: she was born on 30 August, 1797, the child of Mary Wollstonecraft, celebrated as the author of *The Rights of Women,* and William Godwin, the even more celebrated author of *Political Justice*. The infant Mary was herself considered a potential celebrity, as "the only offspring of a union that will certainly be matchless in the present generation".[1] She was the only offspring because her mother died of puerperal fever eleven days later, having been actually married to Godwin little over five months: the anti-matrimonial principles of both gave way to convenience in March 1797. Mary Wollstonecraft also left her three-year-old daughter Fanny, whose father, Gilbert Imlay, had abandoned her two years previously. The two small children were cared for initially by various friends until, in 1801, Godwin married again, taking for his second wife Mrs Clairmont, a middle-aged widow with two children of her own, Charles and Jane. To these were added a son by Godwin, William, born in 1802.

Among those who had a hand in caring for the infant Mary was a neighbour, a Mr Nicholson, an enthusiastic amateur of phrenology, and physiognomy, who examined the baby when she was less than three weeks old, and submitted a detailed report to Godwin, believing, as he said, that "our organisation at the birth may greatly influence those motives which govern the series of our future acts of intelligence, and that we may even possess moral habits, acquired during the foetal state". He saw in the new-born child signs of "considerable memory and intelligence", "quick sensibility, irritable, scarcely irascible, and surely not given to rage"; not much evidence of persistence in "investigation"—"I think her powers, of themselves, would lead to speedy combination, rather than continued research". He could not say very much on the shape of Mary's mouth, it being "too much employed to be well observed"—the baby was evidently crying—but, remarking that "she was displeased", noted in her expression "more of resigned vexation than either scorn or rage". His conclusion was that "her manner may be petulant in resistance, but cannot be sullen".[2] How far this prognosis has any bearing on Mary's actual character we may decide according to our views of fortune-telling and other such arts. But it does tell us something of interest about the milieu in which she was brought up, and the attitude and expectations of the adults around her. To have one's capacity for "research" speculated upon at the age of three weeks may be somewhat of a burden later on.

Mary was brought up with half- 'and step-brothers and sisters, but spent a good deal of her later childhood away from home; from 1812 to 1814 she lived with a Scottish family, the Baxters, in Dundee. She appears to have met Shelley for the first time, briefly, in 1812, when he visited her father with his first wife, Harriet, but did not get to know him until the summer of 1814, when she returned to her home; Shelley was then living in London and a regular visitor to her father's house. They fell in love and ran away together in July 1814, going to France and Switzerland, with Mary's step-sister Jane, or Claire Clairmont as companion. The three returned to England after two months and Mary and Shelley continued to live together, precariously and uncomfortably, during the next year and a half, while Shelley was pursued by creditors and Mary was estranged from her own family. Claire continued most of the time to live with them. In February 1815 the first child of Mary and Shelley was born, a girl who died after a few days. A second child, their son William, was born on 24 January, 1816. The following May, Mary and Shelley, with their infant son and once again with Claire Clairmont, set out on their second trip to the Continent, arriving at Geneva by the middle of the month. Here, in a cottage by the lake, and making various expeditions about the country, they

stayed until the end of August. During this period Mary conceived and began to write the story of *Frankenstein*.

Its immediate origins were described in some detail in the
introduction she wrote for the 1831 edition, at the request, she
says, of her publishers: she was the more willing to comply
"because I shall thus give a general answer to the question, so
very frequently asked me, 'How I, then a young girl, came to
think of, and dilate upon, so very hideous an idea?' "³ So far
as the circumstances of the time went, she did her best to
provide an answer, though, writing fourteen years later, she
was somewhat vague on points of chronology.

Soon after Mary, Shelley, and Claire settled in their cottage
they "became", as she says, "the neighbours of Lord Byron".
Byron, having shortly before left Britain for good, arrived towards the end of May and took up occupation of the Villa
Diodati, a place already sufficiently endowed with poetic associations as the house where Milton had stayed with his friend
and former schoolfellow Charles Diodati. The cottage, the Villa
Chapuis, was close at hand on the shore of the lake, and the
two parties were, it seems, almost continuously together. The
meeting, which brought Shelley and Byron together for the first
time, was in fact a planned one, largely at the instigation of
Claire Clairmont, whose pursuit of Byron (she having briefly
become his mistress in London not long before) was a motive
for the whole expedition, and an addition to the highly charged
emotional atmosphere of the time. Byron himself was accompanied, apart from his usual retinue of servants, by John
William Polidori, brought as his personal physician: an odd
and unhappy young man who was the butt of Byron and was
laughed at by the others as well; he kept a journal which is one
of the supplementary sources of information for the events of
this summer. His subsequent career, though of no further concern to the chief actors in this history, was not less disastrous
than theirs; he eventually went out of his mind and poisoned
himself.

The pleasures of arrival in Geneva, which was also an escape
from many pressing anxieties, are enthusiastically described by

Mary in her letters of the time (later included in the *History of a Six-weeks' Tour*) giving an account of their doings:

> We have hired a boat, and every evening, at about six o'clock, we sail on the lake, which is delightful, whether we glide over a glassy surface or are speeded along by a stormy wind,

and again:

> You know that we have just escaped from the gloom of winter and of London; and coming to this delightful spot during this divine weather, I feel as happy as a new-fledged bird, and hardly care what twig I fly to, so that I may try my new-found wings.[4]

The feelings of release and also of unfolding powers expressed in this letter may be taken as part of the prelude to *Frankenstein*; the lake and town of Geneva and the surrounding mountains, explored in an expedition some weeks later, provided much of the external scenery of the novel. By that time, when Byron had arrived at Diodati and the two parties had joined forces, the story was already begun. The "divine weather" of May had now broken and given way, as Mary says in her Introduction to the novel, to "a wet ungenial summer" and "incessant rain often confined us for days to the house". She elaborates on the weather further in a letter written at the beginning of June in which the rain is "almost perpetual" and accompanied by spectacular thunderstorms:

> . . . the thunderstorms that visit us are grander and more terrific than I have ever seen before. . . . One night we *enjoyed* a finer storm than I had ever before beheld. The lake was lit up, the pines on Jura made visible, and all the scene illuminated for an instant, when a pitchy blackness succeeded, and the thunder came in frightful bursts over our heads amid the darkness.[5]

The summer of 1816 was in fact one of the coldest on record throughout the Northern hemisphere; the reason is believed to have been a great increase in atmospheric dust following a volcanic explosion in the East Indies the previous year. There could hardly have been a more appropriate cause.

Indoors, the company amused themselves with conversation, and telling ghost stories. They had been reading a volume of German tales (in a French translation, *Fantasmagoriana*, published in 1812; at this time neither Mary nor Shelley could read German). She gives the gist of a couple of these "histoires d'apparitions, de spectres, revenans, fantomes, etc." in her Introduction : one concerning an Inconstant Lover who finds he is embracing the ghost of his deserted lady, and another about a father, "the sinful founder of his race", doomed involuntarily to destroy "all the younger sons of his fated house" —both themes, it may be observed, likely especially to have struck Shelley. A good deal of this wet summer seems to have been passed indulging in Gothic terrors : a little later "Monk" Lewis visited Diodati and recounted some shockers recorded by Shelley in Mary's *Journal* [6] ("all grim").

Before that, however (the exact sequence of events is uncertain) they had all agreed, at Byron's suggestion, to write ghost stories of their own. None of the others did anything of particular note, though Byron's unfinished attempt had curious progeny : it was a story about vampires, printed with his *Mazeppa* in 1819, which Polidori later completed and published, trying to pass it off as being altogether Byron's own; it is reckoned to be the source of Bram Stoker's *Dracula*. Polidori's own production at the time was "some terrible idea about a skull-headed lady" which Mary gently mocks. Shelley did nothing that has been preserved; according to Mary, he began one "founded on the experiences of his early life", but she says nothing more about it, or why he gave it up; perhaps, as on other occasions, he frightened himself too much to continue.

The entry in Polidori's journal for 17 June says "The ghost stories are begun by all but me",[7] but according to her own account Mary was lagging behind. She could not "think of a story", but persisted, encouraged by the others and more determined than they were, perhaps, that it should be a good one, "One which would speak to the mysterious fears of our nature and awaken thrilling horror—one to make the reader dread to look round, to curdle the blood, and quicken the beatings of the heart". Among other motives it is clear that her pride, greatly reinforced by her desire to please and impress Shelley, was involved: *"Have you thought of a story?* I was asked each morning, and each morning I was forced to reply with a mortifying negative." She lacked an idea, or rather the animating spark of association: "invention", she observes, following the Humean doctrine already mentioned, and giving it greater depth, ". . . does not consist in creating out of void, but out of chaos; the materials must, in the first place, be afforded: it can give form to dark, shapeless substances, but cannot bring into being the substance itself".

The flashpoint was provided by a discussion between the two poets—"Many and long were the conversations between Lord Byron and Shelley, to which I was a devout but nearly silent listener"—concerning "the principle of life", and whether it might ever be "discovered and communicated". Polidori gives a corroborative note of this same conversation, in which he also seems to have taken part—"Shelley and I had a conversation about principles—whether man was to be thought merely an instrument".[8] By "principle" was evidently meant both the original life-creating force and the essential difference between living and dead matter. According to Mary, the talk encompassed speculation that "Perhaps a corpse would be re-animated; galvanism had given token of such things; perhaps the component parts of a creature might be manufactured, brought together, and endued with vital warmth."[9] It is worth noting here that in these terms the conversation Mary listened to not only suggested a striking subject, but was in itself a description of her own situation as she was trying to "think of a story", at any rate as she spoke of it retrospectively: the effort of "creation . . . out of chaos", the power of invention to "give form to dark, shapeless substances". It was at once a picture of her own state of mind, a paradigm of what she wanted to do, and the idea she was waiting for. Each effect reinforced the others.

She describes how, after listening to this prolonged discussion —"night waned upon this talk, and even the witching hour had gone by"—she eventually went to bed but, her mind stimulated to great activity, could not sleep. Nor, she says, did she think in the ordinary sense, but "My imagination, unbidden, possessed and guided me, gifting the successive images that arose in my mind with a vividness far beyond the usual bounds of reverie". In this hypnagogic state, a condition in which, according to later psychological theory, consciousness, though still retained, is peculiarly open to incursions from the unconscious, she saw "with acute mental vision" the elements of her story.

"I saw the pale student of unhallowed arts kneeling beside the thing he had put together," constructing and animating his synthetic man; "I saw the hideous phantasm of a man stretched out and then, on the working of some powerful engine, show signs of life and stir with an uneasy, half vital motion". She saw the consequences, when the "student" would abandon his work in revulsion and horror but, waking from sleep, would see "the horrid thing" at his bedside looking on him "with yellow, watery, but speculative eyes". She opened her own, she says, in terror: "The idea so possessed my mind, that a thrill of fear ran through me, and I wished to exchange the ghastly image of my fancy for the realities around." Trying to turn her mind on something else, she reverted to her "tiresome unlucky ghost story", her failure and desire to excel; when, "swift as light and as cheering" she realised that "What terrified me would terrify others", and that she had her story to her hand.

Next day she set to work "making only a transcript of the grim terrors of my waking dream". Shelley, who had always been anxious that she should write, encouraged her and urged her to expand; what was to have been "a few pages" grew into *Frankenstein*. She wrote at intervals, recorded in her *Journal*, during the remainder of the stay in Switzerland, and continued after Shelley, Claire, and herself returned to England at the end of August. Though much interrupted by their travels and generally unsettled life, she seems pretty well to have finished the book by the end of the year; by April 1817 the *Journal* is recording work on correction and transcription of the work. After being refused by two publishers it was accepted by a third, to come out the following spring.

The essence of the finished story remains quite simple and true to Mary's originating vision. In its expansion, however, it acquired interesting detail and subdivision into three interlocking narratives, which it may be convenient to summarise at this point.

The tale is begun in epistolary form by Walton, a would-be Arctic explorer, who writes to his sister as he prepares to set off by ship in an attempt to reach the North Pole. Walton, it may be said, is a prefiguration of the hero, a shadow cast ahead by Frankenstein himself : elevated by ambition and curiosity, discounting the prospect of "frost and desolation", and, on the contrary, imagining the Pole as a wonderful "region of beauty and delight". "What," he asks, "may not be expected in a country of eternal light?" He is equally inspired by "ardent curiosity" and the hope of discovery that will confer "inestimable benefit" on mankind; he dismisses all difficulties and declares his supreme self-confidence : "What can stop the determined heart and resolved will of man?" He sets out from Archangel and when his ship is distant from land but surrounded by ice, observes a dog-sledge, the driver of which appears "of gigantic stature" passing over the floe. The next day his sailors bring on board a man cast away on a floe and in the last stages of exhaustion. He had refused help until he learnt where Walton's ship is bound : on being told "the northern pole" he consented to be rescued. He recovers, impresses Walton by his "noble" character and appearance of suffering, and on learning of Walton's high ambitions and determination to pursue his exploration at whatever cost—"One man's life or death were but a small price to pay for the acquirement of the knowledge which I sought; for the dominion I should acquire and transmit over the elemental foes of our race"—shows great agitation and proceeds to tell his own cautionary story.

The stranger, Frankenstein, explains how, driven by similar ambitions and a desire to learn "the secrets of heaven and earth", he has been a student first of alchemy and magic and then of "natural philosophy" : he inquires persistently into the "principles of life" and discovers by means unstated "the cause of generation and life; nay more, I became myself capable of

37

bestowing animation upon lifeless matter". He describes how he then embarked alone and in secret upon "the creation of a human being" and after long labour succeeded; the story now reaches the point of Mary's first beginning and, as she tells us in her Introduction, the first words she wrote, "It was on a dreary night of November, that I beheld the accomplishment of my toils".

Frankenstein gives life to his creation, usually referred to thereafter as the Monster, or the Fiend, and is immediately revolted by the result : it may be noted that he had originally intended the creature to be beautiful and had "selected his features" to that end, but he turns out hideous and terrifying. Frankenstein flees from the room and eventually goes to sleep, but is woken by the Monster as in the scene originally conceived, and flees again; the Monster vanishes. After an interval of time, during which Frankenstein has been prostrated and has recovered, he hears that his infant brother has been murdered and a nursemaid accused of the crime. He returns to his home at Geneva, catches a glimpse of the Monster hiding in the woods, and has the idea that he may be the murderer, but tells no one of his suspicions; consequently the nursemaid is executed as a murderess. Impelled by a "whirlwind passion" Frankenstein seeks solace in the mountains and on the glacier at Chamonix meets the Monster who comes in fact to find him. Frankenstein recoils with hatred from "the wretch whom I had created", but is compelled by the Monster to listen to him : there now follows the third part of the story, which is the Monster's own account of himself.

He describes the gradual growth of his consciousness and awareness of his surroundings, and his first encounters with men, who all run from him in terror and disgust. He hides in the outhouse of a cottage and observes the family within through a crack in the wall, a device which allows him, by watching and listening, to learn first human speech and later reading. Listening, as one of the inmates of the cottage instructs another, he acquires a general idea of the history of civilisation, conveniently potted, and the present state of mankind; he also happens on a portmanteau of books and manages to read them, thus gaining, in Plutarch's *Lives*, *Paradise Lost*, and the *Sorrows of Werther*, the three books in the bag, the elements of a classical and romantic education.

He becomes attached to the family in the cottage and longing for companionship, finally resolves to approach them, but is rejected again and driven out, later burning the cottage and fleeing again to the woods. From papers in the pocket of clothes he took on his original flight from Frankenstein's laboratory he learns the facts of his identity and manufacture, and now resolves to seek out Frankenstein, "my father, my creator". He travels through the countryside hiding from men, but partly restored to feelings of "gentleness and pleasure" by the return of spring; one day he sees a peasant child playing in the woods and, when she falls into the river, rescues her; but her father tears the child away and, when the Monster attempts to follow, shoots and wounds him. Further embittered, he hides until his wound is healed and then completes his journey to Geneva; there by chance he sees a young child and captures him, meaning to "educate him as my companion and friend". The boy tries to get away, and in the struggle speaks of his father : he is Frankenstein's younger brother. Enraged at the name, the Monster strangles him and, in further revengeful impulse, plants incriminating evidence on the sleeping nursemaid.

Having thus brought his own history up to date, the Monster now turns to Frankenstein and demands that, since mankind rejects him he, Frankenstein, must make a companion for him of his own kind, "a female . . . with whom I can live in the interchange of those sympathies necessary for my being". He both appeals to Frankenstein's sense of justice and threatens him with further disaster if he refuses; he also promises that if he is thus provided with a helpmeet he will shun human society and live in "the most savage of places", molesting no one. Reluctantly, Frankenstein agrees : the rest of his own story recounts how he set to work (in "the remotest of the Orkneys", for the sake of secrecy) to make a female monster; how, when the work was almost complete, he changed his mind for fear that male and female would people the world with monstrous offspring, and how the Monster, enraged at his breach of faith,

revenged himself further, first by killing Frenkenstein's best
friend and finally, carrying out a long-standing threat, by
strangling Frankenstein's bride on his wedding night; how
Frankenstein then set off in pursuit of the Monster, who has
led him to the Arctic where Walton has found and rescued
him. He ends by exhorting Walton to take over the task of
destroying the Monster in the event of his own death.

The story is brought to an end in a resumption of Walton's
narrative. He describes further conversations with Frankenstein,
and his growing friendship with him; the increasing danger of
their situation and the demand of his crew that he abandon his
voyage (they are still trying to reach the Pole) and return; his
consent; the death of Frankenstein, and the final appearance of
the Monster, who comes to view the dead body of his creator
and to mourn his "last victim". The Monster then departs into
Arctic darkness with the promise, as yet unfulfilled, of destroying himself.

The background to this remarkable invention has already
been partly indicated. Geneva, the lake, and the mountains
provide much of the setting, especially the *mer de glace* at
Chamonix on which the crucial interview between Frankenstein
and the Monster takes place, and which Mary had seen soon
after starting the story. In July, Mary and Shelley made a
week's expedition to Chamonix together, when the "savage and
colossal character" of mountain, glacier, waterfall and river
made a deep and permanent impression on both of them; she
was often to refer to this experience in later life, and it was the
direct inspiration, in Shelley, of some of his most celebrated
poetry.

She vividly recorded what she saw in her *Journal*, where the
descriptions, together with Shelley's in his letters to Peacock—
both collected later in the *Six-weeks' Tour*—tally closely with
what was incorporated in the novel. Indeed one may suppose
there to have been further direct transcription of immediate
impressions, since her *Journal* also notes that she was working
on the story during this expedition; the sight of the glacier,
"the most desolate place in the world", as the *Journal* calls it,
may directly have suggested the encounter she imagined in the

same place, "a scene terrifically desolate", where the Monster comes bounding over the broken ice, "rising like the waves of a troubled sea", to confront Frankenstein. Shelley's description, written at the same time in a letter to Peacock, fills the picture out further :

> The vale itself is filled with a mass of undulating ice, and has an ascent sufficiently gradual even to the remotest abysses of these horrible deserts. It is only half a league (about two miles) in breadth [Frankenstein's reckoning is "almost a league"] and seems less. It exhibits an appearance as if frost had suddenly bound up the waves and whirlpools of a mighty torrent. We walked some distance upon its surface. The waves are elevated about 12 or 15 feet from the surface of the mass, which is intersected by long gaps of unfathomable depth, the ice of whose sides is more beautifully azure than the sky. In these regions everything changes and is in motion. This vast mass of ice has one general progress, which ceases neither day nor night; it breaks and bursts for ever : some undulations sink while others rise; it is never the same. The echo of rocks, or of the ice and snow which fall from their overhanging precipices, or roll from their aerial summits, scarcely ceases for one moment. One would think that Mont Blanc, like the god of the Stoics, was a vast animal, and that the frozen blood for ever circulated through his stony veins.[10]

This well-known passage, more elaborate than Mary's note in the *Journal*—though missing the characteristically real detail she noticed, the "dirty white" surface of the glacier—stands as a kind of bridge between the part of *Frankenstein* in question and Shelley's own poem, *Mont Blanc*, written at this time. There will be occasion to refer to these famous "lines written in the Vale of Chamouni" later; meanwhile it may be observed that Frankenstein himself, trying to calm his agitation in roaming the same paths as Mary and Shelley—and experiencing the same weather, as "The rain was pouring in torrents, and thick mists hid the summits of the mountains"—partakes not only of Mary's impressions of desolation but something like Shelley's exaltation, at least before the Monster arrives; he remembers how the sight of the "ever-moving glacier", "had then filled me with a sublime ecstasy, that gave wings to the soul, and allowed it to soar from the obscure world to light and joy".

Other elements of the story are related to immediate experience in a more general way. Frankenstein is himself a Genevese, his father, venerable and wise, brought in sorrow to the grave by the deeds of the Monster, one of the syndics, or chief magistrates of the city. Frankenstein's peregrinations include most of the places that Mary, in her young life, had known. His upbringing among the Swiss and French Alps, his journey down the Rhine to Holland—following the route taken by Mary and Shelley on their first Continental escapade in 1814—allow her to describe at first hand the romantic scenery that supplies the most conventional part of the story. London itself, Oxfordshire, the Lake District, Scotland ("I visited Edinburgh with languid eyes and mind", says Frankenstein; "and yet that city might have interested the most unfortunate being") were all familiar ground to her. There is no reason to suppose that she visited the Orkneys, selected by Frankenstein for his second monster-making, but in Dundee, a regular port of embarkation for Orkney, she is likely to have heard about the islands as, what they were at the time, particularly lonely and remote. It is as such that Frankenstein chooses one of them ("It was a place fitted for such a work, being hardly more than a rock, whose high sides were continually beaten upon by the waves"). The Polar seas, where the story begins and ends, were in the news at the time, as has already been noted. Both British and Russian voyages of exploration were being undertaken, and there was much public speculation about what they would find, including the fantasy, which Frankenstein's explorer-rescuer shares, of an ice-free Pole : an idea which goes back to the legend of the Hyperboreans, and was still cropping up in boys' stories in Victorian times.

But though Mary made the most of what she knew to provide the novel's incidental furniture, and though in part—the Chamonix expedition in particular, with its obvious reflection not merely in the setting but the spirit of the story—*Frankenstein* drew some essential features from her immediate outward experience, she was not, of course, really concerned with external verisimilitude. As was asserted in the Preface to the first edition (presented as though by the author, but actually written by Shelley), "the event on which this fiction is founded, has been supposed . . . as not of impossible occurrence", and the story consequently was "exempt from the disadvantages of a mere tale of spectres and enchantment" : in a technical sense it belonged in the same category of romantic fiction as the works of Mrs Radcliffe or the American Charles Brockden Brown, in which a "natural" explanation for apparently super-natural happenings was always provided.

Indeed in this narrow sense it was not a "ghost story" at all, but a forerunner of those tales of the marvellous but possible which we now call science fiction. Nevertheless, the possibility of consistency of her story is in truth an internal rather than an external one : it was psychological, not physical laws, "the elementary principles of human nature" as Shelley's Preface said, that she paid heed to in writing. Thus Walton for example, speaking of the "country of eternal light", the place where "the sun is forever visible" which he expected to find at the Pole, was not talking like any actual explorer. But this curious geocentric error, of which Mary was quite well aware, was allowed to stand in her revision of the book, and, we must feel, rightly so, for Walton was describing no geographical Arctic but an Arctic of the mind.

Whether, indeed, Mary placed her action in scenes that she could view with her own eyes—"the black sides of Jura, and the bright summit of Mont Blanc"—or such as Ingolstadt, Frankenstein's university, where he learns "the secrets of heaven and earth" and sets up his laboratory, a place unvisited by Mary, they belong rather to a metaphorical and symbolic than any actual geography. Ingolstadt, for example, was the university where the revolutionary secret society of the Illuminati, a romantic conspiracy which exercised a strong fascination upon Shelley especially, was formed in 1776; Mary doesn't mention this in the novel, but it was most probably the context in which she had heard of the town.

It is this metaphorical landscape, of course, which is of real and permanent interest. The "excellent descriptions of scenery" which impressed the *Gentlemen's Magazine* we tend now, insofar as they are merely topographical, to skip; but the striking succession of dark, stormy, and barren scenes the novel traverses belong to the atmosphere and indeed to the action itself to a degree uncommon even in the convention of the Gothic picturesque. *Frankenstein* carries to extreme but—because the feelings so reflected are so strong—never absurd degree the use of the pathetic fallacy common to the genre. The emotions of the hero and his physical surroundings continually play on one another in a way that make them in fact one : indeed, he remarks this intimate connection himself, though stating it in naturalistic terms as showing man the creature of his immediate environment :

> Alas! why does man boast of sensibilities superior to those apparent in the brute; it only renders them more necessary beings. If our impulses were confined to hunger, thirst, and desire, we might be nearly free; but now we are moved by every wind that blows, and a chance word or scene that that word may convey to us.

This reflection, forced upon Frankenstein by the fluctuation of his own feelings at the critical point where he is about to encounter the Monster on the *mer de glace*—soothed and elevated at one moment by the sight of the mountain-tops, and cast down the next, when "the summits were hid in the uniform clouds, while rain poured from the dark sky"—formulates the pathetic fallacy back to front, in such a way indeed that it is not fallacious but rational.

Man, a "necessary being"—that is to say one in the grip of necessity—is dependent even for the state of his emotions on the circumstances of the time; just because, unlike the beasts, he cannot live by bread alone but is sensitive to more than simple physical effects, he is the helpless victim of "every wind that blows". The conviction thus borne in on Frankenstein is of great importance in the moral scheme of the novel; the pathetic fallacy here turned upside down is, as we shall see, a way of thinking upon which the story as a whole makes profound comment. But it supplies nevertheless the mode in which, as a work of art, it is written : man, landscape, and the vagaries of weather are bound together, and their interaction in the meta-phorical language of the work is not to be seen in terms of cause and effect.

The climate of *Frankenstein* is an interesting study in itself, and it should be noted that it is not one of continual storm and tempest. Thunderstorms, the stage effects par excellence of Gothic melodrama, have their place, it is true. It is a violent storm witnessed by Frankenstein as a boy that turns his mind, hitherto occupied by alchemy and sorcery, to the "new and astonishing" subjects of electricity and galvanism; in this storm, coming "from behind the mountains of Jura" and in its course shattering by lightning an oak-tree so that "nothing remained but a blasted stump", can be seen not only Mary's immediate experience, the storms described in her letters, but a complex of associations with both Shelley and Byron.

Another Swiss thunderstorm, described in almost the same words as those in the letter already quoted—". . . vivid flashes of lightning dazzled my eyes, illuminating the lake, making it appear like a vast sheet of fire; then for an instant everything seemed of pitchy blackness"—accompanies Frankenstein's return to Geneva after the murder of his brother William, and it is in a flash of this same lightning that he catches a glimpse of the Monster, the first sight since the panic at Ingolstadt of "the wretch, the filthy daemon, to whom I had given life". At the same instant he suspects, and is immediately certain, that the Monster is the murderer : "No sooner did the idea cross my imagination, than I became convinced of its truth." It is as though not only the physical shape but the moral significance of the Monster were revealed in the same lightning-flash; almost as though the lightning once again created them.

But in the main the weather is calm, though gloomy; it is indeed an intensely wintry landscape that Frankenstein moves through. The "dreary night of November" on which he gives life to his creation, while "the rain pattered dismally against the panes" gives way to "morning, dismal and wet" in which he

45

flees from his handiwork, walking the streets and "drenched by the rain that poured from a black and comfortless sky". This was the rain, no doubt, of the "wet ungenial summer" that overtook them at Diodati; but in the story it soon gives way to winter. Winter accompanies the Monster especially : during his first wanderings it soon sets in with frost and snow, his reactions to this "disconsolate" change, and his sensations when, half-naked, he finds his feet "chilled by the cold damp substance that covered the ground", being particularly described. He feels the cold and at first seeks warmth, learning the use of fire like primitive man and looking for shelter; but ice and snow are in truth congenial to him, they are his proper environment. From the beginning, he tells Frankenstein, he has been "better fitted by my conformation for the endurance of cold than heat", and he seems in fact to carry coldness with him.

As he becomes more monstrous, so his surroundings are more frozen; he is at home among the ice-caves of the *mer de glace*, and, of course, finally leads Frankenstein, with deliberate revengeful purpose, towards "the everlasting ices of the north, where you will feel the misery of cold and frost, to which I am impassive". He is not so impassive at the beginning when, as we have just seen, the onset of winter seems "disconsolate" and when in fact he lives through the changes of the season and feels their effects, as part of his new world of sensation, most keenly. The coming of spring especially affects him, filling him with surprise that "what before was desert and gloomy should now bloom with the most beautiful flowers and verdure. My senses were gratified and refreshed by a thousand scents of delight, and a thousand sights of beauty".

This is the time when, as a kind of stowaway amid human society, he hopes for acceptance and companionship; in these hopes and in primitive pleasure in his surroundings, he exclaims, in terms which, if we remember Shelley's *Queen Mab* are unmistakably familiar, "Happy, happy earth ! fit habitation for gods, which so short a time before was bleak, damp and unwholesome".[11] There follows his rejection by the family in the cottage, and it is winter again when, in isolation and despair, he travels to seek out Frankenstein :

Nature decayed around me, and the sun became heatless; rain and snow poured around me; mighty rivers were frozen; the surface of the earth was hard and chill, and bare, and I found no shelter. Oh, earth! how often did I imprecate curses on the cause of my being! The mildness of my nature had fled, and all within me was turned to gall and bitterness.

↣ By the time he reaches Geneva it is spring once more and his hopes return with the idea of kidnapping a child to bring up as his companion; but the frightened child is Frankenstein's brother, and the Monster murders him. The next time we see him is on the glacier. The alternation of seasons responds faithfully to feelings and actions and the echo of *Queen Mab*, the poem of Shelley's youth, produces another from a later period. The Monster experiences spring but belongs to winter : it is the continuation, with the opposite effect, of the apostrophe in the *Ode to the West Wind*. If spring comes for Frankenstein or his creature, winter is not far behind.

What in more general terms this winter meant for Mary Shelley, and in the subsequent career of her myth will be the subject of inquiry in due course. In the meantime examination of the background may be extended from the immediate circumstances in which she conceived and began to write her story to other more distant sources. A large system of derivation and association can be traced; many threads come together in Mary Shelley, trying to "think of a story" and set it down to her satisfaction. We will try to follow them as they converge on her personal situation; where they extend thereafter, through her and beyond, may appear later.

THREE

"THE MODERN PROMETHEUS"

THE SUB-TITLE OF *Frankenstein* is *The Modern Prometheus*. Mary thus associated her story with one of the most powerful, persistent, but also protean of classic legends, for Prometheus has always been able to assume new forms. How many of these, in literature or plastic art, she was acquainted with is doubtful; she was unlikely, for example, to have known much about the curious and as it were underground existence of Prometheus as an adjunct of Christian allegory during the Middle Ages. But it is striking that Frankenstein, her Prometheus, while sharing the impious and agonised qualities that exerted such fascination on the Romantics, is Promethean first and foremost as a maker of man, an aspect of the legend that has tended to be obscured in emphasis on the primary Promethean act of stealing fire from heaven.

The story of *Prometheus plasticator*, who takes a hand in either the original or a supplementary creation of man, seems to have been an early addition to the myth if not part of it from the beginning. It occurs chiefly, however, in Roman or Graeco-Roman examples, in which it had evident connections with ideas of immortality; its best-known representations are on Roman sarcophagi, notably the well-known "Capitoline" sarcophagus, which shows the creation of man in three stages: the shaping of man by Prometheus as sculptor, his endowment with life by a winged being who applies fire to his body, and his animation by Minerva, who brings his soul in the form of a butterfly or bee. (We shall have occasion to refer to this scheme later.) The idea of Prometheus as the creator of mankind in general crops up in various Latin authors, including Ovid, Horace, and Catullus, often with the accompanying notion that the work was ill done : or at least that men's imperfections, and especially his "animal nature", are to be blamed on him.

Prometheus was absorbed along with other pagan personages into Roman Christianity, and again with emphasis on his work as maker and shaper. In the early interpretation of myth in Christian terms he is quite plainly stated to be an aspect or function of God: thus Tertullian (*Apologeticus* XVIII) says *"Deus unius qui universa condiderit, qui hominem de humo struxerit; hic enim est verus Prometheus"*.[1] An early Christian sculpture, the so-called "Dogma" sarcophagus now in the Lateran Museum, shows the creation of man by the three persons of the Trinity in direct adaptation of the stages imagined by pagan artists. In medieval representation Prometheus began, like other co-opted members of the pagan pantheon, to be separated again from the united being of God, but remained his servant and ally, especially as the direct agent (despite the formula laid down in Genesis) in the creation of man.[2]

Typically Prometheus appears in medieval iconography as animating man after the primal creation has been performed by God; he does so by bringing a flame to endow man's body with soul, but there is no suggestion that the flame has been stolen, nor of any conflict between Prometheus and the Almighty. The reassertion of Prometheus's conflict with God seems to have been concurrent with the Renaissance and the rise of humanism. For Erasmus, it is true, Prometheus was an example for all who sought to combat ignorance ("Prometheus est nobis imitandus") without any suggestion that the pursuit of knowledge would bring penalties. But elsewhere the idea that knowledge may be a torment begins again to be attached to the myth: in the writings of the Italian Platonist Marsilio Ficino (1433–99) the story of Prometheus is interpreted as an allegory of the soul seeking after truth and his torture the pain brought by reason : after having stolen one beam of light from heaven the soul is "beset by the continuous gnawing of inquiry, the most ravenous of vultures"; only death can bring release, carrying the soul to the source of all knowledge, where it will "be entirely filled with the whole light".[3]

It is unlikely that Mary Shelley knew any of this, wide though her reading already was, and enlarged by Shelley's own extraordinarily wide-ranging knowledge. It is the more interesting to find resemblances in her own version which are presumably untaught, arising naturally by the logic of myth. Thus in one of the medieval representations of Prometheus mentioned, he is shown, as coadjutor of God, animating Adam, but God is creating Eve; in every case it is man, not woman, that he makes or brings to life. We are reminded that Frankenstein, having made a man-monster, cannot bring himself to finish the task of manufacturing a mate. His reasons are various, and by their very multiplicity rouse the suspicion that they are rather excuses for going back on his promise : to make a female is something he just cannot do.

This crisis in Frankenstein's story will be discussed later; what may be noted now is his (apparently) unconscious agreement with an older view, that though reason and knowledge may put life into man, woman must be the work of God. There is a difference to be seen here between the act of Prometheus and that of Pygmalion, whose overwhelming desire for the woman he has made as a work of art brings her to life (or causes Aphrodite to do so in pity for him). Prometheus is spoken of sometimes as artist—he is credited indeed with the invention of sculpture—and the making of woman, or at any rate her image, is not impossible for an artist. But he is an artist more in the sense of artificer; and in at least one early representation (a Graeco-Roman gem-carving of the third–second century BC) appears, as a bearded sage, making a man not as a sculptor carves a form out of stone, but building it up from a skeleton. Again we are reminded of Frankenstein who "to examine the causes of life" finds that "we must have recourse to death", and seeks the components of his creation in charnel-houses. It is not so much that Prometheus is to be thought of as the original teacher of anatomy, and that Mary Shelley knew as much, as that analytical reason necessarily acts in this way : the human form in dissection is an emblem of analysis in general as readily available to the modern as to the ancient imagination.

An interesting suggestion by the latest editor of *Frankenstein* points to a specific source in which Mary might have come across references to Prometheus as maker of man. These occur in the writings of Shaftesbury. In his *Advice to an Author* (1710) Shaftesbury calls the poet "a second *Maker,* a just Prometheus". In *The Moralists* (1709) references occur in a number of places, and seem to indicate a direct connection with ideas in *Frankenstein*. At one point Shaftesbury, following the Latin writers, speaks of Prometheus as the original creator of mankind, blameable therefore for man's imperfections:

> . . . who with thy stol'n Celestial Fire, mix'd with vile Clay, dids't mock Heaven's Countenance, and in abusive Likeness of the Immortals, mad'st the Compound Man; that wretched Mortal, *ill* to himself, and Cause of *Ill* to all.

Later he turns this proposition back on itself in discussing the ancients' treatment of the problem of evil—"They fairly made Jove a Stander-by"—pointing out that the question of divine responsibility is by no means solved thereby:

> For the Gods . . . either cou'd have hinder'd Prometheus's Creation, or they cou'd not. If they cou'd, they were answerable for the Consequences, if they cou'd not, they were no longer Gods being thus limited and controul'd. And whether Prometheus were a Name for *Chance, Destiny,* a *Plastick Nature,* or an *Evil Daemon*; whatever was design'd by it; 'twas still the same Breach of Omnipotence.

The actual phrase, modern Prometheus, occurs in speaking of "our modern Prometheus's, *the Mountebanks,* who perform'd such Wonders of many kinds, here on our earthly Stages". Here again the reference is rather to artistic than scientific creation; but a nearby passage makes a direct link with scientific or at least alchemical discovery:

> We have a strange Fancy to be Creators, a violent Desire at least to know the Knack or Secret by which Nature does all. The rest of our Philosophers only aim at that in Speculation,

which our Alchymists aspire to in Practice. For with some of these it has been actually under deliberation how to make Man, by other Mediums than Nature has provided.

Mary's record of her reading in her *Journal* makes no mention of Shaftesbury, but several years later she referred in a letter to the *Characteristicks* as a familiar work.[4] It is extremely tempting to think that these highly suggestive passages were known to her in 1816, either in her own reading or through Shelley's. But there is no need to suppose a single, or any specific literary source. As Shelley was to remark a little later, "a certain similarity all the best writers of any particular age are marked with, from the spirit of that age working upon all".[5] The spirit of the age may include certain images: the idea of Prometheus was in the air.[6]

Mary may or may not, again, have known Goethe's poem *Prometheus*: at this time, as we have seen, both she and Shelley were confined to reading German in translation; Shelley's own version of parts of *Faust* comes later and neither may actually have read *Faust* or much else of Goethe by 1816. They are likely, however, to have heard not only about the play but also of the poem. In the same way they may well have known of Beethoven's Promethean ballet, performed at Vienna in 1801, which from its title, *The Creatures of Prometheus*—all that remains of whatever story the music illustrated—must presumably have dealt with *Prometheus Plasticator*. But where Mary must have heard Promethean themes discussed was at Diodati itself, in the talk of Byron and Shelley. The part of her *Journal* in which these conversations may have been recorded has unfortunately not survived. But they must have been extraordinary, and extraordinarily enthralling for such a young woman as Mary: more continuous and free, probably, than at any subsequent time in the uneasy relationship of Shelley and Byron, the rivalry of which they were both aware, even while denying it, being still not inhibition but stimulus.

Byron, having just exiled himself from England, and enjoying the double sensation of freedom from restraint and luxurious remorse which served to produce his characteristic poetic impulse, was writing at full flood, working on the continuation of *Childe Harold* and *The Prisoner of Chillon*, and producing various occasional pieces besides. As the third canto of *Childe Harold* proceeded he read or showed parts of it to other members of the party, "clothed" as Mary said, "in all the light of harmony and poetry", and also well touched with local colour. The mountain scenery, the trips on the lake, the thunderstorms —including the interesting simile, in an apostrophe to Rousseau, of "a tree/ On fire by lightning", both "kindled" and "blasted"/, an impressive phenomenon also mentioned, as we have seen, in *Frankenstein*—all figure largely in this section of the poem. There is one direct Promethean echo here, rather grotesquely attached to thoughts on Voltaire and Gibbon :

> Mortals, who sought and found, by dangerous roads
> A path to perpetuity of fame :
> They were gigantic minds, and their steep aim
> Was, Titan-like, on daring doubts to pile
> Thoughts which should call down thunder, and the flame
> Of Heaven. . . .

There is also, of course, the poem *Prometheus* itself, dated "Diodati, July 1816", a fairly ordinary exercise in what we have come to think of as the Byronic attitude—

> The rock, the vulture, and the chain,
> All that the proud can feel of pain,
> The agony they do not show—

but proof that the subject was in his mind. Some of the suggestions, or counter-suggestions in it turn up in Shelley's *Prometheus Unbound*. But the principal source of these—of elements, that is to say, in Byron's work which provoked Shelley to answer —and at the same time of parallels with *Frankenstein*, is in *Manfred*, which was begun in Switzerland the same summer.

Byron himself had ambiguous feelings about this "drama"— which, as he hastened to point out at the same time, was "*quite impossible* for the stage".[7] In the same and subsequent letters to John Murray concerning the poem he describes it as "of a very wild, metaphysical, and inexplicable kind" and repeats more than once that he has "really . . . no notion whether it is good or bad". Clearly it had some special associations for him. The semi-jocular hints in which he spoke of it to Murray—"the hero [is] a kind of magician, who is haunted by a species of remorse, the cause of which is left half-explained"—may be taken as Byronic flirtation with personal revelation. What these private associations were—they seem to have had to do with his half-sister Augusta, and have been guessed at as bearing on the "incest" theory—belongs to Byron biography and need not concern us here. But the Promethean character of *Manfred* is of present interest.

Manfred, the doomed hero, haunting the "Higher Alps", either in his castle or on the mountain-tops themselves, partakes in some degree of Goethe's Faust—elemental spirits are at his beck and call in much the same way—and also of Milton's Satan, the prototype of all these heaven-defying figures, but most, and without contradiction, of Prometheus. He meditates at the beginning how

> Philosophy and science, and the springs
> Of wonder, and the wisdom of the world,
> I have essay'd, and in my mind there is
> A power to make these subject to itself—

and also how he has "done man good". He has sought "conclusions most forbidden" in "the caves of death" (seeking, exactly like Frankenstein, "its cause in its effect" and, like him drawing "From wither'd bones, and skulls, and heap'd up dust,/ Conclusions most forbidden"). He has studied "sciences untaught,/ Save in the old time"; in his youth, he tells the Abbot who tries in vain to save him, he has had "noble aspirations . . . To make my own the mind of other men,/ The enlightener of nations; and to rise/ I knew not whither . . ." Here again he speaks in almost the same words as Frankenstein in the intoxication of his first discovery.

He has also, however, found that "The Tree of Knowledge is not that of Life" and ".   science/ But an exchange of

ignorance for that/ Which is another kind of ignorance". Consequently he now looks for oblivion or death, but cannot die
until the end of the poem, when "a dusk and awful figure"
"like an infernal dog"—a hybrid of Goethe's and Marlowe's
Mephistopheles—comes to drag him away. Even then, it is not
the Devil who takes him, but he himself who casts himself away
—he will, he declares, be "my own destroyer, and . . . My own
hereafter" : he has no prospect of forgetfulness. He is baffled,
in fact, by his own powers : when he calls up the spirits at the
beginning he boasts himself their equal, if not actually their
master :

> . . . Slaves, scoff not at my will !
> The mind, the spirit, the Promethean spark,
> The lightning of my being, is as bright,
> Pervading, and far darting as your own. . . .

The last quotation is the only point in the poem where Prometheus is named; but Byron owned, again in a letter to Murray,
that the legend was in the background : "The *Prometheus* [of
Aeschylus] if not exactly in my plan, has always been so much
in my head that I can easily conceive its influence over all or
anything that I have written."

Manfred was only begun in Switzerland, and was not finished
until early in 1817; whether any of it was shown to the others
at Diodati we don't know. It seems almost as likely that first
drafts of *Frankenstein* influenced the poem as the other way
about. What seems reasonably certain in any case is that the
subjects and feelings that play so important a part in both—
the search for "forbidden" knowledge, the lofty aspirations, and
consequent downfall—will have been talked about that summer;
and talked about, perhaps, not only in abstract speculation but
in association with personal affairs. For all the young men and
women who met at Diodati the expedition was, as has already
been indicated, an escape : for the two poets especially, each
leaving behind a rejected marriage, both hounded in greater or
lesser degree by private and public opinion at home, it must
have seemed so.

The flight to a warmer and outwardly more tolerant climate, a more exuberant spring, was for both a liberation. It was not altogether an escape, of course. Shelley's cares pursued him, if not in other form, in letters from London concerning his precarious finances which cast them (as Mary recorded in the *Journal*) into "very bad spirits".[8] Byron found himself spied on by English visitors and, more vexatiously, haunted by Claire Clairmont, determined to re-attach herself to him and already pregnant by him. The past might be dismissed in words, his marriage already written off ("And here's exactly what 'tis worth", he wrote in the *Endorsement to the Deed of Separation*) but could scarcely be exorcised.

The weather broke. In the brilliant sunshine of May it was easy, perhaps, to think of the marvellous daylight that Mary's Arctic explorer hoped to find made eternal at the Pole—and which turns up as a simile of youthful beauty in *The Prisoner of Chillon*, "A polar day, which will not see / A sunset till its summer's gone". But that poem was written, in June, 1816, after the sun had gone, and is pervaded, of course, with dark and damp. It was followed a little later by the transcription of "a dream which was not all a dream" dated at Diodati that July, and subsequently given the title *Darkness*. This vision of universal desolation following the extinction of the sun—the earth left without light and abandoned to chaos, destruction, and decay—is one of the most concentratedly black pieces Byron ever wrote : inspissated gloom indeed. The effects of entropy imagined therein are strongly reminiscent of Mary's own full-length picture of world disaster, *The Last Man,* written many years later; she may well have picked up suggestions from it. But the point is rather that the poem expresses some of the feelings of the time, feelings which Mary must certainly have been aware of, could very well understand and even, though for reasons of her own, partake of.

In this poem, the sun being extinguished, creation is reversed. Fire, the Promethean element, is used for a time, adding to the general destruction, until it gives out; men starve and perish merely at the sight of each other—"Even of their mutual hideousness they died"—and the earth is finally empty and formless as it was in the beginning.

> ... The world was void,
> The populous and the powerful was a lump,
> Seasonless, herbless, treeless, manless, lifeless—
> A lump of death—a chaos of hard clay.

A "lump of death", of clay, is a man either before he is fired with life or after the spirit has fled, according to the point of view. Frankenstein's Monster, the "filthy mass that moves and talks", combines the two : shows a further stage in the feelings from which such images naturally arise, and finds a new and potent form for them. There is no need, again, to suppose a direct relationship between the poetry Byron was producing at this time and the novel; it is rather that in him then and there, as the poems bear subsequent witness, there was a compendious exhibition, almost a caricature, of attitudes that contributed to it. Byron was not in his person the primary source, as we shall see. But he was certainly important as, so to speak, part of the background : almost a conventionally neces- sary component of the Romantic paraphernalia so abundantly provided, from the grotesque extreme of "Monk" Lewis and his ghost stories in one direction to the sublime of the sunlit or tempestuous lake, the thunderstorms, the towering actual pre- sence of Mont Blanc in the other.

Part of the furniture was Miltonic, by association with Dio- dati itself; and Milton himself, standing formidably at the back of all the Romantics, must be the next taken into account. His influence is extensive and acknowledged by Mary, Miltonic references occurring repeatedly through the novel, and Miltonic examples being followed, with many permutations, in the development of its moral drama. The originals were fresh in Mary's mind as she wrote. Her book-list gives *Paradise Regain'd* as read in 1815, and in 1816 she and Shelley were both reading *Paradise Lost* at intervals through the year. One entry in the *Journal* (for 20 August, shortly before their return to England) notes that "Shelley and I talk about my story"; after their return, when the terse entry "write" refers to continuing work on the novel on days in succession, Shelley read *Paradise Lost* aloud to her, finishing the whole poem in a week between 15 and 22 November.

It may indeed be said that Mary had as intensive a course in Milton as the Monster himself when, having taught himself to read, he rapidly acquired a world-view and general outline of human nature and history ready-made from *Werther*, Plutarch's *Lives*, and *Paradise Lost*, so conveniently picked up in somebody's portmanteau. The effects are fully transmitted. The first two of these books, the Monster says, moved him in different ways, *Werther* producing sympathetic grief ("I wept, without precisely understanding it", a neat criticism) and thoughts of suicide, Plutarch elevating him again with heroic examples. " 'But *Paradise Lost* excited different and far deeper emotions' " he says, causing him to refer " 'the several situations, as their similarity struck me, to my own.' " " 'Like Adam'," he reflects, " 'I was apparently united by no link to any other being in existence'," but unlike him, under the love and care of his Creator and provided with a mate, " 'I was wretched, helpless, and alone.' "

Presently he discovers another and, he thinks, closer parallel: " 'Many times I considered Satan as the fitter emblem of my condition; for often, like him . . . the bitter gall of envy rose within me.' " It is at this point that, being now literate, he deciphers Frankenstein's own papers that he has brought along with him, and learns not only how he was made, but Frankenstein's disgust with his own handiwork : " 'the minutest description of my odious and loathsome person is given, in language which painted your own horrors, and rendered mine indelible.' "

The Monster as a parody of Adam, and Frankenstein as parody of God are here openly proposed. But the uses of Miltonic-Scriptural machinery do not end there. *Paradise Lost* is, of course, the great guide-book of spiritual rebellion, repeated in various forms, human and Satanic. The powerful attractions of the rebellious Satan were keenly felt by Shelley, who ascribed to him not only the "grandeur and energy" undoubtedly due to the most interesting character in *Paradise Lost,* but moral superiority to God :

> . . . as far superior . . . as one who perseveres in some purpose which he has conceived to be excellent, in spite of adversity and torture, is to one who in the cold security of undoubted triumph inflicts the most horrible revenge on his enemy—not from any mistaken notion of bringing him to repent of a perseverance in enmity but with the open and alleged design of exasperating him to deserve new torments.[9]

Shelley here, and again later in the *Defence of Poetry,* in which he speaks of Milton's Satan in the same words, was saying no more than was, and is, the common observation of most readers of *Paradise Lost,* that, as Blake put it, "Milton was of the Devil's party without knowing it". There is no evidence that Shelley knew *The Marriage of Heaven and Hell* or indeed anything at all of Blake but his conclusion was here, at any rate, the same, that Milton's partiality for Satan was the very sign that he was "a true poet". But for Shelley this partiality was conscious and based on clear-cut moral distinctions : a simple reversal, in fact, of moral virtue between God and the Devil, which does Milton less justice, perhaps, than did Blake. For Shelley it was simple : Satan, the justified rebel, was virtuous, God the tyrant was evil. But the moral ambiguity was restored by Mary.

The epigraph to the original edition of *Frankenstein* was taken from Book X of *Paradise Lost*; Adam's expostulation to God :

> Did I request thee, Maker, from my clay
> To mould me Man, did I solicit thee
> From darkness to promote me—?

The Monster is thus identified from the start, it seems, with Milton's Adam, a bad copy of the first man—although, as Frankenstein says, he, like God, "had selected his features as beautiful". The result is quite different, but clearly related to the original : instead of "fair large Front and Eye sublime", the

59

Monster's "yellow skin scarcely covered the work of muscles and arteries beneath"; his hair, "of a lustrous black, and flowing", might be like Adam's "hyacinthine locks", his teeth "of a pearly whiteness" but "these luxuriances only formed a more horrid contrast with his watery eyes . . . his shrivelled complexion and straight black lips". The same distorted equivalence continues when the Monster, in his glacier-meeting with Frankenstein, gives like Adam an account of his first awakening: apologising in advance and in almost exactly the same terms, for the uncertainty of his memory: " 'It is with considerable difficulty that I remember the original era of my being: all the events of that period appear confused and indistinct.' " (As Adam explains to Raphael, "For Man to tell how human Life began/ Is hard; for who himself beginning knew?")

But instead of coming to life in the unsullied environment of Eden, where "all things smiled", the Monster wakes in a charnel-house and finds even his first sensations painful, the darkness troubling, the light oppressive, hunger and thirst a torment. The world into which he wanders, though it affords some of the same facilities as Paradise (" 'I ate some berries which I found hanging on the trees, or lying on the ground. I slaked my thirst at the brook' ") is for the most part unpleasant and bewildering. Without his maker to instruct him as God instructs Adam he understands nothing and, a crucial difference, has no God-given language. In Adam's case, though "who I was, or where, or from what cause" he does not know, he has only to attempt speech "and forthwith spake", naming everything in sight. In the Monster's, Frankenstein has already described his apparition at the bedside, how he could only mutter "inarticulate sounds", although trying to communicate. He does not know the name of anything, and can hardly be said to think (" 'No distinct ideas occupied my mind; all was confused' "). When he comes in contact for any length of time with human beings (the family in the cottage next to which he hides himself) he doesn't know what they are saying and has to teach himself language by careful listening; with the fortunate circumstance, it is true, that one of the cottagers is herself learning from another. The whole cottage episode is in fact inserted in order that the Monster should learn speech, letters, and the rudiments of human culture *without being taught*, either by a human or a divine agency: nothing, and it is essential to the story that it should so be, is allowed to break his isolation.

Much of this business is simply in accordance with the principle already mentioned, that events however extraordinary should have a "natural" explanation. But Mary's adherence to this rule was less the negative one, of excluding "supernatural" mechanisms by no matter what improbabilities, than the positive one of "delineating . . . human passions", as Shelley said, according to "the elementary principles of human nature". It was necessary for her plot that the Monster should learn to speak and read; but it was necessary much more fundamentally for her purpose that he should do so without a teacher.

One can see at work here the speculation, much indulged in by men of Enlightenment, what would be the effects upon a human being of complete severance from human society from infancy: would a child thus cut off learn to talk at all, would he speak (as Lord Monboddo supposed) the "language of our first parents", what would his behaviour be? Mary's Monster, though full-grown—or rather, a ready-made adult—is in the situation of Monboddo's child, and her answer is the reasonable one, that child or man so deprived of the normal means of learning will be quite inarticulate. But the Monster's education also demonstrates (and here Mary showed her grasp of processes and capabilities which modern learning theory is only now returning to recognise) that even without any of the ordinary, and necessary circumstances of "socialisation", a human being, born or made, has innate potentialities that allow him to make use of them far beyond mechanically rational expectation. The Monster cannot learn speech without hearing others speak, he cannot read without at least indirect instruction, but he has a "natural" aptitude, even though an artificial creature, which enables him to pick up these human accomplishments with extraordinary rapidity. Thought, one may say, was already present in him, though confused, and logical deduction (learning about fire) was possible for him before language, which expresses but does not originate it, was available to him. The Monster's feats of learning are extra-ordinary, or far-fetched; but seem less so to anyone who seriously thinks (as Mary may well have thought, watching her baby son exploring and learning about his world) what it is for an infant to learn speech, not as one may acquire another language, but as an absolute beginner.

The Monster, however ill-made, has the potentialities of a child, though starting off, like Adam, fully-grown; and one of Mary's more obvious aims was to show, in accordance with quite un-Miltonic views—those rather of Rousseau, and even more of her father, William Godwin—that an Adam without any of the advantages of the original, and without direct in-spiration from God or anywhere else except his own nature, was nevertheless capable of happiness and virtue. Though a monstrosity, something worse than a *lusus naturae*, he has an inbuilt affinity with the natural world : even in his wholly un-enlightened state, knowing nothing of himself or his surround-ings, he feels pleasure at the sight of the rising moon, though he doesn't know what it is; he listens, again with pleasure, to the song of the birds; and he is immediately attracted by the first human beings he sees, though rejected by them.

Like the ethologist's duckling he is primed for attachment; but being a conspicuously Ugly Duckling is spurned from the beginning. His longing for society and "sympathy" and his deprivation of them are main themes of the story, of which more will be said. The point at the moment is the Monster's potentiality as a new, completely uninstructed being who not only shows remarkable resource and intelligence, but has a "feeling heart". He responds at once to the music played by the inhabitants of the cottage, and to the spectacle of their mutual affection; the girl listening to her father was, he says, " 'a lovely sight, even to me, poor wretch! who had never beheld aught beautiful before' ", and the emotion they show powerfully affects him. The girl weeps and the father smiles on her and comforts her, whereupon the Monster watching from his hiding place feels " 'sensations of a peculiar and overpowering nature: they were a mixture of pain and pleasure, such as I had never

62

before experienced, either from hunger or cold, warmth or food' ".

He feels them moreover before he can put words to them; it is only later, after learning a collection of nouns and proper names, that he begins to grasp at abstractions: " 'I distinguished several other words, without being able as yet to understand or apply them; such as *good, dearest, unhappy*'." He grows, though still in hiding, to "love and reverence" his "protectors", as, pathetically, " 'in an innocent, half-painful self-deceit' ", he likes to call them. He is like a lonely child creating an ideal fantasy-family for himself; alternatively, he is in the happy state of pre-lapsarian Adam: " 'My spirits were elevated by the enchanting appearance of nature; the past was blotted from my memory, the present was tranquil, and the future gilded by bright rays of hope and anticipation of joy'."

What goes wrong? Superficially, of course, it is simply a matter of bad luck and misunderstanding. The Monster schemes to ingratiate himself with the cottagers by speaking first to the old man who, as well as being gentle and benevolent, is blind and therefore won't know him as a monster. But just when he is about to reveal his identity and throw himself on the old man's mercy, the others return, think that he is attacking their father, and drive him out; shortly afterwards, in fear and disgust they leave the place and the Monster never sees them again. From this time things go from bad to worse for him, he is rejected on all sides, fled from, shot at, and so he becomes by degrees what the others have taken him for, a malignant outcast.

" 'I was benevolent and good'," he says to Frankenstein on the glacier; " 'misery made me a fiend. Make me happy and I shall again be virtuous'." The same Godwinian formula appears at other points, and was naturally singled out by Shelley himself as the chief moral of the story: the crimes of the Monster, he said in his first appreciation of the book, were not due to "any unaccountable propensity to evil, but flow irresistibly from certain causes fully adequate to their production . . . Treat a person ill and he will become wicked."[10] Shelley did not inquire why it should be necessary to invent a Monster to demonstrate

ARIEL LIKE A HARPY

this—"perhaps the most important and of the most universal application of any moral than can be enforced by example"— nor what the implications were for the character of those who so ill-treated him. Writing as a confirmed Godwinian he was disinclined to push his analysis so far. For the interdependence of virtue and happiness are only a small part of the moral structure of *Frankenstein*, which deals in uncertainties much more difficult to resolve than any to be found in Godwin or, for that matter, in Milton.

It has already been seen how the Monster, reading *Paradise Lost* and discovering parallels, likens himself not only to Adam but to Satan; a little later he reverts to this when he finds out that Frankenstein himself had found his own handiwork not, as God did, good, but revolting. " 'Accursed creator! Why did you form a monster so hideous that even you turned from me in disgust? God, in pity, made man beautiful and alluring, after his own image; but my form is a filthy type of yours, more horrid even from the very resemblance. Satan had his companions, fellow-devils, to admire and encourage him; but I am solitary and abhorred.' " The Monster is worse off than Adam, exiled from the start, and he is also a Satan, but more wretched than Milton's, who not only had his hellish host to support him, described by Milton in such grandiose terms, but was conscious also of belonging in some way, even though a rebel, within God's universe. The Monster belongs nowhere and to nobody. As the story progresses so he becomes progressively more Satanic, his powers growing to positively fiendish capacity (he is alluded to more often as "the Fiend" in the later part of the book) and his ill deeds multiplying accordingly, but also taking on some of the Luciferian majesty so striking in Milton's Satan. In his second confrontation with Frankenstein, in Orkney, he addresses him as "slave"—" 'You are my creator, but I am your master' ", and threatens him: " 'Beware; for I am fearless, and therefore powerful. I will watch with the wiliness of a snake, that I may sting with its vemon'." Not surprisingly, Frankenstein in reply calls him simply "Devil".

And at the end, Monster-Adam has become quite explicitly Monster-Satan. He speaks of his last murder and act of revenge, and says, " 'then I was not miserable. I had cast off all feeling, subdued all anguish, to riot in the excess of my despair. Evil henceforth became my good.' " ("So farewell Hope, and with Hope farewell Fear,/ Farewell Remorse: all Good to me is lost;/ Evil be thou my Good," says Milton's Satan.) The Monster is now exactly like Satan remembering his once angelic status, but unable to comprehend it: " 'I cannot believe,' " he says, " 'that I am the same creature whose thoughts were once filled with sublime and transcendant visions of the beauty and majesty of goodness. But it is even so: the fallen angel becomes a malignant devil.'

The last sentence touches the centre of the whole theme; but there is some distance to go before we can hope to see what, if more than a commonplace of mythological moralising, it signifies in the Monster's history. It may be observed now that not only the Monster is a fallen angel: so is Frankenstein. He is so by definition, if we allow Prometheus to be identified in some respects with Lucifer. His attributes and aspirations are angelic: he is extraordinarily gifted, the particular darling of his family, even in ruin described (by Walton, after his death) as a "glorious spirit". He is "reserved" to discover the "astonishing secret" of the generation of life, and himself expresses surprise that he should be so singled out; but such humility soon gives way to unlimited ambition—" 'I will pioneer a new way, explore unknown powers, and unfold to the world the deepest mysteries of creation.' " In his discovery of the "secret" (which means in effect that he has eaten the fruit not only of the Tree of Knowledge, but the Tree of Life as well) he is exalted: " 'Life and death appeared to me ideal bounds, which I should first break through, and pour a torrent of light into our dark world' "; he speaks at this point like Prometheus indeed.

But he is brought low, to remorse, despair, and death, and again the question may be asked, What went wrong? Within the Godwinian scheme, though it may be made to account for the Monster's depravity, it is extremely difficult to answer. Frankenstein has suffered no deprivation, on the contrary he has been doted on, and his upbringing by parents equally loving and judicious, in an atmosphere uniformly high-minded,

3—ALAH * *

approaches the Rousseau-Godwin ideal. He certainly cannot
say that he is wicked because he has been ill-treated : nor does
he. Neither he nor any of the various commentators on his fate
in the novel considers that he is wicked at all. Calamity nevertheless overtakes him, and he is at least enough conscious of the
moral mechanisms at work to believe that he has brought them
on himself. Yet though he may be blamed, and does indeed
blame himself, it is not the sort of blame which carries with it
any moral reproach, for of course he never intends evil; his is a
perfect instance of a well-paved road to hell.

There is a puzzle here, proverbially described but not elucidated : why *should* good intentions lead to hell? Neither the
moral schemes of Milton nor Godwin can solve it; in Godwin's
case it is simply denied, in Milton's avoided, for Satan, however
noble, does not have good intentions. Mary Shelley did not
"solve" it either, for it is of course the sort of puzzle incapable
of solution by any formula. Mary was not a one for formulas
and made no attempts in that direction, but on the other hand
she did not avoid the puzzle; as does the proverb, she described
it. In place of Milton's rigid and brilliant categories, of Satan
and God Almighty, embattled forces locked in everlasting conflict and eternally separate, Mary introduced what looks like a
moral confusion. The Monster has potentialities for good but
becomes satanic; his maker is perfectly good—or at any rate
has no reason not to be—but produces evil. Neither has a
monopoly of angel—or devil—identification : they share both,
exchange them, and transform them. *Paradise Lost*, for all its
stupendous action, is a static drama; whether one is "of the
Devil's party" or not, it is impossible to see it otherwise. Satan
is fixed in his damnation from the beginning, and his rage is in
fact a striving against these negative swaddling-bands. Mary
breaks out of this bondage to immutable categories; indeed she
shows, though she does not explain it, that such segregation
of moral attributes produces reversals and catastrophes so
thoroughly paradoxical that evil may at least appear to grow
from good.

There is naturally no need to suppose that Mary Shelley set
out, in writing *Frankenstein*, to embody in it a critique of

Paradise Lost. It was simply present, thanks to her reading and Shelley's, as one of the cluster of suggestions bearing upon her germinal idea, and how Milton's imagination seemed to her own, and how hers reacted to it were no more than functions of that idea. Her perceptions were not theoretical, but intensely personal : it is the contact made between her personal insight and such very general ones as are contained in the Miltonic cosmology and theodicy—as well as others as remote from her personal concerns—that gives her work its peculiar force. Where her personal concerns were involved we shall try to understand; but first there are other literary influences to be examined, closer and more directly affecting her habits of thought.

FOUR

GODWIN AND GODWINISM

FRANKENSTEIN IS DEDICATED to "William God-
win, author of *Political Justice, Caleb Williams,* etc". The
book thus declares itself (as the *Quarterly* remarked, disparag-
ingly) to be "of his school", and was assumed to be by the
most fervent of his disciples, Shelley. His daughter was not
his disciple in the same sense, but she was certainly not less
influenced by him, in her opinions and also in the many less
obvious ways in which a father can, heredity aside, touch and
enter into the character and outlook of a devoted daughter.
Mary was deeply devoted to her father, although he, a remote
parent—partly on principle, partly from pure selfishness, the
two going conveniently together—had little to do with her
upbringing. Immediately after her birth and her mother's
death he was writing, concerning Mary and her three-year-
old half-sister Fanny, ". . . the poor children! I am myself
totally unfitted to educate them. The scepticism which perhaps
sometimes leads me right in matters of speculation, is torment
to me when I would attempt to direct the infant mind. I
am the most unfit person for this office; she [Mary Wollstone-
craft] was the best qualified in the world. . . ."[1] Godwin's
genuine grief at the death of his wife might have accounted for
this feeling of helplessness, but it was, or became, a settled
habit. After a short time during which Mary and Fanny were
looked after by a succession of friends, Godwin married again
(in 1801) and their care passed to their stepmother, who, if not
entirely the stepmother of tradition, never had either Mary's
love or respect. Her childhood was by no means altogether
unhappy, but must have been full of much strain and conflict.
Godwin seems to have done little to interfere, except in
making arrangements for Mary to live away from home, for

68

the sake of her health, for which he was solicitous, and also perhaps because he felt unable to age with her. By the time she was nearly fifteen he was sending her off to live with Scottish friends, the Baxters, in Dundee, a curious letter to William Baxter serving as introduction and explanation :

> There never can be perfect equality between father and child, and if he has other objects and avocations to fill up the greater part of his time, the ordinary resource is for him to proclaim his wishes and commands in a way somewhat sententious and authoritative, and occasionally to utter his censures with seriousness and emphasis.
> It can, therefore, seldom happen that he is the confidant of his child, or that the child does not feel some degree of awe or restraint in intercourse with him. I am not, therefore, a perfect judge of Mary's character. I believe she has nothing of what is commonly called vice, and that she has considerable talent . . . I am anxious that she should be brought up in this respect like a philosopher, even like a cynic. It will add greatly to the strength and worth of her character. . . I wish, too, that she should be *excited* to industry. She has occasionally great perseverance, but occasionally, too, she shows great need to be roused. . . .[2]

This letter provides the best account we have of Mary as a child, more reliable at least than the prognostications of the physiognomist already quoted. It is interesting to see that whatever the fanciful Mr Nicholson may have expected of the baby Mary's "persistence in research", by the time she was in her teens she was already showing the perseverance that, both as a writer and in life, she could call on thereafter. In a shorter letter to an unknown correspondent, written a little later, Godwin called her perseverance "invincible" : a quality he liked to attribute to the human mind at its most heroic. It is also interesting to see that she needed "rousing", and credit must be given to her father at least for noticing it and worrying about it. It is possible of course that he was really talking about himself : he said almost exactly the same thing about his own mentality in referring to the influence upon him of

Thomas Holcroft : "My mind, though fraught with sensibility and occasionally ardent and enthusiastic, is perhaps in its genuine habits too tranquil and unimpassioned for successful composition, and stands greatly in need of stimulus and excitement."[3] It was perhaps a hereditary trait, which in Mary, reinforced by the unhappiness and loneliness of much of her childhood, emerged in a tendency to depression.

The most striking thing about Godwin's letter to Baxter, however, is its acceptance—though owning to "a thousand anxieties in parting"—of the distance between parent and child; which was, indeed, a matter of principle. It was perfectly consistent with his views, expressed in *Political Justice* and elsewhere, that the upbringing of children was not necessarily the job of parents. Like most rationalists of his time he regarded infants as mere parcels, to be handed from one person to another without adverse effect : "The mature man seldom retains the faintest recollection of the incidents of the two first years of his life. Is it to be supposed that that which has left no trace upon the memory can be in any eminent degree powerful in its associated effects?"[4]

In an ideal state infants would "probably", but not necessarily be cared for by their mothers, and their support would be communal—"supplies . . . will spontaneously flow, from the quarter in which they abound, to the quarter that is deficient." Education in any formal sense, or by particular persons, will cease : "No creature in human form will be expected to learn anything, but because he desires it, and has some conception of its value; and every man, in proportion to his capacity, will be ready to furnish such general hints and comprehensive views, as will suffice for the guidance and encouragement of him who studies from the impulse of desire." These principles seem not a bad foundation for a free and enlightened upbringing, and it may be said that Mary, left largely to pursue the knowledge she desired and thought valuable, made good enough use of her capacities. But they do also reflect the peculiar detachment from personal responsibility of Godwin and Godwinism, in which "Justice" was elevated to a kind of self-acting regulator of behaviour, scarcely demanding the active participation of anyone. General hints and comprehensive views, though doubtless useful, are a poor substitute for the close attention which is a sign of love.

Godwin's extraordinary detachment from other people (which did not, of course preclude his acceptance of their aid, as, notoriously, in the case of Shelley) undoubtedly helped him to the lofty impartiality and originality in considering moral questions which gives *Political Justice* its uncommon force. It must have made him a most inadequate father, but it did not lessen Mary's strong and, it may be said, passionate feeling for him—a feeling to be expected, in any case, in a motherless girl. That Mary suffered to some extent what would now be called a father-fixation is not surprising : it is more surprising, perhaps, that it did not affect her more, or more cripplingly interfere in her relations with other men. In later years she could herself be somewhat detached about her father, though affectionate ("poor old fellow", she calls him) and protective—Shelley while he lived and she afterwards were the old man's principal support. She was deeply affected by his death : but had been able shortly beforehand to speak of her feelings towards him with insight—"my excessive and romantic attachment to my Father".[5]

To his cool regard she brought her enterprises, hoping for his approval, and, even after long experience, her personal griefs : the relations between them, at any rate after her marriage to Shelley and settlement in Italy—where Godwin's communications reached them chiefly in the form of requests for money—are well illustrated by a letter from him in 1818, on learning of the death of her baby daughter Clara :

I sincerely sympathise with you in the reflections which form the subject of your letter, and which I may consider as the first severe trial of your constancy and the firmness of your temper that has occurred to you in the course of your life; you should, however, recollect that it is only persons of a very ordinary sort, and of a pusillanimous disposition, that sink long under a calamity of this nature. We seldom indulge long in depression and mourning except when we think secretly that there is something very refined in it, and that it does us honour.[6]

That Mary was indeed severely depressed at this time can be seen in her own letters and *Journal*. She continued, even after the response just quoted, to write to her father and to receive letters from him; though a little later, seeing how much she was affected by them, full of his own distresses, Shelley asked Godwin to write no more.

In writing *Frankenstein* Mary was opening her mental life for the first time to general view. As a child (she says, in her Introduction to the 1831 edition) she wrote stories and even more indulged in "waking dreams", the natural habit of an imaginative and lonely child "following up trains of thought, which had for their subject the formation of a succession of imaginary incidents. My dreams were at once more fantastic and agreeable than my writings." Her writings, she goes on to say, were "intended at least for one other eye—my childhood's companion and friend; but my dreams were all my own; I accounted for them to nobody; they were my refuge when annoyed—my dearest pleasure when free." It is a reasonable assumption that she did not tell her day-dreams to her father, or even show him what she wrote down. *Frankenstein* must have had something of the quality of a declaration, to the world in general, and to some persons in particular : in it, her first serious literary undertaking, Mary was possibly as eager for her father's approval as Shelley's—the hope of both combining with her own exacting internal standards to drive her on. ("To be something great and good was the precept given me by my Father," she wrote many years later in her Journal; "Shelley reiterated it"—and *Frankenstein* was the first public attempt to live up to it.)

That it should be a Godwinian book she must have wished, worthy of him and also of the idealised mother she never knew. Some of the reflections of Godwin's ideas in the character of the Monster have already been noted, and some other echoes of *Political Justice* in particular may be added. Godwin's educational notions, and his general view, at that time (he was later to modify it) that education determines character can be seen in the unhappy effects of the Monster's "upbringing", as again quite simply his succinct statement that "hate engenders hatred".[6] Godwinian precepts in education turn up elsewhere, in the oddly assorted family in which Frankenstein grows up, and especially in the adoption and upbringing of his "cousin" and future bride, the foster-child Elizabeth.

It is of course a common romantic device, an acceptably disguised form of brother-sister incest which can be found in many other places (notably in Shelley's own works); in the original edition of the novel Elizabeth is actually Frankenstein's cousin, but this was altered in the 1831 edition in which she becomes a foster-sister, though still addressed as "cousin". Her adoption can also be seen as a strong, though it may be thought rather forced effort to put into practice the Godwinian dictum, "It is of no consequence that I am the parent of a child, when it has been ascertained that the child will live with greater benefit under the superintendence of a stranger".[8] Elizabeth is not unlike Mary herself, fair of face, the daughter of "a Milanese nobleman" imprisoned for revolutionary activities and of a mother who dies at birth. She is in the care of a Swiss peasant family, but is adopted by Frankenstein's mother, her "rustic guardians" reflecting that though she is "a blessing" to them, "it would be unfair to her to keep her in poverty and want, when Providence afforded her such powerful protection".

Her upbringing by the Frankenstein family is described with a somewhat strained emphasis on its felicity (the young Frankenstein is told that the new child in the house is a "present", as has many a child in an attempt to forestall jealousy; he takes it literally, from then on looking on Elizabeth as "mine—mine to protect, love, and cherish"). They grow up together in perfect harmony—"I need not say that we were strangers to any species of disunion or dispute." It is curious to think of this transaction against the background of Mary's own childhood among half- and step-sister and brothers, or in a quite unrelated family; also to think of Shelley's wild schemes for adopting children at Oxford, and of the harshly ironic way the children of his first marriage were taken from him, for their own good. Neither Shelley nor so far as one knows anyone else quoted Godwin during the Chancery case which placed them to "live with greater benefit under the superintendence of a stranger".

The effects on Frankenstein of a complete Godwinian education, and on the Monster of the lack of it are equally disastrous; it may be that the Monster's fate illustrates the maxim in *Political Justice* that "a slave and a serf are condemned to stupidity and vice, as well as to calamity", but the converse, that a firm mind having the benefit of good example and fortified by virtue and truth, can endure adversity and "look down with pity on my tyrant", is certainly not borne out by Frankenstein's behaviour. But this sort of sentiment, which shows Godwin at his most platitudinous, is not in truth what Mary chiefly took from his writing and his thought. For he was a subtle and resourceful thinker, who was by no means incapable of modifying his views or even of reversing them, even within the compass of the same work; and who was always aware, not only of the power of thought but of its deviousness. It was perhaps from this, even in his theoretical writings —the sense at once of the overriding importance of human motives in shaping the world, and of their ambiguity—that Mary absorbed most. Godwin observed that "pure" motives, good or ill, do not occur ready-made, so to speak, but are arrived at developmentally and by degrees, reaching sometimes the most widely separated forms from the same beginning. He laid down his own version of the Pleasure Principle to account for all human behaviour, but showed how differently it might operate: "Pure malevolence is the counterpart of disinterested virtue. . . . Both the one and the other are originally chosen with a view to agreeable sensation; but in both cases the original view is soon forgotten." Such an insight, as remarkable as Godwin's rational obtuseness in other ways, is implicit throughout *Frankenstein.* There is another maxim in *Political Justice* which appears at first to contradict it, but on examination does not: Godwin is speaking of the

74

difficulty, or, more strongly, the fallaciousness of judging actions by intentions :

> We shall overturn every principle of just reasoning, if we bestow our applause upon the most mischievous of mankind, merely because the mischief they produce arises from mistake : or if we regard them in any other light, than we would an engine of destruction and misery, that is constructed of very costly materials.

In other words, loftiness of motive is not an absolute standard for assessing human good and—the wording rather seems to suggest—may even be an aggravation of evil : for the "costly materials" might have been put to better use. The whole sentence, with the metaphor it embodies, might be taken as a motto for *Frankenstein*.

The same man, indeed, who made the enormous blanket assumptions in *Political Justice* about the future possibilities of human nature was capable of the most original and dexterous psychological analysis in the present. But on the whole he reserved these latter gifts, his penetration of "things as they are", for his fiction. *Things As They Are* was the alternative title of his most famous novel, written immediately after *Political Justice,* and mentioned with it in Mary's dedication to her father : *Caleb Williams.* Its influence upon her was clearly very great, and not only, of course, upon her; as a political statement it had an effect only second, perhaps, to *Political Justice,* but even more, probably, has it held readers, in Godwin's own day and since, as a drama of psychological conflict, the conflicts which arise in the very pursuit of Godwin's sovereign objects, of justice and truth. To appreciate his achievement, and to see how it affected Mary, it will be necessary to look at the book in some detail. Other of Godwin's works of fiction, notably *St Leon* and *Mandeville,* illustrate the theme; but it is *Caleb Williams* that most powerfully shows some of the images and thoughts at work in *Frankenstein.*

Caleb Williams was published in 1794, a year after the

appearance of *Political Justice,* and sharing its notoriety, with a preface to the first edition so boldly challenging the establishment that it was prudently suppressed for a year. Godwin, a slow writer, produced the whole novel—three volumes—in less than a year, working by his own account in an almost continuous burst of mental activity and under inspiration : "I wrote only", he said, "when the afflatus was upon me."[9] The "excitement" that he felt he needed was present, and his imagination was powerfully at work.

Mary read *Political Justice* in 1814, no doubt encouraged by Shelley. But her book-list records that she read *Caleb Williams* twice, in 1814 and again in 1816, the year of Frankenstein, and there can be little doubt through which book more of her father's thought entered into her. The two belong together, as Goodwin said : "*Caleb Williams* was the offspring of that temper of mind in which the composition of *Political Justice* left me." It was an unruly offspring; in important respects it seems to have been in revolt against its parent.

It is a story of crime, pursuit, terror and injustice in which the promised demonstration that under the present state of affairs "man is the destroyer of man" ("of all other beings", as *Political Justice* puts it, "the most formidable enemy of man") is amply fulfilled; one may suspect a fascination of the author by the things he deplores. Caleb Williams is a young man of humble origins taken into the employment of a gentleman, Falkland, and much favoured by him. Falkland is a man of refinement, high principle, and honour : it is his fervid attachment to personal honour that is his undoing. Some time before Caleb Williams joins his household he has been in dispute with another local landowner, Tyrrel, a brutal overbearing squire-arch who insults him, acts despicably in driving a tenant from his farm, and a girl, his ward, to her death. This last incident produces hysterical hatred in Falkland, described in detail : "he raved, he swore, he beat his head, he rent up his hair." Tyrrel goes from bad to worse in misbehaviour until one night, having again publicly insulted Falkland, he is set upon and murdered. Suspicion falls on the ejected tenant, who is tried and executed together with his son; but some is also cast upon Falkland himself, resulting in a public inquiry at which he asserts his innocence and, being a gentleman, is believed. Thereafter, however, he shuns society and becomes morose and secretive: thus rousing in Caleb Williams the curiosity which is his reigning passion. He discovers incriminating evidence, and finally draws from Falkland a confession that he indeed was the murderer; but at the same time becomes Falkland's prisoner, since Falkland is determined that no one else shall know, for the sake of his "honour", and will stop at nothing to preserve his reputation—" 'I love it more than the whole world and its inhabitants taken together.' "

The novel now becomes a story of escape and pursuit. Caleb Williams, though not intending to betray Falkland, tries to escape his surveillance, is overtaken, brought to trial on a trumped-up charge, and expects to be condemned to death, but escapes again, temporarily joins a band of robbers, and moves on, employing various disguises, but with Falkland's emissaries, now joined by the most sinister of the robbers, Gines, constantly at his heels. Overtaken and again arrested, he decides to break his resolution of not giving Falkland away, and denounces him to a magistrate, but is disbelieved: this time he is released at the instigation of Falkland himself, who wants to make him swear away his own accusation; he refuses. The pursuit continues, assuming more and more the aspect of nightmare, until Williams again approaches a magistrate and obtains a hearing: confronted with Falkland, he puts his case and Falkland, dying, repents, and falls into his arms.

Such an outline of this melodramatic and indeed preposterous plot cannot of course give any idea of the power of the story, or elucidate its connection with *Frankenstein*. That will become more apparent if we look more closely at the relationship between Williams and Falkland, and consider some of the very curious transformations of character brought about in the course of the entire novel. That it exposes "things as they are" in the public realm, in the tyranny of the rich and the oppression of the poor, the venality of the law and its inadequacy to achieve justice even on its own terms—let alone those ideal ones proposed in *Political Justice*—is undoubtedly true. The sense of helplessness of a poor man up against wealth and "position", and the way the rich support each other against a troublesome claim—the whole operation of what was later to be called the solidarity of the ruling class—are made exceedingly vivid. The prison scenes are especially powerful, and there is no question that Godwin, who was not himself ever imprisoned (though some of his friends were) felt the horrors of an eighteenth century jail deeply, quite apart from his theoretical standpoint that deprivation of liberty was the worst evil, short of death, that one man could impose on another. All this is cogently, forcefully, and (allowing for the extreme improbability of some of the events in themselves) naturally conveyed in the course of the story, and it is easy to understand why, in the still early years of the French Revolution, it should have been thought by many seditious.

But it was seditious in another way more readily apparent, perhaps, to us today, though even then no doubt it was this other sort of subversion—its disturbing penetration into the structure and dynamics of human nature—that made it so exceedingly gripping to read ("No one", said Hazlitt, "ever began Caleb Williams that did not read it through"). The effect is made principally, as has been suggested, in the relationship of the two principals, Caleb Williams and Falkland. These two represent two sides of a single personality, or rather two forces which, at work within a personality, act and react upon each other. The changes of their struggle, and its reproduction and extension in subsidiary characters, give the whole great dramatic force; but it is the peripeteia of an internal drama. It is indeed the drama of a dream, in which the same transformations and multiplications commonly occur—one element turning up in different shapes and changing shape "before our eyes". Indeed it is characteristic of this type of fiction that the principal actors repeat themselves or have understudies, so to speak, in subsidiary roles : it can be seen in *Frankenstein,* it appears continually in the poetry of Shelley; it may be detected, in the elaboration and grand multiplication of the infernal host, within the formal framework of *Paradise Lost.*

Caleb Williams, the narrator, and therefore the conscious

mind of the whole, represents above all the rational faculties, reason and calculation, foresight, self-consciousness or *conscience* itself. It is significant that the chief motive of Caleb's actions, or at any rate the one that sets the whole story in motion, is "curiosity": the desire to know, to pry into secrets or, to describe the same thing in loftier terms, to conduct rational inquiry. It is a passion, insofar as Caleb can be said to have one:

> The spring of action which perhaps more than any other characterised the whole train of my life, was curiosity. It was this that gave me my mechanical turn; I was desirous of tracing the variety of effects which might be produced by given causes. It was this that made me a sort of natural philosopher; I could not rest till I had acquainted myself with the solutions that had been invented for the phenomena of the universe. . . .

His curiosity is diverted from these general objects to the mystery surrounding Falkland, his employer: was he or was he not guilty of "enormous crime", was he a murderer? Caleb pursues his detection passionately, with a zeal that "drank up all the currents of my soul", but it must be observed that he does so without either personal animus towards Falkland or with regard for justice in any ordinary sense. "No spark of malignity had harboured in my soul. . . . My offence had merely been a mistaken thirst for knowledge." Or, as it might be said, in the pure impartial spirit of scientific inquiry; nevertheless one which can actually be described by Caleb as a "demon".

On the other hand Falkland, whose "ruling passion" is "honour", the overweeningly high standards of conduct that he has attached to himself—he is not so much guided by them as in possession of them—repudiates Caleb's persistent questioning with extraordinary vehemence and ferocity; he too becomes positively demonic in denial. He seeks solitude and avoids Caleb, upon whom he turns, when followed, with extravagant fury: "there was something inconceivably, savagely terrible in his anger." Falkland in fact, clambering among the "rocks and precipices" to avoid Caleb, enacts the dangerous state of an impossibly refined or idealised notion of oneself under threat of exposure by reality and defended with a violence familiar in modern psychological terms as over-compensation. Naturally the two are mutually exasperating—"we were each of us a plague to the other"—locked in the impasse of neurotic conflict; but in the same way quite inseparable.

There is such an affinity between them that much of their dealings with one another can take place without speech : there is a "magnetical sympathy" between them so that the dire effect on Falkland of Caleb's hints and allusions simultaneously produce their effect on himself, as though indeed they were working on his own mind. He knows so well what Falkland is thinking that, as he explains, he need not differentiate in his narrative between "the silent" and "the articulate part of the discourse between us". Falkland for his part is aware of Caleb's suspicions, "frequently before I was myself aware, sometimes almost before they existed". This does not in the least tend to reconciling the two, indeed it exacerbates their antagonism, which is brought to a crisis—Caleb's decisive conviction of Falkland's guilt—in the midst of a fire, a symbolic *mis-en-scène* that, again, is familiar to psychoanalysis. The proof is, Caleb supposes, hidden in a certain trunk always kept locked : the house goes on fire and, on a sudden impulse, Caleb seizes the opportunity to force the trunk open. "I have always been at a loss to account for my having plunged thus headlong into an act so monstrous," he says, going on to connect it directly with the fire itself :

One sentiment flows by necessity of nature into another sentiment of the same general character. This was the first instance in which I had witnessed a danger by fire. All was confusion around me, and all changed to hurricane within. . . . I by contagion became alike desperate.

The fire produces "a kind of instant insanity". It precipitates crisis, but produces no solution. Caleb, interrupted, never actually sees the contents of the trunk (too frightening to be looked at?), but Falkland, assuming that he has done so, con-

fesses the murder to him. To him alone : Falkland is determined to preserve his "honour" still : in a curious formula,
necessitated by the transference of an internal dialogue to
external persons, but thereby making it extraordinarily vivid, he
declares :

> Though I be the blackest of villains, I will leave behind me a
> spotless and illustrious name. There is no crime so malignant,
> no scene of blood so horrible, in which that object cannot
> engage me.

He forces Caleb to swear secrecy and makes him virtually a
prisoner : guilt and conscience are compelled to live together.

Such a situation, of course, soon becomes intolerable, and
Caleb escapes, to begin the long succession of chase and pursuit, capture and escape which makes up the rest of the action.
Falkland's men catch him and he is cast into prison, the equivalent of an attempt at complete mental suppression. But he
breaks out—in physical terms, most improbably, in psychological, one may say, inevitably. The stone walls and iron bars
of the will can't be relied on to confine even the most unwel-
come thought in consciousness. On a later occasion Falkland
actually helps Caleb to get out of jail : the enmity of the two,
the "implacable hatred" with which Falkland persecutes Caleb,
is of that mutually supportive and cherishing kind typical of
neurotic illness.

The indissoluble bond between them does however undergo
a change, of an interesting kind. There are no more con-
frontations until the end; instead, Falkland pursues Caleb, and
keeps watch on him by means of his servants, and in particular
of the villain named Gines (or, originally, Jones). Gines has
been a member of the robber-band with whom Caleb at one
time consorts—a sort of Robin Hood fraternity engaged in a
justified "war with their oppressors", like twentieth century
guerrillas—but is far too wicked for them, and comes into the
employment of Falkland as a willing tool. He is an out-and-out
monster of evil and malice, strongly resembling the first villain
in the book, the tyrannical squire Tyrrel. Tyrrel is a powerful

man, of the flesh fleshly, compared with "that hero of antiquity whose prowess consisted in felling an ox with his fist and
devouring him at a meal. Conscious of his advantage in this
respect he was insupportably arrogant, tyrannical to his
inferiors, and insolent to his equals." Gines, cruel and brutal, a
robber turned thief-taker, in whose face "habit had written the
characters of malignant cunning and dauntless effrontery in
every line", is the lower-class equivalent.

Each, beside Caleb and Falkland, seems a comparatively
realistic portrait; but Gines at any rate acquires attributes of a
nightmarish or even numinous kind, which he shares with
Falkland. He, in the background, begins to appear endowed
with supernatural powers : Caleb tells himself that his persecutor "acts by human and not by supernatural means", but
nevertheless admits that "I could with difficulty think anything
impossible to him". His powers remind Caleb, in one of the odd
reversals characteristic of this relationship, of "what has been
described of the eye of Omniscience pursuing the guilty sinner";
and a little later Caleb ascribes to Falkland the all-presence of
God in the 139th Psalm, and in almost the same words,
as one of whom it may be said that if his "victim fled to the
rising of the sun . . . the power of the tyrant was still behind
him. If he withdrew to the west, to Hesperian darkness and
the shores of barbarian Thule, still he was not safe . . ." If
Falkland thus becomes like the Psalmist's Lord, Gines, his
emissary, is like Satan sent to harry Job.

Both Tyrrel and Gines supply something missing, or denied
by Falkland and Caleb : a crass animal element, markedly
anti-intellectual. Tyrrel, who despises poetry and learning of all
kinds (Falkland writes an Ode of which Tyrrel contemptuously
asks, "do you think he would write poetry if he could do anything better?") feels himself slighted as the "rude and genuine
off-spring of nature". Falkland, his physical and moral
opposite, of "small stature", "delicate, gallant, and humane",
actually corroborates this when, learning of the latest of Tyrrel's
ill deeds, he can "not prevent himself from reproaching the
system of nature for having given birth to such a monster as

Tyrrel". Nature in a word, has offended him in his "notions of virtue and honour" :

> He was ashamed of himself for wearing the same form. He could not think of the human species with patience. He foamed with indignation against the laws of the universe, that did not permit him to crush such reptiles at a blow, as he would crush so many noxious insects.

So, unable to tolerate the "laws of the universe", he commits murder.

Caleb also rejects the "brute part" of creation, chiefly in the abhorred and disgusting person of Gines; though it is remarkable that in his extreme fair-mindedness, something in which he certainly represents Godwin himself, he allows Gines to be "enterprising, persevering, and faithful". Caleb, or Godwin, is able in spite of himself to see that there is some connection between the animality of a Gines, or the other robbers, and, "energy", "perhaps of all qualities the most valuable" Since it is Godwin speaking and not Blake the conclusion drawn is political-economic rather than poetic-religious : "a just political system would possess the means of extracting from it [energy] its beneficial qualities, instead of consigning it as now to indiscriminate destruction."

But here there is no redemption, harnessing, or "extraction" of energy (Godwin's psychological analysis always tended to chemical or mechanical analogies). Nor, one may say, is one possible. Consciousness of evil and frantic denial of it, high-mindedness and protestations of innocence together with conviction of guilt are chained together in an unceasing round, seeming to allow no conceivable resolution. In fact Godwin had great difficulty in bringing the novel to an end. Writing out of "a high state of excitement," as he said, and at what was for him breakneck speed, he approached his finish and then stuck; by his own account he wrote nothing for more than three months. Even when he had devised an ending he was dissatisfied with it and in revisions substituted another, entirely different. The manuscript of the first version has recently come to light, and is printed in an appendix to the latest edition of the novel; it is very interesting to compare the two.

In his first essay Godwin made in fact no attempt at a solution. There is a final confrontation between Caleb and Falkland, producing no change in their position: Falkland, now a dying man, continues to deny all Caleb's allegations (made this time before a magistrate) and Caleb is not believed. He goes mad, and is shut up with Gines, or Jones, as keeper, the latter now assuming a positively fiendish aspect—"I am persuaded that no distracted slave of superstition ever annexed such painful ideas to his dreaded Beelzebub, as I annexed to the figure and appearance of this man." He has a lucid interval during which he makes this communication, and then lapses (with some suggestion that he is being drugged) into final helpless insanity. Such, one may say, is indeed a logical and probable end to the unresolved conflict. Falkland before his death is already virtually insane; the suppressed knowledge and the grossly overstrained resistance to it push the entire composite mentality into the last refuge of entire alienation.

But it can hardly be called a satisfactory end, artistically or otherwise, and Godwin's recasting of his catastrophe, by a bold and imaginative stroke, undoubtedly achieved something more. This time he started with the same hearing before a magistrate. Caleb, in the presence of Falkland, now desperately ill, repeats his accusation and the whole history of his persecution, but this time, moved to pity by Falkland's wretched state, also expresses remorse at having forced this exposure. He actually praises Falkland for his high principles and reproaches himself: "I came to accuse, but am compelled to applaud. I proclaim to all the world that Mr Falkland is a man worthy of affection and kindness, and I am myself the basest and most odious of mankind!" Falkland, touched by this evidence of sincerity and charity, relents, confesses to the murder, and throws himself into Caleb's arms. This reconciliation is, one may say, a genuine solution to the problem, or conflict: in psychoanalytic terms the suppressed knowledge is at last recognised and allowed to surface, or perhaps more accurately one part of the composite personality Caleb-Falkland acknowledges the existence of the other. The highly emotional atmosphere of this mutual recognition is quite consistent with what, in such terms, would be called abreaction.

But though, considered in this way, Godwin's second thoughts provided an apt, consistent, and artistically coherent conclusion, it can hardly be called satisfactory in a human sense. In fact, it is a tragedy : Falkland dies, and Caleb now considers himself a murderer, pledging himself to spend the rest of his life in remorse and mourning; so indeed may neurotic conflict, even though brought into the light and forcibly resolved, leave nothing behind but depression and despair.

In truth the sympathy between Falkland and Caleb is too close, and their opposition is almost a fake. Both, as has been remarked, represent the intellectual man, the man of rationality and "fine feelings". Both actually share the same obsession with innocence. Falkland's whole life and energies are taken up in maintaining his "reputation", or guiltlessness; Caleb Williams begins the entire story with a protestation of the same kind :

> My life has for several years been a theatre of calamity. I have been a mark for the vigilance of tyranny, and I could not escape. My fairest prospects have been blasted. My enemy has shown himself inaccessible to intreaties and untired in persecution. My fame, as well as my happiness, has become his victim. Every one, as far as my story has been known, has refused to assist me and has execrated my name. I have not deserved this treatment. My own conscience witnesses in behalf of that innocence my pretensions to which are regarded in the world as incredible.

He continues this vehement protestation right up to the point of the final reversal—". . . if these be the last words I shall ever write, I die protesting my innocence !"

Technically, of couse, he actually *is* innocent, Falkland is the only guilty one : but if it is allowed that both are inhabitants of the same mind, the distinction does not lose all importance, but shifts its ground. Each is pushing off his guilt onto the other : both therefore regard themselves as persecuted, and their persecution manias—it is not too strong a term—are so to speak interchangeable. The idea of persecution pervades the whole story, and no doubt by intention, since it illustrates the theme of man as wolf to man; herein lies Godwin's didactic purpose in exposing the horrors of "things as they are" under the "system of selfishness" in which "every man is fated to be more or less the tyrant or the slave". But the form it takes, and the inference of a malicious plot in every case—a whole overlapping series of plots, practically everyone being either the victim or perpetrator of some malign machination, and in some cases being both—have the force of obsession. (It is common, of course, to this type of novel, and may be to some extent discounted as conventional; though the ubiquitousness in turn suggests the question why it should be so common, and what in the climate of the time made both the purveyors and admirers of Gothic melodrama so prone, like Catherine Morland, to fantasies of persecution.)

In Godwin anyway it goes far beyond literary fashion, to become systematised as a permanent substratum of his own highly original thinking. In *Caleb Williams* all the characters held up for admiration are in some way or other the innocent victims of an evil plot; even Falkland, the murderer and persecutor, who is declared to have been brought to final disgrace and death by error (his idea of "honour", or chivalry) and the evil state of society, a "corrupt wilderness". Tyrrel himself, the villain disposed of before the real story begins, reacts to censure of his behaviour with a fantasy of his detractors being "under the influence of a fatal enchantment" so to turn against him; though he to be sure is usually too busy plotting against someone else to notice plots against him. Before long he is murdered, the only character in the book, apart from the father and son whom Falkland allows to be wrongfully executed for the crime, actually to suffer the extreme of persecution and oppression, a violent death. His murder is the mainspring of the story but he himself, except insofar as he is reproduced in Gines, is abolished as a factor in its moral mechanism. He is in a strong sense wiped out; his murder is referred to but he himself is completely forgotten; at the end, amid the extravagant self-reproaches of both Falkland and Caleb for persecuting each other, neither has a word of remorse or regret for his murder, which has become for Falkland no more than "one act of momentary vice".

Such is the power of Godwin's narrative, the force of his, or his spokesman's obsession, that one scarcely notices at first this astonishing moral hiatus. Tyrrel has too long and too thoroughly been removed from the scene. But because he is not present—that is to say neither in himself nor in any memory or acknowledgment of his being or having been—the dénouement lacks a vital element. The repentance of Falkland, ignoring the object which most calls for it, is the more violent for being in essence false; the result is not regeneration but destruction. Falkland and Caleb are reconciled but, as has been said, their reconciliation only brings together things scarcely different from each other, two versions of the same attitude.

The real problem, that "innocence and guilt are too much confounded in human life", remains unsolved, not dealt with at all; and Falkland's original reaction to this "confusion", that life is therefore intolerable—" 'Detested be the universe, and the laws that govern it! Honour, justice, virtue are all the juggle of knaves! If it were in my power, I would instantly crush the whole system to nothing!' "—is unchanged, or rather is now more extreme than ever. There is nothing left for him but to die, and for Caleb to spend the remainder of his life in impotent regret, in permanent depressive self-denial. "I began these memoirs" he says, "with the idea of vindicating my character. I have now no character that I wish to vindicate." He is, in a word, nothing.

The bearing of this extraordinary first novel of her father's upon Mary Shelley's own work will be at least in part apparent already, and will emerge more fully shortly. (It can be called Godwin's "first novel", although he had previously produced several others, because he himself so described it, dismissing his earlier published stories as trivia, of "obscure note". Like *Frankenstein, Caleb Williams* was the first, overwhelming overflow into fiction of an accumulated store of imagination.)

Before leaving *Caleb Williams*, however, one or two discrete points may be noted or re-emphasised.

One is the way that Caleb, though the embodiment of rational faculties, is in the grip of them to an extent which is, one may say, highly irrational. His "curiosity" is a compulsion, a passion, at its height taking complete command of him : the fatal attempt to look into the trunk is described as an act not simply of rashness but of "infatuation", or madness, "an instantaneous impulse, a short-lived and passing alienation of mind". The pursuit of his investigation is in itself intoxicating : a little earlier, on arriving at his first conviction (though still unproved) of Falkland's guilt, he is thrown into extraordinary excitement :

> My blood boiled within me. I was conscious to a kind of rapture for which I could not account. I was solemn, yet full of rapid emotion, burning with indignation and energy. In the very tempest and hurricane I seemed to enjoy the most soul-ravishing calm. I cannot express the then state of my mind than by saying, I was never so perfectly alive as at that moment.

Caleb's state of mind hardly seems appropriate—especially since he claims to be devoid of malice—in one merely engaged in detection, tracking down someone else's "guilty secret". The point is rather than it *is* a secret, hidden and forbidden knowledge, the discovery of which affords power but is in itself a satisfaction of Caleb's most urgent passion, of "curiosity". Had the truth of Falkland's guilt been what is still popularly called a "scientific secret" (who or what has hidden them?) his violent joy in discovering it, combined with the "soul-ravishing calm" of intellectual control, would seem natural enough. The whole description reminds us strongly of Frankenstein's exaltation of spirit when he makes his really momentous discovery, of "the principle of life".

The same elevation by the powers of his own mind and will is felt by Caleb later when he escapes from Falkland's house and again when he is in prison expecting to be sentenced to **death** :

I feel that I am free. . . . What power is able to hold in chains
a mind ardent and determined? What power can cause that
man to die, whose whole soul commands him to continue to
live.

In gaol, looking only for an "ignominious death", he resolves
to escape by a pure act of will :

Adamant and steel have ductility like water to a mind sufficiently bold and contemplative. The mind is master of
itself. . . .

Mind, he reflects, was "never intended by nature to be the
slave of force. . . . These limbs and this trunk are a cumbrous
and unfortunate load for the power of thinking to drag along
with it; but why should not the power of thinking be able to
lighten the load till it shall be no longer felt?" "No", Caleb
exclaims to himself, "I will not die !" (One can't help thinking
here of the ludicrous account of Thomas Holcroft, Godwin's
friend and fellow-Perfectionist, insisting that death, even by
having one's head chopped off, is simply an "error" : "chopping
off heads is error, and error cannot exist."[10] But in *Caleb
Williams* this megalomaniac conviction of the power of mind
over matter is, one may say, no joke.) It remains to be
observed again that such overweening faith in the powers of
his own mind do not preclude Caleb's being quite unable at
crucial moments to control his impulses. At each turn of the
plot, which is therefore in a special sense *his* plot, he acts "wilfully" but also involuntarily.

The second point to which attention may be drawn is the
extent to which Falkland, of such elevated sentiments and fine
sensibilities, a compendium of "beauty, grace, and moral excellence", who "began life with the best intentions and the most
fervid philosophy", turns into a devil, assuming more and
more of a fiendish aspect in Caleb's eyes. When first induced
by Caleb to speak of the crime (which he denies) "there was
something frightful, almost diabolical in his countenance". As
his persecution continues, Caleb comes to regard him as wholly

evil: "I saw something so fiendlike in this hunting me round the world . . . that henceforth I trampled reverence and the recollection of former esteem under my feet." In the penultimate meeting between the two, Falkland appears to Caleb 'like nothing that had ever been visible in human shape", "haggard, emaciated, and fleshless", his complexion, "of a dull and tarnished red", suggesting "the idea of its being burnt and parched by the eternal fires that burned within him". In other words, the Devil incarnate; and a little later his state is in so many words compared with "the imaginary hell, which the great enemy of mankind is represented as carrying everywhere about with him". We return, in fact, to Satan in *Paradise Lost*.

Finally, the two—the absolute supremacy of "mind", the same "torrent of mind" united in "enquiry after the beautiful and true" that Holcroft speaks of through Anna St Ives in his novel of that name, and the fiendish destructiveness—are united in Falkland when he contemplates history and the progress of mankind. Before trouble arises between them, he and Caleb are speaking of Alexander the Great, one of Falkland's heroes, and Caleb ventures to point out the slaughter and devastation wrought by his conquests. Falkland replies:

> The way of thinking you express, Williams, is natural enough, and I cannot blame you for it. But let me hope you will become more liberal. The death of a hundred thousand men is at first sight very shocking; but what in reality are a hundred thousand men more than a hundred thousand sheep? *It is mind, Williams, the generation of knowledge and virtue, that we ought to love.* (My italics.)

Caleb (and doubtless Godwin behind him) is sceptical of this way of "making men wise", and goes on to ask whether "this great hero was [not] a sort of madman?" What sort of madman has already partially appeared, and may presently be studied further in direct relationship to *Frankenstein*. First, however, something must be said about another extension of these ideas, also owing much to Godwin and standing to some extent as mediator between him and Mary Shelley, in the works of one of her favourite authors, the American novelist already mentioned, Charles Brockden Brown.

Brown (1771-1810) is a figure of importance in early American literature, hardly known now except to literary historians, but of some popularity on both sides of the Atlantic in the early nineteenth century, particularly in radical circles; those who liked Godwin would like Brown. He was himself a disciple, or at least an imitator of Godwin; to "equal *Caleb Williams*" was his highest ambition. The degree to which he actually espoused Godwinian ideas, rather than merely making use of them for the moral-intellectual machinery of his novels, is an interesting question, but with only slight bearing on the matter in hand. What does touch it is to see his own additions to the drama of intra-psychic conflict in Godwin's stories; though nothing like so accomplished a writer as Godwin—careless, at times barely coherent, and capable of shattering bathos —he did contribute to the *personae* of this drama images of striking force and originality. Even more than Godwin was he an "inspired" writer, writing when the "afflatus" was upon him; his best work—four novels in two years, besides many fragments—was produced, like Godwin's, in a concentrated outpouring of creative activity.

His romances, as has already been remarked, follow the rule also observed in *Frankenstein,* of avoiding "supernatural" agency for the extraordinary happenings recounted and of elucidating them, if at all, in terms of "the mysteries of our nature, the effects of which we have all witnessed, or may witness, and to which we are all subject" (to quote an early comment on his work).[11] Men of strange but "natural" gifts or afflictions bring about improbable and surprising events: in *Ormond* (1799) the mysterious hero-villain is a consummate master of impersonation, which enables him to "gain access, as if by supernatural means, to the privacy of others"; in *Wieland* (1798) the apparent villain—nearly all Brown's villains are ambiguously so, just as his heroes are villainous—has a similar talent of ventriloquism, or "biloquy"; in *Edgar Huntly* (1799) the narrator-hero is a somnambulist in pursuit of another somnambulist whom he suspects of murder. It may well be said, indeed, that all Brown's characters are sleep-walkers, since their actions, transformations, and frequently baffling duplications—even cropping up with the same name in different stories—are only understandable as dreams, often reading like direct and undigested transcription of dream-experience. Within the dream-like or phantasmagorical (but not preternatural) framework of his highly confused plots the joined and opposed ideas of Reason, an omnipotent questing rationality or "curiosity", and of forces quite outside reason's control, are constantly in play, embodied sometimes in different characters, sometimes within a single person.

Ormond is perhaps the most unmixed example of rational man, a walking compendium of *Political Justice,* believing that "In order to the success of truth [sic] . . . nothing was needful but opportunities for a complete exhibition of it", and devoted to improving the world; but with a sinister or even Satanic aspect arising if not logically, naturally from his rationality. (Brown observes that "in no case, perhaps, is the decision of a human being impartial, or totally uninfluenced by sinister and selfish motives"; it is characteristic of his scepticism concerning human nature, which he takes further than Godwin's grasp of its complexities.) Though inspired by a love of mankind, Ormond has no faith whatever in philanthropy: "Efforts designed to ameliorate the condition of an individual were sure of answering the contrary purpose. The principles of the social machine must be rectified before man can be beneficially active."

But even believing thus that "the system" must first be changed, he holds (in this again a good materialist and "necessarian", caught in the same trap that Marxist logic finds it hard honestly to escape) that man is himself "part of a machine, and as such had not the power to withold his agency". His way out of the dilemma is himself to be in some way outside the "machine" and in control of it; as such, by implication, super-human. His aim is to manipulate the social machine by means of "opinion", but scarcely as Godwin hoped to influence it, by open argument; like almost all Brown's active characters, he goes to work in secret. He will "exercise absolute power over the conduct of others, not by constraining their limbs or by exacting obedience to his authority, but in a way of which his subjects should be scarcely conscious". He is indeed the "hidden persuader" : in the name of rational consciousness he works through unconsciousness, his means being his mastery of disguise; this, of course, despite the supreme value he places, as a good Godwinian, upon "sincerity". We see in fact little of these sophisticated aspirations in action; his aims rapidly boil down to pursuit of the heroine, Constantia (herself a rationalist, impregnably virtuous, a kind of irreligious Pamela) who finally only wards off rape with a penknife.

Edgar Huntly, or The Sleep-Walker is appropriately the most dream-like of all these stories; its seemingly arbitrary sequence of events only makes any kind of sense as a product of unconscious association. The action, as in many dreams in which the dreamer first watches a happening in which he has no part, and then moves into it himself, begins with the history of a man, Clithero, whom the narrator, Huntly, suspects of murder; after a distinct but quite unexplained break Huntly begins a series of adventures on his own. Both characters are somnambulist, and both very clearly in the grip of forces they cannot control.

The first part introduces a remarkable set of incest-fantasies, merging with one another. The speaker, Clithero, has been the faithful—virtually filial—servant of a gentlewoman of spotless virtue, widowed and with a grown daughter, but indissolubly tied to her twin brother, who thus takes the place of her husband. He is an exception to the general rule noted above that Brown mixed good and ill in his characters; he is as wholly bad as his twin-sister is good, being indeed devilish—he "exceeded in depravity all that is imputed to the arch-foe of mankind" and "seemed to relish no food but pure, unadulterated evil". Clithero kills him, in circumstances almost exactly corresponding with the killing of Laius by Oedipus, on the highway and mistaking him for a robber; to make the identification unmistakable (though there is no reason to believe Brown was conscious of it) Clithero says, "I had meditated nothing; I was impelled by an unconscious necessity; had the assailant been my father the consequences would have been the same". Having slain the brother-father he feels impelled to kill the sister-mother, his beloved patroness (he even describes himself as her son) in order to spare her the pain of learning the fatal news; he visits her bedroom in a scene strongly reminiscent of *Hamlet,* and is only just prevented from stabbing the woman in the bed. In fact she is not his "patroness" but her daughter, his own betrothed; thus as it were compressing Hamlet's impulses towards Ophelia and Gertrude economically into one. Clithero's resemblance to Hamlet, stricken by the revelation of evil, is so close—he is "fettered, confounded, smitten with excess of thought, and laid prostrate with wonder"—that one is tempted to assume a memory of the play; but if so it seems likely to have been unconscious. What is most interesting in the present context is Clithero's feeling that his thoughts themselves bring about the things he foresees and fears:

> I seemed to have passed forward to a distant era of my life; the effects which were to come were already realised—the foresight of misery created it, and set me in the midst of that hell which I feared.

In his own person Edgar Huntly falls into a more primitive level of fantasy—quite literally, tumbling into a pit and exploring a cavern which brings him out into the primeval American wilderness, to fight with wild beasts and wild men. The novel has earned commentary as the prototype of the Red Indian adventure tale, in this case a formidable running fight in which the indestructible hero kills off dozens of redskins; but it is more remarkable perhaps as the dream-exploits of a pacific and pious young man who might have been brought up, as was Brown himself, as a Quaker. The whole affair is a delirium of violence which suddenly ceases when the novel emerges abruptly and inconsequently into daylight and its various elements are dispersed: Clithero to final madness and suicide, Huntly taking his place, betrothed to the daughter of his "patroness", the original murder mystery swept back under the carpet of the unconscious as the work of savage Indians. The self-revelation promised by Huntly at the start—"What light has burst upon my ignorance of myself and of mankind! How sudden and how enormous the transitions from uncertainty to knowledge!" is not brought about except as a function of the dream-experience itself: there is no "interpretation". At the end Huntly is only able to reflect on the universality of ignorance and self-delusion: "Disastrous and humiliating is the state of man! By his own hands is constructed the mass [*sic:* maze?] of misery and error in which his footsteps are for ever involved." The expression is incoherent, but the idea of man as a being who does not lead his life but is led by it comes out strongly enough and gives meaning to the extravagant jumble of unexplained accident and coincidence.

The most successful and fully worked out of these stories, however, is the first of them, *Wieland, or The Transformation*. Transformation is of course the principal business of all Brown's novels, in which disguise and deception (whether or not explicitly self-deception) is more or less satisfactorily shown growing to discovery; in this case with very powerful effect. It is an account of religious mania, operating through two generations. The elder Wieland, a German emigrant to America (supposed to be related to the poet Christoph Wieland) is an extreme Calvinist, or "Albigensian", haunted by scruples and obsessionally engaged in "ceaseless watchfulness and prayer" and finally literally burned up by his religious fervour: he dies of "spontaneous combustion".

Wieland the younger inherits his father's enthusiasm with interest, and falls an easy prey to the deceptions of Carwin, the ventriloquial joker whose "biloquism" represents the promptings of unconscious wishes, or more simply the split in Wieland's own nature. There are other sides to the character of Carwin, but here it is only needful to note that though introduced as an unutterable villain, credited with devilish malignity —one who "wages a perpetual war against the happiness of mankind, and sets his engines of destruction against any object that presents itself"—he is more mischievous than malicious. Nevertheless he leads Wieland to suppose that he is the object of direct communication (by disembodied voices) from God; the delusion takes immediate hold and continues an autonomous existence without further assistance from Carwin. Wieland, convinced that, like Abraham, he is called on to prove his faith by sacrifice of his own flesh and blood, murders his wife and children, and is only just prevented from murdering his sister (whose letters recount the whole story).

Seized and imprisoned, he confesses, but with pride rather than repentance, his manner showing "less of humanity than godhead", and his prayers being strongly reminiscent of the antinomian ecstasy of such as James Hogg's Justified Sinner— " 'Thou, Omnipotent and Holy! Thou knowest that my actions are conformable to thy will. I know not what is crime; what actions are evil in their ultimate and comprehensive tendency or what are good. Thy knowledge, as thy power, is unlimited. I have taken thee for my guide, and cannot err.' " Exalted, he addresses God, "the object of my supreme passion", as an equal: having fulfilled his part of the test-bargain—" 'What have I witheld which it was thy pleasure to exact?' "—he calls on God, thus magically controlled, to perform his: " 'Now may I, with dauntless and erect eye, claim my reward, since I have given thee the treasure of my soul.' " The latter phrase is, of course, the usual formula for one who has sold his soul to the Devil.

Quite insane, Wieland is closely confined, but cannot be kept in prison; combining in himself the demoniacal fury of a Falkland and the omnipotent determination of Caleb Williams, he breaks out and immediately seeks out his sister to complete his "submission" to God by killing her. The murderous wish cannot be suppressed, and Wieland is entirely absorbed or transformed into it: he "is no more. A fury that is rapacious of blood, that bends all his energies to the destruction of what was once dear to him, possesses him wholly." His sister, who has in the meantime learnt of Carwin's machinations, tries to save herself by telling him that what he took for God's command was no more than a "biloquial" trick. He refuses at first to listen to "reason", the possibility that his "voices" were deceivers; even if he was deluded, he says, with perfect, though insane logic, he was bound to obey, since "If a devil has deceived me, he came in the habit of an angel". He himself, believing that "God was my mover", is blameless, "pure from all stain".

He is about to strangle his sister when Carwin himself intervenes; he speaks to Wieland not with the voice of reason but directly to the unconscious, using his "biloquial" powers to recall him to himself: " 'Shake off this phrenzy, and ascend into the rational and human. Be lunatic no longer.' " Wieland is cured, his final transformation being thus effected in a highly dramatic but coherent and emotionally consistent way; he understands what he has been and what he has done and is devastated by self-knowledge. His repentance is described in explicitly Christian terms, an interesting point in a work generally reckoned and, one may assume, intended to be a demonstration of the dangerous delusions of faith. He is urged to "ascend into the rational and human", yet this ascent necessarily involves a descent from the megalomaniac heights of his delusion. In his exaltation he has identified himself with Christ or, more precisely, has set up as Christ's rival: " 'Thou' ", Carwin addresses him, " 'who hast vied with the great preacher of thy faith in sanctity of motives and in elevation above the sensual and selfish.' " His fall reduces him to the opposite but still Christ-like state, in which he is described, in his repentance, as "a man of sorrows".

The first of Brown's novels to appear on Mary Shelley's reading list is *Edgar Huntly*, recorded as having been read by both Shelley and herself in 1814. She read *Ormond*[12] and *Wieland* in 1815. It may be assumed that it was Shelley who introduced Brown to her in the first place, as a writer he rated on the same level as Schiller and Goethe. He was so struck by the character of Constantia in *Ormond* that he wrote two poems inscribed to her: one of these, *To Constantia, Singing* (1817) shows a remarkable cluster of Shelleyan identifications and aspirations roused, given wings, and projected into "voluptuous flight" by the image of that (to our eyes) insufferably priggish heroine.

On Mary the influence of Brown is apparent both in the general form of *Frankenstein* (as well as, to a lesser extent, her

97

ARIEL LIKE A HARPY

later novels) and in particular incidents and phrases. We may find significant, for instance, the complaint of Clithero, in *Edgar Huntly,* when, haunted by the consequences of his "innocent" crime, he says that " 'the demon that controlled me at first is still in the fruition of power; I am entangled in his fold and every effort that I make to escape only involves me in deeper ruin' " : the "brawny and terrific figures" of the Indians in the later parts of the story and Huntly's "shuddering loathing" of them may perhaps have contributed another element in the make-up of the Monster and Frankenstein's reaction to him. Some of the suggestions in *Ormond* have already been noted; the self-consciousness of Ormond himself, almost the only one of Brown's agents who knows quite well what he is doing, allows him to combine both within himself : when he is telling Constantia, with sadistic deliberation, of his designs on her virtue, he asks almost gloatingly, " 'Catch you not a view of the monsters that are starting into birth here ?' "

Many more direct hints can be found in *Wieland.* Carwin seems initially an entirely sinister being, and notably monstrous, "ungainly and disproportioned", his feet "unshapely and huge", his features very like those of the Monster in Frankenstein's first description : "His cheeks were pallid and lank, his eyes sunken, his forehead overshadowed by coarse, straggling hairs, his teeth large and irregular, though brilliantly white, and his chin discoloured by a tetter. His skin was of coarse grain and sallow hue. Every feature was wide of beauty." Nor is it incompatible with the Monster that he also possesses "a mind of the highest order". The heroine's revulsion from Carwin and fear of him, as "setting his engines of destruction" to work with indiscriminate malice, proves partly to have misjudged him; but Carwin himself (again combining Monster and Frankenstein in his own person) is frightened by what he has started by his "curiosity" and mischief : " 'had I not rashly set in motion a machine, over whose progress I had no control, and which experience had shown me was infinite in power ?' "

Some have seen in this rhetorical question "the germ of *Frankenstein*". It may be thought that other parts of these novels are not less suggestive. The real point is less a question of identifying precise derivations—in a work bringing together so many diverse threads, at second and first hand, it is hardly possible to name any one as pre-eminent or original—than of observing parallels and resemblances which must have been apparent to Mary herself. It would probably be truer to find in both Mary's and Brown's creations, a common debt to Godwin and beyond Godwin, to an "intellectual climate" impossible to particularise.

Mary's imaginative response was in many respects similar to Brown's, but what she got from him was not so much perhaps any specific elements of her story as a readiness to accept what her imagination offered. Indeed, she went much further than he did. In Brown the unconscious material so profusely thrown up remains disorganised, much of the time incoherent, and this was paradoxically an effect of his failure to allow it full force, to trust the products of his imagination. A pervasive scepticism or, at bottom, a moral timidity caused him to shy away from their full development and consequently to land as often as not in the most ludicrous banality. Mary, of far greater resolution and single-mindedness—without the provincial vanities and self-regard of the "first professional American author", or the curious collector's attitude to ideas which, it may be said, has affected professional American authors ever since—was able to bind many strands into a single whole, and to give her creation a life outside and beyond herself in a way Brown never achieved or even approached. His inventions were par excellence the products (like Godwin's) of introspection. Mary's, if one may so put it, were not extracted from herself but encountered there; they came from elsewhere, and she had the courage and determination, like Fair Janet in the ballad of *Tam Lin,* to wait and meet them.

FIVE

SHELLEY AND FRANKENSTEIN

THE TWO PEOPLE directly responsible for Mary
Shelley's writing *Frankenstein* were Byron and Shelley himself. It was Byron who suggested that everyone in the
party at Geneva should "write a ghost story". It was
the conversation between Byron and Shelley about "the principle of life" that gave Mary her starting point. For Byron the
ghost story project was a diversion, and one he soon tired of.
("The illustrious poets", says Mary in her Introduction, ". . .
annoyed by the platitude of prose, speedily relinquished their
uncongenial task".) But for Shelley no kind of writing, least of
all Mary's, could be regarded merely as a diversion. His own
story aborted, but he took the keenest interest in hers; it was
he who encouraged her, gave her the continued stimulus that
(if Godwin was right) she needed, and helped her at every
point up to and including negotiation with the publishers and
provision of the original anonymous Preface. How far his help
went in actual composition we cannot be sure. According to
Mary, she owed her expansion of the idea into a novel to his
"incitement". ("At first I thought of but a few pages . . . but
Shelley urged me to develop the idea at greater length".) But
she was clear and insistent that not "the suggestion of one
incident, nor scarcely of one train of feeling" was his. Shelley's
own references to the book, in dealing with the publishers,
indicate that he did nothing more than make a few corrections
in proof[1] and some earlier corrections in his hand appear in the
original manuscript. The actual writing seems to have been
done mostly when Shelley was not there. Entries in Mary's
Journal show that she usually worked on the story when he was
out of the house; two years later, when they were living in Italy
and Shelley, being away for a few days, wrote to Mary

urging her to employ the time on another work, he spoke of *Frankenstein* as "fruits of my absence".[2] It is curious that he should describe it in such a way; for he did very much more than push Mary into writing. He provided the subject.

Frankenstein himself is clearly and to some extent must intentionally have been a portrayal of Shelley, and Shelley can scarcely have been unaware of it, if only on account of his name. Frankenstein's first name is Victor, the same (presumably in earnest of a life of mental fight and spiritual conquest) that Shelley took for himself on a number of occasions in boyhood and later. His first published work was the volume of poems shared with his sister Elizabeth (and also, if inadvertently, with "Monk" Lewis) printed as by "Victor and Cazire"; the hero of another poem of this time, *"The Wandering Jew"*, was called Victorio; even the pseudonymous "editor" of the anti-monarchical burlesque, *The Posthumous Fragments of Margaret Nicholson,* published while Shelley was at Oxford, was "John Fitzvictor". To these may be added a feminine version, Victoria, who briefly appears as a murdered sister in the early prose-romance, *St Irvyne.*

Shelley dropped the pseudonym soon, of course, and nearly all his published work, these juvenilia apart, appeared either anonymously or under his own name. But the name Victor was absorbed, so to speak, into the work itself. "Victory" is a word that occurs with striking frequency in his poetry, especially in the later period. Almost every one of what may for the moment—if very roughly—be called his "political" poems includes at some point aspiration towards or invocation of "Victory". It is the last word of *Prometheus Unbound,* and it sounds, though more ambiguously, all through *Hellas,* of which the epigraph is a line from Sophocles, the *Oedipus Coloneus* : "I am a prophet of a victorious contest." What it meant for him we shall try to see later; in the meantime it can be asserted that anyone who knew Shelley or his writings well could scarcely have thought of victory or a victor without thinking of him.

But it is not only in name that Frankenstein resembles Shelley. It cannot be said, perhaps, that their characters are alike, since Frankenstein has scarcely any character in the ordinary sense, and the very fact of his inadequacy in this respect, his want of solidity in fictional terms, is something that must be taken into account. But if he does not appear in the story as a "real" human being, he very vividly is there (if one may make such distinctions within a work of art) as an "ideal" one; and the ideal he represents is in many very striking ways a Shelleyan one. If he is not Shelley he is a dream of Shelley, and one that he would not have been averse to dreaming himself, as an improvement, up to a point, on experience.

Frankenstein, like Shelley, is an ardent and high-spirited youth, of early promise and "vehement passions". If his up-bringing does not much resemble what we know of Shelley's early years at Field Place, it is possible to see in it, in its atmo-sphere of perfect love, harmony, and parental indulgence—"I was their plaything and their idol, and something better—their child, the innocent and helpless creature bestowed on them by Heaven . . . to bring up to good"—not only a stock model of romantic family principles but also an idealised and trans-formed version of Shelley's childhood, the childhood that he felt and must often have said that he ought to have had. No doubt it was also a compensation for some of Mary's depriva-tions as a child : as in this beginning, so throughout, the story of Frankenstein serves for both, he is a visible sign of their identifi-cation with each other.

There is no physical description of Frankenstein, and again one might say that he has no physical body, he is all spirit and restless, inquiring mind. These are sufficiently described, in childhood and later. As a child, he says, "my temper was some-times violent, and my passions vehement; but by some law in my temperature they were turned, not towards childish pursuits, but to an eager desire to learn, and not to learn all things indiscriminately". Compare the impressions of Shelley's boy-hood collected by Hogg and given in his *Life* :

From his earliest years, all his amusements and occupations were of a daring and, in one sense of the term, lawless nature. He delighted to exert his powers, not as a boy, but as a man. . . . His understanding and early development of imagination never permitted him to mingle in childish players. . . . But he was always actively employed; and although his endeavours were prosecuted with puerile precipitancy, yet his aim and his thoughts were constantly directed to those great objects which have employed the thoughts of the greatest among men.[3]

Frankenstein is brought up with his "more than sister", Elizabeth, the name also of Shelley's mother and of his favourite sister. Frankenstein's elderly father, on the other hand, the revered, high-principled learned Syndic, entirely mild and benevolent, is an exact reverse image of the tyrannical father who, to whatever extent he existed in real life, haunted Shelley's imagination. In fact this sort of wise, kindly, silver-haired old man, altogether un-authoritarian, the somewhat enfeebled counter-balance to the hated Lord God Father Almighty—too old, it may be observed, to be any sort of rival to a young man —crops up again and again in Shelley's writings, most notably in *The Revolt of Islam* (1817): the aged "hermit", "grand and mild" who rescues the hero, Laon, from prison, cares for him and instructs him, though only as his "passive instrument".

In the biographical (apart from the psychological) ancestry of this ideal father William Godwin undoubtedly had a share; but more probably was owed, both in Shelley's and Mary's representations of him, to Dr Lind, the elderly savant who befriended Shelley at Eton and who, in one of the ill-attested stories of his schooldays—one can never be sure how far Shelley's accounts of persecution were founded on fact—is said to have intervened with his actual father to prevent his being sent to a madhouse. Whether or not this incident was pure fantasy on Shelley's part is immaterial in the present context; it clearly established a connection between the "hermit" and Dr Lind, and that the "hermit" was a "memorial" to him is indeed testified in Mary Shelley's own notes to *The Revolt of Islam*. Dr Lind, "exactly what an old man ought to be. Free, calm-spirited, full of benevolence and even of grateful ardour", as Shelley described him, according to Hogg, is also very like the elder Frankenstein, of "upright mind" and calm integrity, whom his son loves and reveres. He also enters into the person of Waldmann, the second of Frankenstein's professors at Ingolstadt, of "mild and attractive" manners, dignity and kindliness, who is chiefly responsible for engaging Frankenstein in the study of science.

At this point the parallel between Shelley and the young Frankenstein becomes even more evident. Shelley, like Victor Frankenstein, had an early passion to learn "the secrets of heaven and earth" : one may say that in both the drive was inherent (like Caleb Williams's "curiosity", and possibly of the same unconscious origins), although in Frankenstein's case the particular direction it takes is the result of small original accidents, "ignoble and almost forgotten sources". Oddly enough, and with a logic by no means immediately apparent, the first of these is a chance exchange between Victor and his father which confirms him, not in scientific pursuits but in his interest in magic and alchemy. It seems less odd when we remember that Shelley too had the same interest : when Frankenstein describes his compulsion to penetrate the "secrets" both of the material and immaterial worlds—"whether it was the outward substance of things, or the inner spirit of nature and the mysterious soul of man that occupied me, still my enquiries were directed to the metaphysical or, in its highest sense, the physical secrets of the world"—it might be Shelley speaking.

Shelley's "passionate attachment" to "the study of the occult sciences, conjointly with that of the new wonders, which chemistry and natural philosophy have displayed to us" is amply testified by Hogg : both at Eton and at home, "Shelley's pocket money was spent in the purchase of books relative to these darling pursuits—of chemical apparatus and materials. The books consisted of treatises on magic and witchcraft as well as those more modern ones detailing the miracles of electricity and galvanism". As a child, at Field Place, he made up stories about alchemists, and his home was later "the chief scene of his experiments. He there possessed an electrical machine, he contrived a galvanic battery, and amused himself with experiments, which might well excite delight and wonder in so ardent a mind". Shelley's interest in "the miracles of electricity and galvanism" remained with him all his life, furnishing a recurring metaphor in his poetry, where it occurs in a "metaphysical or in the highest sense physical" manner as a symbol of thought and life. We may reasonably guess that his interest in and knowledge of the subject came out, if not at other times, in the crucial conversations at Diodati, which included galvanism. Frankenstein's own interest in electricity is traced to an accident when, during a violent thunderstorm, he sees "an old and beautiful oak" completely shattered by lightning, "entirely reduced to thin ribands of wood"; a "man of great research in natural philosophy" happens to be present, and improves the occasion with a dissertation on electricity and galvanism which profoundly impresses Frankenstein.

A number of sources seem to be combined in this story: the tremendous electrical storms the Geneva party saw and "enjoyed" have already been noted; there may also be a connection with an anecdote of Byron's of having seen a dead tree *restored* to life by a "thunder-bolt". There is also a likely association with the story of Shelley's schooldays when he himself either exploded with gunpowder or set "on fire" with a burning glass a tree at Eton. The *Quarterly Review*, telling the story, aptly saw in it an adumbration of Shelley's opposition to tyranny and superstition—in a word his Promethean aspirations.

Shelley's double preoccupation with occult and scientific "secrets" remained with him, moving one with another, though magic became for him gradually more of a joke. By the time Hogg met him at Oxford he was, or professed to be, wholly devoted to "science", putting it far above the humane studies. " 'The study of languages' ", Hogg remembers him saying during their first conversation, " '. . . is merely the study of words and phrases, of the names of things; it matters not how they are called; it is surely far better to investigate things themselves.' " (One recalls here Frankenstein's close friendship with Henry Clerval, whose interests are literary, historical, and linguistic; though Clerval may be said principally to represent another aspect of Shelley himself, there seems here to be something derived from Hogg and also possibly from Peacock.)

Continuing the conversation on this first meeting between himself and Shelley—an occasion which remained extremely vividly in Hogg's mind—Hogg asked how "things" were to be investigated, and Shelley, in great animation, "his face flushing as he spoke", replied " 'through the physical sciences, and especially through chemistry' ". Hogg goes on to describe the resumption of this talk a little later, when Shelley enlarged on his enthusiasm for science as the benefactor of mankind; admitting that recent discoveries were "rather brilliant than useful" but "asserting, however, that they would soon be applied to purposes of solid advantage" (the cant-term "spin-off" had not yet been invented, but the line of argument was well established). Shelley then went on, according to Hogg, to speak fervidly of the future prospects opened by scientific discovery: an end to toil, an age of plenty, aerial transport and exploration, the synthetisation of food, the irrigation of the desert and transformation of climate and geographical regions: all the ordinary marvels of science fiction at its most optimistic. We may suppose Hogg's memory to be substantially correct, since Shelley himself was soon to be writing these visions of the vast benefits of science into his first long poem, *Queen Mab*.

Nor, to be sure, should we be too ready to dismiss them as fiction, or fantasy; apart from those which were reasonable projections from general knowledge of scientific advances at the time, others can hardly now be treated, as Hogg tended to treat them, merely as the vapourings of youth. A particular passage in his account of Shelley's discourse is worth giving more fully:

The generation of heat is a mystery, but enough of the theory of calorific has already been developed to induce us to acquiesce in the notion that it will hereafter, and perhaps at no very distant period, be possible to generate heat at will, and to warm the most ungenial climates as readily as we now raise the temperature of our apartments. . . . We could not determine, without actual experiment, whether an unknown substance were combustible; when we should have thoroughly investigated the properties of fire, it may be that we shall be qualified to communicate to clay, to stones, to water itself, a chemical recomposition that will render them as inflammable as wood, coals, and oil, for the difference of structure is minute and invisible, and the power of feeding flame may perhaps be easily added to any substance, or taken away from it. . . . These speculations may appear wild, and it may seem improbable that they will ever be realised, to persons who have not extended their views of what is practicable by closely watching science on its course onward; but there are many mysterious powers, many irresistible agents, with the existence and with some of the phenomena of which we are acquainted.

Shelley knew nothing, probably, even of the then state of atomic theory, and can hardly have had any theoretical view of its subsequent development and results; he argued from "phenomena with which all are acquainted". But the shadow of some things to come is hardly, now, to be ignored in this speech; nor the Promethean zeal of the young hypothetical fire-bringer who spoke of the way "electrical kites" could "draw down the lightning from heaven" and who exclaimed, " 'what a terrible organ would the supernal shock prove, if we were able to guide it; how many of the secrets of nature would such a stupendous shock unlock!' "

In the same part of Hogg's descriptions of Shelley as he first knew him at Oxford occurs the further curious detail of his "contempt" for mathematics; Frankenstein also will have nothing to do with mathematics. Or rather, he takes them up for a time, and later looks back on their abandonment with regret as bringing "unusual tranquillity and gladness of soul". Mathematical studies, and his temporary abandonment of the "tormenting" pursuit of occult knowledge, represented—so he believes in retrospect—the suggestion of his "guardian angel", the last and unavailing "effort of the spirit of good". He subsequently gives up mathematics, and is thus doomed to "utter and terrible destruction".

Finally we may remember Frankenstein's general desire to penetrate both "inner" and "outer" secrets, the "metaphysical" and "physical", and place it beside Shelley's reply when Hogg asked him his view of metaphysics:

"Ay, metaphysics", he said, in a solemn tone, and with a

mysterious air, "that is a noble study indeed! If it were pos
sible to make any discoveries there, they would be mor
valuable than anything the chemists have done, or could do
they would disclose the analysis of mind, and not of mer
matter!"

Frankenstein's intellectual development, if one may so call it
his progress from one branch of study to another, is more syste
matic, but in essence the same as that of the young Shelley. I
is also a kind of model of the history of science. He starts with
alchemy and the occult, reading Cornelius Agrippa, Paracelsus
and Albertus Magnus. He dreams of finding the Philosopher'
Stone and even more the Elixir of Life—"Wealth was a
inferior object; but what glory would attend the discovery, if
could banish disease from the human frame and render ma
invulnerable to any but a violent death!" At this time he als
studies necromancy and dealing with spirits: "The raising o
ghosts or devils was a promise liberally accorded by m
favourite authors, the fulfilment of which I most eagerl
sought." Shelley also went in for ghost and devil raising, a
home and school, at least half seriously, as Hogg recount
("Sometimes he watched the livelong nights for ghosts") and a
Shelley himself admitted to Godwin in the letter of 1812 i
which he introduced himself, "ancient books of Chemistry an
Magic were perused [in his childhood] with an enthusiasm o
wonder, almost amounting to belief"; it was *Political Justice*
according to this account, that, like Frankenstein's meeting wit
his professors, "opened to my mind fresh and more extensiv
views".

Frankenstein is turned from magic first by the incident of th
lightning-stroke already described, which leads him temporaril
to mathematics, the Pythagorean or perhaps the Newtonia
phase of his development, but one which, as we have seen, h
subsequently abandons. When he goes to the University o
Ingolstadt "Chance—or rather the evil influence, the Angel o
Destruction, which asserted omnipotent sway over me from th
moment I turned my reluctant step from my father's door" (
most curious mixture of filial deference and emancipation fror

parental restriction of knowledge) leads him to the physical sciences. He first interviews the professor of "natural philosophy", the rude and unattractive Krempe, but is referred by him to Waldman, and there is immediately seduced—the word is not too strong—to the study of "true science". Waldman's "benevolent" aspect, and his kinship with Dr Lind and the ideal wise and kindly old men of Shelley's imagination, have already been mentioned. It is worth noting in addition that his particular attraction lies in his voice, "the sweetest I had ever heard", says Frankenstein. There seems likely here to be a memory of Carwin in *Wieland*, who deludes and draws his victims to destruction by his "biloquial" and alluring voice; but behind both can be seen Milton's Tempter who

> . . . with Serpent Tongue
> Organic, or impulse of vocal air,
> His fraudulent temptation thus began

This version of the Snake in Eden, disguised as natural philosopher, delivers a lecture which is itself a general "history of chemistry", and concludes with "a panegyric upon modern chemistry the terms of which", says Frankenstein, "I shall never forget" :

The ancient teachers of this science . . . promised impossibilities, and performed nothing. The modern masters promise very little, they know that metals cannot be transmuted, and that the elixir of life is a chimera. But these philosophers, whose hands seem only made to dabble in dirt, and their eyes to pore over microscopes or crucibles, have indeed performed miracles. They penetrate into the recesses of nature, and show how she works in her hiding places. They ascend into the heavens; they have discovered how the blood circulates, and the nature of the air we breathe. They have acquired new and almost unlimited powers; they can command the thunders of heaven, mimic the earthquake, and even mock the invisible world with its own shadows.

Such were the professor's words—rather let me say such the words of fate, enounced to destroy me. As he went on, I felt as

if my soul were grappling with a palpable enemy; one by one
the various keys were touched which formed the mechanism of
my being; chord after chord was sounded, and soon my mind
was filled with one thought, one conception, one purpose. So
much has been done, exclaimed the soul of Frankenstein, more,
far more, will I achieve : treading in the steps already marked,
I will pioneer a new way, explore unknown powers, and unfold
to the world the deepest mysteries of creation.

The resemblance of Professor Waldman's claims and Frankenstein's eager projection of them to Shelley's rhapsody in his
talk with Hogg is striking enough. Shelley's fervour as Hogg
describes it was when he was at Oxford, at the age of eighteen.
He did not go on to become a natural scientist, and there does
not seem any real likelihood that he might have done. He
retained a keen interest, however, in scientific discovery and
technical advance, on which in a strong sense of the word he
let his mind *play*. His delight in playing with fire-balloons—at
once potent symbols of fiery aspiration, vehicles for dissemina-
tion of the revolutionary word, and pure toys—is famous, and
was still with him years after the time when he hoped to broad-
cast his political pamphlets by their means; Mary records
making "a balloon for Shelley" during their Geneva stay.[5] A
more practical piece of engineering was the proposed steamboat to ply between Genoa and Leghorn, a project in which
Shelley invested and lost a considerable sum of money in 1820;
its significance for him, of which more will be said later, was
not perhaps very different from that of the fire-balloons.
Much more copiously, however, Shelley's writing provides
evidence of exactly the kind of quasi-scientific speculation
expressed by Frankenstein in his words and his history. It can
be found throughout his work, and must be examined in greater
detail later, not only as it touches the question of a model for
the character of Frankenstein but as illustration of the whole
theme we are following. A few examples may be given at this
point from *Queen Mab*, the long visionary poem Shelley wrote
in 1812 and which in 1816 still represented the most extensive
and systematic statement of his beliefs. He had, it is true, come

to dislike it (he was to describe it, when trying to suppress the pirated edition of 1821, as "villainous trash"[6] but more, probably, for personal reasons and on account of its technical immaturity, than because of any substantial changes in his thinking.) The dedication, with its pledge of unchanging fidelity to his first wife, Harriet, was certainly something he preferred later to forget; but otherwise, except for modification of the extravagant hostility to Christianity which gave *Queen Mab* its first notoriety, it contains, though in undisciplined and juvenile form, much of the subject-matter of all the poetry he was subsequently to write.

An important part of this subject-matter, and the main theme of *Queen Mab* itself, was of course a projected vision of mankind's future, when human life should be transformed, in good Godwinian terms, by technical advance and political enlightenment. The Spirit of Ianthe—an earthly girl a good deal like Harriet—is transported in sleep to a point outside time and space where the Fairy Queen instructs her in all things past, present, and to come. She is given a panorama of human history to date in a series of horrific scenes of war, pestilence, and tyranny; the Fairy then turns to where "Futurity/ Exposes now its treasure" and shows what better things lie ahead. Expressed now in high poetic terms we have again the expectations Shelley spoke of to Hogg, and more: the desert fertilised by science, the climate transformed, the Poles unfrozen (a favourite hope of Shelley's, echoed perhaps in Walton's notion at the beginning of *Frankenstein*, that the North Pole may prove a temperate zone) and the oceans bearing "bright garden-isles" for the surplus population, a charming idea that may be recommended to present science-fiction practitioners. Disease is abolished and death become no more than a "slow necessity" if not postponed altogether, as Godwin forecast in *Political Justice*; man's nature itself is transformed as "happiness/ and science dawn, though late, upon the earth". "Reason and passion" are no longer in conflict but together subdue all matter, though themselves subject to "necessity". Such a resplendent vision of sublunary perfection—"O happy Earth, reality of heaven!"—may be reckoned Shelley's special personal contribution to politico-social optimism, and though it is not original in him, the combination of something like the expectation of Isaiah (the lion, now ostentatiously vegetarian, lies down with the lamb in *Queen Mab*, indeed becomes a lamb himself) with the scientific hope has never, perhaps, been put at higher pitch. It is Godwinism illuminated and given wings; but the means, it must not be forgotten, are just what Godwin prescribed, the discovery and recognition of "truth", by which is meant factual or scientific truth.

The actual process of scientific discovery was something that concerned Shelley very little; despite his reverence for Bacon, he seems to have absorbed almost nothing from him of the idea of experimental method. Frankenstein himself, needless to say, has no more notion of it; neither his crucial discovery nor his exploitation of it is stated in such terms, although the terms in which they are stated, both the sudden light, "so brilliant and wondrous, yet so simple", and its subsequent application in slow but "pointed" research, are not incompatible with the way many scientific discoveries have been described subjectively. Frankenstein, in a word, is not a real scientist any more than Shelley was; but he represents a man's surrender to something in the spirit of scientific inquiry that Shelley was aware of and that fascinated him as Frankenstein himself is fascinated by the intellectual allurements of Waldman.

Fired by these, Frankenstein is prepared to "dabble in dirt", or more specifically in decay. "To examine the causes of life, we must first have recourse to death", he concludes, and in his search for "the principle of life" he studies not only anatomy but "the natural decay and corruption of the human body", spending "days and nights in vaults and charnel-houses". Shelley similarly associated the attempt to discover "secrets" of almost any kind with "the secrets of the tomb". That is of course a stock phrase of Gothic romance and horror-story, and something must be allowed for the effects of mere literary fashion. But even taking it into account and reckoning on a certain natural contagion, the extent of Shelley's preoccupation with tombs and charnel seems extraordinary. If we go back to his juvenilia—writings dating perhaps from about the time when, according to Hogg, he planned to spend a night in the vaults of a church, watching the piled bones in case they should produce a ghost—we find them concerned almost to the exclusion of all other matter with graves and corpses. The early poems in the *Esdaile Notebook* are a catalogue of such matters; one in particular, a first version of what appears in later collections as the lines *On Death* ("The pale, the cold, and the moony smile") makes an interesting association between "mortality" and the secrets of life :

> The secret things of the grave are there,
>   Where all but this body must surely be,
> Though the fine-wrought eye and the wondrous ear
>   No longer will live to hear and see
> All that is bright and all that is strange
> In the gradual path of unending change.

There is an echo here, no doubt, of Ariel's song in *The Tempest*; there is also a curious parallel with what Frankenstein says of the work immediately leading to his great discovery :

I saw how the form of man was degraded and wasted; I beheld the corruption of death succeed to the blooming cheek of life; I saw how the worm inherited the wonders of the eye and brain. I paused, examining and analysing all the minutiae of causation, as exemplified in the change from life to death, and death to life, until from the midst of this darkness a sudden light broke in upon me.

Frankenstein, in fact, succeeds where Shelley was left asking only "Who telleth the tales of unspeaking Death?"; but they were looking in the same place. Another poem in the *Esdaile Notebook*, simply called *The Tombs*, begins :

> These are the tombs. Am I, who sadly gaze
> On the corruption and the skulls around,
> To sum the mass of loathsomeness,
> And to a mound of mouldering flesh
> Say—"Thou wert human life !"

ARIEL LIKE A HARPY

The words are almost exactly those used by Frankenstein when he looks on the "filthy mass" of his creation; but in his case life has returned to answer the question in a way that adds to his horror and disgust.

Life, death, graves, worms, apparitions and suchlike paraphernalia are found in abundance in the short prose romance *St Irvyne*, written and published, anonymously, by Shelley at Oxford in 1811. This is a wild farrago of flight, persecution, seduction, and supernatural encounters (handled with considerable skill of the cliff-hanging kind); but it contains a character of interest for the present purpose in the double personage of Nempere-Ginotti, alternating aspects of satanic villainy. Ginotti says of himself, "From my earliest youth, before it was quenched by complete satiation, *curiosity* [Shelley's italics] and a desire of unveiling the latent mysteries of nature, was the passion by which all the other emotions of my mind were intellectually organised". (Curiosity, the reigning passion of Caleb Williams, is here explicitly directed to the discovery of general, not merely personal secrets; although pursued by extravagantly unscientific methods, it may be called a kind of scientific curiosity.)

The chief "mystery of nature" again, is death, which Ginotti simply rejects: "I must either dive into the recesses of futurity" —an odd, but most suggestive refuge—"or I must not, I cannot die." He explains that when he formed this resolution, "about 17 years of age" he was an atheist: "I had dived into the depths of metaphysical calculations. With sophisticated arguments had I convinced myself of the non-existence of a First Cause and, by every combined modification of the essences of matter, had I apparently proved that no existence could possibly be unseen by human vision." (It was soon after *St Irvyne* appeared that Shelley was sent down from Oxford for publishing his *Necessity of Atheism*.) Ginotti, whose alter ego Nempere pursues a supplementary career of seduction, turns out to have concluded a Faustian pact with Satan, gaining the secret of eternal life in return for his soul; the story ends among dead bodies in the vaults of a castle, with full chorus of horrors and the final dragging off of Ginotti, "mouldered to a gigantic skeleton" to an eternity of torment.

The preoccupation with death and decay, and the persistent idea that "the tomb" held momentous secrets remained with Shelley when some at least of the Gothic furniture of his juvenile writing had been discarded; what was left was perhaps more truly his own. *Alastor*, the poem written in 1815, he certainly took very seriously indeed, and, as "allegorical of one of the most interesting situations of the human mind" (as he describes it in his Preface) is an important source for his internal or mental biography. The introductory lines apostrophise nature as earth-goddess, "Mother of this unfathomable world!" and go on :

> . . . I have watched
> Thy shadow, and the darkness of thy steps,
> And my heart ever gazes on the depth
> Of thy deep mysteries. I have made my bed
> In charnels and on coffins, where black death
> Keeps record of the trophies won from thee,
> Hoping to still these obstinate questionings
> Of thee and thine, by forcing some lone ghost,
> Thy messenger, to render up the tale
> Of what we are. In lone and silent hours
> Like an inspired and desperate alchymist
> Staking his very life on some dark hope,
> Have I mixed awful talk and asking looks. . .

He is still waiting, half conjuring, half cajoling—very much indeed like a child with his mother—for his "Great Parent" to "unveil" or allow him to enter her "inmost sanctuary". Frankenstein is more successful; he is also, of course—and here we see an inescapable difference between him, imagined by Mary, and Shelley himself—less prone to think of "secrets" as feminine possessions and penetration of them as the incestuous relationship of son with mother. It is remarkable, however, how little difference this makes. Nature is still for Frankenstein a feminine embodiment to be "pursued to her hiding-places"; that these are underground, or only to be reached by subterranean ways,

holds good for one as much as the other. "I was like the
Arabian," says Frankenstein, speaking of the stages of his discovery and thinking of one of the tales of Sinbad the Sailor,
"who had been buried with the dead, and found a passage to
life, aided only by one glimmering, and seemingly ineffectual,
light."

When Frankenstein returns "to life" from his underground
labours among dead bodies he brings a monster with him. His
motives remain, however, what they have been from the beginning, of the loftiest kind, inspired by exalted philanthropic
ambition. When he makes his "discovery" and embarks on its
application, "the creation of a human being", he is uplifted,
and his enthusiasm carries him along "like a hurricane"—a
characteristically Shelleyan simile—as he thinks, in truly
Promethean terms, of the benefactions he will bring:

> Life and death appeared to me ideal bounds, which I should
> first break through, and pour a torrent of light into our dark
> world. A new species would bless me as its creator, and source;
> many happy and excellent natures would owe their being to
> me.

Such noble, if also impious thoughts sustain him through "the
horrors of my secret toil, as I dabbled among the unhallowed
damps of the grave, or tortured the living animal to animate
the lifeless clay". Very soon, of course, he loses all joy in the
pursuit, but his high ideals and general philanthropy remain, to
influence further turns in the story. Even in his ruin he recalls
these ambitions not so much in irony as continuing sources of
self-esteem:

> "When younger . . . I believed myself destined for some great
> enterprise. My feelings are profound; but I possessed a coolness
> of judgment that fitted me for illustrious achievements. This
> sentiment of the worth of my nature supported me, when
> others would have been oppressed; for I deemed it criminal
> to throw away in useless grief those talents that might be
> useful to my fellow-creatures. . . . Even now I cannot recollect,
> without passion, my reveries while my work was incomplete.

I trod heaven in my thoughts, now exulting in my powers, now burning with the idea of their effects."

He is now sunk, "never, never again to rise"—" 'Oh! my friend' " he says to Walton, " 'if you had known me as I once was, you would not recognise me in this state of degradation.' " Walton, however, has already seen that "He must have been a noble creature in his better days, being now in his wreck so attractive and amiable"; and, completely captivated by him, returns again and again to dwell on his extraordinary qualities and attainments. "Even now", Walton writes to his sister, having just taken Frankenstein aboard, and learning his history,

. . . his full-toned voice swells in my ears; his lustrous eyes dwell on me with all their melancholy sweetness; I see his thin hand raised in animation, while the lineaments of his face are irradiated by the soul within. He is so gentle and yet so wise; his mind is so cultivated, and when he speaks, although his words are culled with the choicest art, yet they flow with rapidity and unparalleled eloquence. Even broken in spirit as he is, no one can feel more deeply than he does the beauties of nature. The starry sky, the sea, and every sight afforded by these wonderful regions, seems still to have the power of elevating his soul from earth. Such a man has a double existence : he may suffer misery, and be overwhelmed by disappointments; yet, when he has retired into himself, he will be like a celestial spirit, that has a halo round him, within whose circle no grief or folly ventures.

In similar terms more than one of the many people fascinated by Shelley described him. Trelawny's story of his first encounter is famous : his observation in the shadow of "a pair of glittering eyes steadily fixed on mine", followed by Shelley's entry, or apparition, "gliding in, blushing like a girl", and then the effect of his extraordinary eloquence as he spoke about the book he had been reading.[7] Hogg, describing Shelley's torrential talk, dwells on the shrillness of his voice—something that does not seem to have struck anyone else so disagreeably—but also on his features, which "breathed an animation, a fire, an enthusiasm, a vivid and preternatural intelligence, that I have never met with in any other countenance". Hogg's attitude to Shelley was highly ambivalent at all times, and he is notoriously unreliable; but just because he is often crabbed, his enthusiasm when he shows it may be taken as the more genuine, as he remembers "the slender beardless stranger speculate concerning the march of physical science : his speculations were as wild as the experience of 21 years [Hogg was writing in 1832] has shown them to be; but the zealous earnestness for the augmentation of knowledge, and the glowing philanthropy and boundless benevolence that marked them, and beamed forth in the whole deportment of that extraordinary boy, are not less astonishing than they would be if the whole of his glorious anticipations had been prophetic; for these high qualities at least I have never found a parallel."

Like Frankenstein, whose "double existence" allowed him to be like a "celestial spirit" even in the midst of his own miseries, Shelley, in Hogg's memory overcame scepticism; his "anticipations" were glorious even if they were not true. Frankenstein is also visited in his despair by "one comfort, the offspring of solitude and delirium : he believes that, when in dreams he holds converse with his friends, and derives from that communion consolation for his miseries, or excitement to his vengeance, that they are not the creations of his fancy, but the beings themselves who visit him from the regions of a remote world. This faith gives a solemnity to his reveries that render them . . . almost as imposing and interesting as truth." Shelley shared the same belief (attested by one of Hogg's informants on the basis of a single day's acquaintance with Shelley, which seems to indicate that it was something he spoke readily about) that "the surrounding atmosphere was peopled with the spirits of the departed".

Finally, what Mary herself said about Shelley may be looked at. She did not say much, except on practical matters, while he was alive, and until many years after his death preserved his memory in private. Her grief was expressed in her *Journal* and in letters to intimates, but was more a record of her own emotions than any description of him; naturally enough. She did however make one entry in her *Journal*, not long after his death, which may be mentioned here, both because it refers directly to the time at Geneva and because it is perhaps the most poignant expression of her feelings of loss that she allowed herself. In October 1822 she saw and talked with Byron for the first time since the immediate aftermath of the drowning, and found that the sound of his voice particularly recalled Shelley to her, with "unspeakable melancholy that yet is not all pain", since it was so vivid. "I have been accustomed," she said, "when hearing it, to listen and to speak little; another voice, not mine, ever replied." Especially it reminded her of the "nightly conversations at Diodati" in which "incapacity and timidity always prevented my mingling"; now, listening to Byron alone, "it is as thunder without rain—the form of the sun without heat or light—as any familiar object might be, shorn of its best attributes . . .". This, she said, explains what otherwise would be an "enigma", the power of Byron "by his mere presence and voice" to rouse "such deep and shifting emotions within me".[8] Her feelings about Byron himself, always conflicting, may be thought to have been a part of the cause; but there seems no reason to doubt what she said, that it was the association with Shelley, and Shelley particularly at the time when *Frankenstein* was conceived and begun, that had such a profound effect on her. It was his voice she remembered and his voice she longed to hear again.

Apart from that, even at this time, her recollection was not particularised, but was rather a general brooding on the qualities of one "brave, wise, gentle, noble-hearted, full of learning, tolerance, and love" who is not to be likened to any other under the sun.[9] Her memories and struggles with her grief had already set into the form, gradually to become something like observance of a cult, of invocation of a being too good to live, having indeed "but one defect—which was his leaving his life incomplete by an early death".[10] Even here, however, the extravagant but conventionalised expressions of mourning have very distinct echoes in *Frankenstein*. It is rather startling to read in her *Journal*, on the last day of the year in which Shelley was drowned, her address to the "glorious spirit" with which she looks to be reunited after death, and then to turn to Walton's elegy for Frankenstein : "what comment can I make on the untimely extinction of this glorious spirit? What can I say, that will enable you to understand the depth of my sorrow?"

To sum up : that the character, or idea of Frankenstein was not at least strongly coloured by what Mary knew of Shelley's boyhood as well as their life together, and by her feelings about him, is hard to believe. It is also hard to believe that Shelley, reading the work he had pushed Mary to write, did not recognise in it a comment on himself. Perhaps he did; perhaps on the other hand he managed to dissociate himself as he often did in argument, even when the object of attack. In the case of Peacock's highly personal satire on him and his marital entanglements in *Nightmare Abbey* we have Peacock's word for it that he took the character of Scythrop to himself and managed to find it flattering; and he himself asked, "looking deeper into it, is not the misdirected enthusiasm of Scythrop what J. C. calls 'the salt of the earth?' ".[11] But whether he found anything personally congenial in Victor Frankenstein there is no knowing, nor even whether he saw himself there at all, though he can hardly have missed the name. If he did notice it, it throws an interesting light forward on the composition of *Prometheus Unbound*.

But in any case, that is not to the present purpose. Once again, it would be a large mistake, if the preceding arguments are allowed weight, to think of Frankenstein as a "portrait" of Shelley in a literal sense : certainly not in the sense in which Shelley turns up as a recognisable figure in Mary's later novels, for instance as Adrian in *The Last Man*, or in the more closely autobiographical *Lodore*. These are quite ordinary transpositions of an individual, or parts of an actual individual, into fiction. *Frankenstein* is in essence something different, an imaginative realisation not of an individual, however much in detail it may resemble him, but of the intellectual and emotional associations of a person. If it is objected that such is all any person is to others, at least degrees of abstraction may be allowed. Frankenstein is an abstract : he has, as has been said, scarcely any physical body or material being, and consequently no "character". He does not need them : it is precisely in being without them that he most closely combines with Shelley.

For one should not say that Frankenstein *is* Shelley, he is the Shelleyan Idea; when he is seen as such his meaning becomes clearer and the linked feelings and thoughts concentrated in him greatly enlarge their scope. They can include all that went to nourish Shelley's mind and fix his opinions, from Godwin back to Plato. They can include what others thought about him and what he thought about himself. They can include, and certainly should include, Mary's own thoughts and character : that there is a great deal of herself in Victor Frankenstein is not to be doubted, and that there should be in no way contradicts the assumptions that have been made. In "objective" fact, if one can speak in such terms, Mary did resemble her lover in a remarkable degree. ("The important thing," as her chief modern biographer has said, "is that in essentials Mary and Shelley were the same."[12]) Much more importantly, the extent of her identification with him—and his perhaps with her—is one of the most striking things about their whole relationship.

But our view of Frankenstein can also include the Shelleyan Idea as it has grown up since Mary wrote, in the past 150 years. Once we see Shelley in Frankenstein and Frankenstein in Shelley two myths or mythological complexes come together, as many elements came together, "swift as light", in Mary's half-conscious mind at Geneva. The connections that make a new combination, the approach of poles that produces a spark, are present : it does not seem accidental that a recurrent image in the story of Frankenstein, itself a typically Shelleyan one, is the meeting of clouds and the flash of lightning.

SIX

ARIEL AND CALIBAN

FOR THE SHELLEYAN idea we already have an image, in Ariel. But Ariel implies Caliban.

By himself Victor Frankenstein is only one half of the composite metaphor presented by the novel. He requires the Monster to complete him. Nowadays indeed the two are commonly confounded, and the Monster, originally nameless, has taken on his maker's name so that people talk of "creating a Frankenstein", a literary error that contains an obvious psychological truth. Now if Victor Frankenstein is based on Shelley or, as has been said, is an embodiment of the Shelleyan Idea, he is still only a partial representation, a portrait of, so to speak, the visible side of the Shelleyan nature. The Monster portrays the other or invisible side, the part that being Shelley necessarily creates or conjures up. To Ariel it adds Caliban—though not, one must immediately say, Shakespeare's Caliban, any more than the Shelley–Ariel is Shakespeare's. They are related, that is all, evidence of the spontaneous congeneration of the imagination. What these double images, winged and "airy spirit" and misshapen monster, mean in Shelleyan terms, how the first belongs to the poet "above the surface" and the second below, we need to examine in more detail. The evidence is partly in Shelley's actual life and what other people thought and said about him, and partly—the greater part—in his works. There is no need rigidly to separate them; for, as many have said, Shelley's life and his thoughts as they speak in his writings are one to a most uncommon extent: few poets have so much lived their poetry as did Shelley. It is a common observation, but what it means that life and art should be so confused is less often looked at.

At what point in his life Shelley acquired Ariel as his exhalation is difficult to say; it is a matter of dispute among Shelley scholars. One recent writer has discovered an Ariel, not directly Shakespeare's, in *Le Vieux de la Montagne*, a French translation of the romance by Ludwig Tieck which is said to have been the starting point of Shelley's unfinished novel *The Assassins*, and which is on Mary's reading list for 1816.[1] In this work "a beautiful boy of 15", named Ariel, magically encounters an ancient, a mage and prophet of "revolution" such as was practised and preached by the Assassins, followers of the Old Man of the Mountains, "to free mankind from the tyranny of power usurped by kings and priests".

Ariel, originally nameless, born on a mountain and suckled by a hind, is first called Angel (by a girl): Ariel is, of course, one of the Hebrew angels or messengers, his name signifying "valiant for God". The boy is renamed Ariel by the magician because he or it of all angels deserves homage: *"il joint à l'âme la plus expansive le corps le plus svelte et leger; il vivifie tout, depuis l'homme jusquà l'atome; la mythologie Grecque l'a un peu defiguré sous le nom d'Amour, mais dans notre théologie c'est Ariel."* The description is certainly suggestive, and may very well have added something to Shelley's notion of Ariel, though it still seems more likely that he took its first form from where Tieck, a Shakespearean scholar, found it himself. It is worth mentioning chiefly because it restores to Ariel the exalted quality of his angelic origins, something which Shakespeare's more modest spirit did not aspire to.

By the time of the last months at Lerici and the acquisition of the boat Shelley and his friends called the *Ariel* it certainly seems to have been Shakespeare's they were thinking of. Without getting too involved in these minor points, it is worth recalling the great excitement caused by this fatal boat—misconceived and ill-designed from the start, according to Trelawny, very "crank" in a breeze and needing much ballast to "bring her down to bearings"—and Shelley's delight in it, and the fuss about the name. The boat, long and eagerly awaited, having been built to Shelley's order, arrived at Lerici in May, and was received with enthusiasm recorded in letters and journals of the time, but also with much annoyance when it was found to bear the name of *Don Juan*, given in compliment to Byron by Trelawny. It was to have been changed to the *Ariel*, but "Lord Byron took fire at this", said Mary in a letter, and ordered the original name to be painted on the mainsail; "she arrived thus disfigured".[2] Shelley's own comment on the affair was only to remark that "we must suppose the name given to her during the equivocation of sex which her godfather suffered in the harem"[3] (the episode in Byron's poem in which the young Don Juan is introduced into the seraglio disguised as a woman).

Without making too much of it, it seems an odd thing to say, since boats, though feminine, are frequently given masculine names; and also as implying that Ariel would not be so paradoxical. Ariel, of course, is a sexless creature; or rather hermaphrodite. In any case Shelley appears to have been greatly put out: Mary records the trouble taken by him and Edward Williams, his friend and fellow-boatsman, to get rid of the offending name, eventually letting in a new piece of sail. If it seems a trivial matter, we must remember the rivalry and jealousy between Byron and Shelley at this time ("I have lived too long near Lord Byron", Shelley wrote bitterly to a friend, "and the sun has extinguished the glow-worm").[4]

We may also consider the strong emotional investment most people have in boats, and the magical importance attached to their identity; in Shelley these feelings were such as to provide one of the main components in his symbolic language. His lifelong passion for boating is well-known; and his poems are full of boat-imagery, usually frail enough craft, quite often winged, the aerial and storm-driven vessels of his soul. Boats are, of course, soul-carriers; and if that is borne in mind we can understand the outrage at seeing his turned, as Mary said, into "a coal barge". It was an interesting choice of phrase; one doesn't think of the elegant Don Juan as a collier, but a coal barge, black, squat, and ugly, might well be called the Caliban.

There appears to have been a good deal of talk about *The Tempest* during the last months at Lerici and Leghorn. Trelawny (who had only just joined the "Shelley Circle") mentions that it was Shelley's "favourite play"; describing a particular occasion when Shelley and Byron were together, he likens the latter, playing billiards and talking trivia, to "Prospero without his book and magic mantle", or as "an ordinary mortal"; adding that Shelley "never laid aside his book and magic mantle; he waved his wand and Byron, after a first show of defiance, stood mute".[5] We will remember this comparison later. Trelawny also makes the interesting observation that reactions to first encounters with Shelley and "the charm of his simple, earnest manner" were apt to be coloured by his general reputation at the time for extreme wickedness and profligacy: remembering "the rancorous abuse heaped on Shelley . . . in which he was described as a monster more hideous than Caliban—the revulsion of feeling on seeing the man was so great that he seemed as gentle a spirit as Ariel". That Shelley connected Ariel with himself quite consciously there seems little doubt, but he doesn't seem to have spoken or consciously thought about Caliban at all; though there is a remark of his in a letter to Hogg years earlier (1811) which shows him associating Caliban with everything odious. It was before his elopement with Harriet Westbrook and when he was spending most of his time in her company and that of her elder sister Eliza, later a most persistent "member of the wedding" and someone on whom he vented the most violent dislike. At this time he was trying to persuade himself that he liked her, that she was "amiable, not perhaps in high degree, but perhaps she is". He went on to say that even this extremely faint and hesitant praise was prejudice, "for you cannot breathe, you cannot exist if *no* traits of loveliness appear in co-existent beings. I think, if I were compelled to associate with Shakespeare's Caliban, with any wretch [he makes exceptions of his particular enemies, including his father] that I should find something to admire."[6]

At first sight Shelley seems here to be saying that you must take people as you find them, or in Godwinian terms that motives and qualities in individuals are always mixed. In fact, however, that was what all his life he found it most difficult to do, and he made of the difficulty a virtue. According to Mary, writing long after his death, he took as his guide the dictum from *Wilhelm Meister*, " 'When we take people merely as they are, we make them worse; when we treat them as if they were what they should be, we improve them as far as they may be improved' ".[7] What he was saying in truth was rather that he determined, even against his will and judgment, to see good in Eliza Westbrook that he did not really believe in; he would do the same even for Caliban, but it must be noted that Caliban is used as the extreme case, the most nearly impossible creature to find "amiable". It is interesting to follow the same letter to Hogg a little further and pursue the association of ideas. For, again, it was the mixture in men and things that he could not tolerate: a strong expression of his recoil from it is to be found in a poem in the *Esdaile Notebook*, probably written about the same time as the letter to Hogg, allegorising on a plant, presumably the wild or spotted arum:

> Fair are thy berries to the dazzled sight,
> Fair is the chequered stalk of mingling hues
> And yet thou does [sic] conceal
> A deadly poison there,
> Uniting good and ill. . . .

The letter to Hogg continues:

What a strange being I am; how inconsistent, in spite of all my boasted hatred of self: this moment thinking I could so far overcome Nature's law, as to exist in complete seclusion, the next starting from a moment of solitude—starting from my own company, as if it were that of a fiend—seeking anything rather than a continued communion with *self*. Unravel this mystery, but—no, I tell you to find the clue which even the bewildered explorer of the cavern cannot reach.

There is a great deal in this passage, in which, with the preceding reference to *The Tempest*, one can guess at a train of associations. Caliban lived on an island, was indeed its original inhabitant; thoughts of isolation, the "complete seclusion" of all island dreams: but *sharing* it with Caliban: with Caliban as admixture in oneself, with whom one is forced therefore to keep company: an unbearable thought, since one does indeed hate oneself, not in the conventional sense in which the thought-train starts, of "unselfishness" and altruism, but hating oneself-as-Caliban: the only solution, flight. Shelley seldom went further, perhaps in exploring to its full depths his own labyrinth, but he could not reach the "clue", or else he would not follow it. The Minotaur was not to be encountered, or even mentioned (though Hogg mentions it elsewhere, in his *Life*, as a "figment" of Shelley's poetic imagination). Daedalus the maker of the labyrinth supplies Shelley with one of his recurrent and most potent images (the "Daedal earth") of art and artifice making and remaking the complex fabric of life. Daedalus and Vulcan have affinities as makers and engineers with Prometheus; the underground mazes or natural caverns, labyrinths of earth, which abound in Shelley's verse are extremely familiar ground. But he never explored them to the Minotaur's lair. He was always in too much of a hurry.

Flight was notoriously Shelley's characteristic mode of loco-motion. In his poetry he is always flying, over sea, over land, a veritable Ariel, and even through caves, a difficult thing to do unless one is a bat. His actual appearance suggested the same thing, flying or flitting, suddenly coming and going. A well-known passage in Hogg provides a picture which, drawn upon by many since who have tried to capture the "Shelleyan essence", has been disputed by others as misleading, and doubt-less it is partial; but it remains a remarkably vivid statement of the impression he made on Hogg himself. The very fact that in it Hogg is saying how hard the impression was to catch and hold makes it the more convincing:

Shelley was fugitive, volatile; he evaporated like ether, his nature being ethereal; he suddenly escaped, like some fragrant essence; evanescent as a quintessence. He was a lovely, a grace-ful image, but fading, vanishing speedily from our sight, being portrayed in flying colours. He was a climber, a creeper, an elegant, beautiful odoriferous plant; he could not support him-self; he must be tied up fast to something of a firmer texture, harder and more rigid than his own pliant, yielding structure; to some person of a less flexible formation: he always required a prop.

His "hasty steps" and continual activity (alternating with inter-
ludes of sudden sleep, something like narcolepsy) were observed
by Hogg at Oxford; again he notes that though Shelley was
often extremely awkward in his movements, he was capable
also of great agility: ". . . he would often glide without collision
through a crowded assembly, thread with unerring dexterity a
most intricate path, or securely and rapidly tread the most
arduous and uncertain ways": just so, in fact, would he fly
through a labyrinth. Others noticed the same thing: "Oh,"
said Jane Williams to Trelawny, "he comes and goes like a
spirit, no one knows when or where." The same thing, of
course, was true of Shelley's whole physical existence, which
was a continual peregrination, it might well be called a flight,
from the time of his expulsion from Oxford and his decisive
breach with his family until his death.

The question is what it was flight to, or after, and what from.
The answer to the first part of the question is commonly recognised. Shelley was in flying pursuit of the unattainable, the
perfect, the ever-receding absolute of love: the soul-mate or
soul within the soul, the *cor cordium*, the "Antigone loved in a
previous existence", the goddess embraced by Ixion, the veiled
maid speaking with the voice of his own soul, the silver spirit's
form, the nymph grasped and turned to a reed of a dozen
different poems and other writings; "the invisible and unattainable point to which Love tends; to attain which it urges forth
the powers of man to arrest the faintest shadow of that without
possession of which there is no rest nor respite to the heart over
which it rules".[8] For Shelley there was no rest nor respite either
in imagination or life: the unattainable was also, of course,
present in the succession of women in whom he saw his nymph
embodied for a greater or lesser time—especially when, though
an actual person, she was not met in the flesh at all, but could
be pursued by letter or poem—to become, as often as not, something as vehemently rejected. These are the well-known parts
of his legend and his life, the composite notion of Shelley
expressed in the title (though that is not the only place where it
is to be found) of Maurois' *Vie d'Ariel*.

Less attention has been directed to whatever it was that

Shelley fled; though there are possibly even more numerous instances to go by, both in his life and works. For his imagination *was* haunted by monsters; they were quite often visible to him.

The record may be traced from his childhood onwards; it can be seen, indeed, as a remarkably consistent development. There are the memories of Shelley's early childhood collected by Hogg from his sisters, of their brother looking for secret chambers and caverns, reading and telling ghost stories, teaching his infant brother to pronounce the name of the Devil; from his time at Eton there are more, of ghost-watching and "raising the Devil" which have already been mentioned. They were the common games and terrors of childhood, no doubt, and nothing much out of the ordinary in themselves—though not many boys would go so far, perhaps, in their half-daring, half-terrified ghost-ploys. The point is rather that at this stage they were enjoyable; Shelley was on good terms, so to speak, with his own fantasy, and his boyhood fiends had not the powers of terror they were later to assume.

The acted fantasies of Shelley's adolescence had their counter-part in the more fully worked out Gothic horrors of his juvenilia; where, again, they seem excessive even for his years and the literary fashion of the age. They are also much more frightening, and though in disorganised and sufficiently crude form, can clearly be seen as the ancestors of much in his later work. A few examples may be given. The early poem *The Wandering Jew* has already been mentioned. In it is seen, in the Jew himself, Ahasuerus, the accursed wanderer who cannot die, a personage who continued to inhabit Shelley's mind and who turns up in different forms, under his own name again in *Queen Mab* and in *Hellas*, and more or less disguised elsewhere, in much of his later poetry. He is closely associated, of course, not only with the idea of immortality as a curse, a punishment for despising God, but with the notion of secret knowledge.

The early poem arrives presently at a characteristic scene of raising the Devil. Victorio, the hero, first conjures a witch who then performs the rite (again, an interesting early appearance of a witch as embodiment of the unfettered imagination, an image to be elaborated and perfected in *The Witch of Atlas*):

> Victorio shrunk, unused to shrink,
> E'en at extremest danger's brink . . .
> Inspired and wrapt in bickering flame
> The strange, the awful Being stood,
> Words unpremeditated came
> In unintelligible flood
> From her black tumid lips. . . .
> Satan, a shapeless hideous beast,
> In all his horrors stood confest . . .

and so forth.

Another poem of the same period tells an odd and fairly incoherent story of a man who, in revenge for some injury done to his mother, comes as a ghost to carry off the bride of a friend to the underworld :

> A mantle encircled his shadowy form
> As light as a gossamer borne on the storm,
> Celestial terror sat throned in his gaze
> Like the midnight's pestiferous meteor's blaze. . . .

One may note the combination of lightness or airyness and terror in the ghost that comes to steal someone else's bride. The fearful or awful presence clothed in gossamer or vapour has many descendants, some unexpected : Mont Blanc itself, the "unknown omnipotence", is similarly swathed in the "veil of life and death" of its own unfurling, and is equivalent—the question is left open where the subject of this creation is located, the mountain or the solipsist imagination—to the dreaming poet.

The same terrific elements turn up in slightly more organised form, together with even more of fiends, charnel, and bloody revenge, in the prose romance *Zastrozzi*, published by Shelley at his own expense while still at Eton. *St Irvyne,* already mentioned, is a similar early source, and it is worth taking a more detailed look at these productions, of which Shelley was obviously proud, even going to the trouble to see that copies of both were sent to Godwin when he introduced himself to him, by letter, two years later. (Each was, he said, "quite uncharacteristic of me as I now am, yet serves to mark the state of my mind at the period of their composition."[9])

Zastrozzi, the eponymous villain of the first of these tales, is a mysterious giant of a man (his "towering form" is several times mentioned; was it one reason why Frankenstein had to make the Monster eight feet high?) who carries out an elaborate persecution of the hero Verezzi (or Truth). Verezzi is a compound of all virtue, with Justice and Heaven on his side, but quite unable to resist the machinations of Zastrozzi, who is "alive to nothing but revenge". He is subject, like Shelley, to a kind of narcolepsy, and while sunk in "extraordinary sleep" is kidnapped by Verezzi. He is chained up, and attempts are made to drive him mad by telling him that he is so (we remember Shelley's persistent fear, or fantasy, that his father was going to have him locked up as insane), but later is released and introduced to Matilda, a wicked female who nevertheless falls in love with him and woos him with extravagant devices.

He resists, being himself in love with the virtuous Julia, but eventually succumbs: "A Lethean torpor crept upon his senses; as he lay prostrate a total forgetfulness of every former event in his life swam in his dizzy brain. In passionate exclamations he avowed unbounded love" and, being falsely assured that Julia is dead, marries Matilda to enjoy "the roses of licensed voluptuousness". (The association of "swooning" with sensual love recurs, of course, throughout Shelley's work; here the effect, which amounts to somnambulism, embarking in an unconscious state on a forbidden course, is stated very clearly.) Verezzi then sees Julia, still living (all arranged by Zastrozzi) and rejects Matilda, his "Lethean torpor . . . dissolved"; meets Julia; stabs himself; Julia is then stabbed by Matilda. The bloody affair is investigated by an Inquisitor who is softened by Matilda's beauty ("he little thought that under a form so celestial . . . lurked a heart depraved, vicious as a demon's") and she repents: a reversal, one notices, of what happens when Beatrice Cenci is confronted by her accusers and judges. Zastrozzi, however, is defiant to the last; he explains that the whole business has been engineered by him, in revenge for the debauching of his mother. He himself is illegitimate; so, having first killed his father (an event too terrifying, perhaps, to enter the tale; it is mentioned almost casually at the end) he completes his revenge by driving his half-brother to suicide in the manner described. He is condemned but, although a declared atheist, looks forward to death in the belief that it "will but render the soul more free, more unfettered".

As has been noted, Shelley's "atheism" and simultaneous belief in ghosts was the subject of argument at Diodati, where "Monk" Lewis and Byron maintained that rejection or acceptance of the supernatural ought to be consistent, an attitude that seems to have annoyed Shelley a good deal; he made use of Mary's *Journal* to register protest against what seemed to him to fly "in the very face of reason".[10] Reason, one may observe, scarcely enters into it : but the desire to abolish supernatural authority in God the Father at the same time as claiming limitless, or supernatural liberty for oneself, the freedom of a wandering spirit, is made very clear in *Zastrozzi*. The entire story reads like a direct transposition of incestuous nightmare; it was intended, in Shelley's words, to deal in "the incalculable horror which a terrible dream is wont to excite".

St Irvyne or *The Rosicrucian* has already been mentioned; some further details may be found in it to add to this early account of Shelley's demons. Ginotti-Nempere, the atheist villain, is again of "gigantic stature", adding to this the Wandering Jew element of possessing eternal life, or at least of being unable to die (it is this secret which he has obtained as a "Rosicrucian"; he can obtain release, and death, only by handing it on to another, a scheme borrowed by Shelley from Godwin's alchemist-novel *St Leon*). The story begins during a thunderstorm in the Alps, when the hero, Wolfstein—exiled from his country for a crime "not wilful or deliberate" but nevertheless "almost too dreadful for narration", the crime perhaps of Oedipus—writes a poem to "the murder'd Victoria" and scares himself by his own fancy of seeing "her form the whirlwind upholding". Overcome by "ideal horror" he himself tries to follow, calling "on the tempest to bear me".

A double plot of inextricable complexity and inconsequence ensues, introducing three heroines. Megalina, wicked and also given to apostrophising the ghosts of the dead as they pass "yelling" on "the eddying whirlwind", is seduced by Wolfstein, who overcomes her slight reluctance with arguments against "prejudice", but soon grows tired of her—his love being "not of that nature which was likely to remain throughout existence; it was like the blaze of a meteor which glares amid the darkness for a while, and then expires". Olympia, beautiful, accomplished, and virtuous, is next to fall in love with Wolfstein, but is driven to suicide. Eloise, the third heroine, appears in time to be seduced, with further arguments against "prejudice", by Ginotti as Nempere. Ginotti ends by relating his history, his "curiosity", atheism, and meeting with the Devil in a dream, "on the brink of a most terrific precipice, far, far above the clouds".

It is an odd dream, not so much of seduction by the Devil as rape. In it Ginotti is at first wooed by a "form of most exact and superior symmetry", and refuses to worship it; the Devil then reappears in a "form more hideous than the imagination of mankind is capable of portraying", who drags him to the precipice and forces his consent. What exactly he consents to, or what bargain is made, is not clear; but soon afterwards Ginotti succeeds in finding a "method by which a *man* might live for ever, and it was connected with my dream". The catastrophe, already noted, soon follows: in the vaults of a castle Wolfstein finds the body of Megalina and is about to retreat, but is kept by "curiosity, resistless curiosity" until Ginotti arrives, "wasted almost to a skeleton", but retaining "loftiness and grandeur". Ginotti, trying to hand on his "secret" and pact with the Devil, demands that Wolfstein should "deny thy Creator"; Wolfstein refuses and the Devil, "he himself, the frightful prince of terror", manifests in a flash of lightning. Wolfstein is struck dead, expiring in convulsions, and Ginotti, with the promise "Yes, thou shalt have eternal life", is dragged off to spend it in hell. The affair ends abruptly, with a brief "explanation", that "Ginotti is Nempere, Eloise is the sister of Wolfstein", and the pious exhortation, like the final trio in *Don Giovanni*, "Let . . . the memory of these victims to hell and malice live in the remembrance of those who can pity the wanderings of error; let remorse and repentance expiate the offences which arise from the delusion of passion, and let end-less life be sought from Him who alone can give an eternity of happiness".

It is not necessary to spend more time on these tales, juvenile extravagances which appear in great part a pastiche, almost a parody of the Gothic horrors of the time; though it would be a mistake to regard them merely as exercises. Before leaving them, however, two Miltonic quotations may be noted. The epigraph to *Zastrozzi* is taken from Book II of *Paradise Lost* :

> . . . that their God,
> May prove their foe, and with repenting hand,
> Abolish his own works. . .

—the lines occurring where Beelzebub in high council with Satan in Hell reckons up the prospects after the Fall, in par-ticular the chances offered by God's new creation, Man. It will be remembered that he finds there hope of a weak point in the defences of Heaven: an ingenious enemy may so go to work that the Omniscient and Almighty will be induced to cut off his nose to spite his face. It is a fine piece of satanic reasoning; what is interesting in the present context is the assumption that Man, once shown to be imperfect, must from Heaven's point of view be annihilated.

Another quotation from Book II of *Paradise Lost* is placed at the head of Chapter III of *St Irvyne,* introducing the first appearance of the "gigantic" Ginotti :

> Whence, and what art thou, execrable shape,
> That dar'st, though grim and terrible, advance,
> Thy miscreated Front athwart my way?

The question is asked by Satan when he takes a first trip into God's newly rearranged universe and finds, to his surprise and

momentary dismay, his own progeny, Death and Sin, guarding
the gate both ways between Hell and the rest of the Cosmos.
The answer, of course, is that it is Death, the Monster, as
Milton calls him, begotten by Lucifer himself, upon his
daughter Sin, and his only son.

It is one of the most bizarre episodes in the whole epic, and
it may well be asked what Shelley found in it worthy of such
special notice. A partial answer may perhaps be found in the
intimate relationship of the different beings involved—Lucifer,
from whose forehead sprang his parthenogenetic daughter Sin
like Athene from the head of Zeus; she, a part of him and
seeming his "perfect image", seducing him and conceiving
Death; Death in turn raping her, his mother, and engendering
with her the brood of Hell-hounds who, the third generation of
incestuous offspring, "howle and gnaw/ My Bowels, their
repast", devouring their own mother, who thus is in the position
of the vulture-torn Prometheus. This extraordinary extension
and multiplication of incest must be taken as expression of a
family relationship between ideas or states of mind, and the way
one may beget another or turn into its opposite: as Sin,
originally beautiful, "shining heav'nly fair", becomes a revolting hybrid, half snake and half woman, by mere inbreeding.
And Satan, ruler of Hell, still considers himself a superior being
to the Monster, Death; though fallen and damned, he is a
Spirit of Heaven and will have no truck with the grossly Hell-
born, his own son. The ironies of such infernal snobbery are not
very likely to have struck Shelley; but Satan's rejection of death
and corruption, his proper creation, may well have held a
strong meaning for him. It is Ginotti's refusal to accept mortality ("I must not, I cannot die") that is the mainspring of the
story.

Shelley, though he began at least one other novel (*The
Assassins,* to which further reference will be made) never wrote
anything more in the manner of *St Irvyne* and *Zastrozzi*. But
ghosts, phantoms, and monsters continued to haunt his work,
almost as much as the more agreeable airy spirits, the vaporous,
cloud-like, wind-driven creatures that give us our more usual

notion of Shelley as Ariel. One, indeed, produces or is followed by the other.

Examples in the main body of Shelley's verse are extremely numerous, and only a selection need be given. Perhaps one may start with *Epipsychidion*, generally reckoned the most refined expression of etherealised Shelleyan love, the desire of the moth for the star or soul within the soul, fixed for the time being in the actual person of Emilia Viviani. It is a curious poem, not only in the confusing flow and plasticity of its imagery, common in Shelley, nor even on account of its possibly deliberate obscurity, but even more perhaps because of our conventional attitude towards it. It is supposed to express the very essence of love and yet is filled to a quite remarkable degree with coldness and exhaustion, the "death of ice" which freezes the waters of the poet's heart, and the "ruins of unseasonable time" into which his emotional life has fallen.

The exciting causes of these lapses into lethargy are given, seriatim, as one "veiled Divinity" succeeded another in Shelley's mind, and much energy has been spent in trying to identify them. Undoubtedly there are references to individuals, Emilia and others, and undoubtedly that was a principal reason why Mary (who may be identified in it as one of those responsible for the frost in the poet's heart) disliked it. But Shelley himself, in his teasing "Advertisement" to the poem, warns readers that it is "sufficiently intelligible . . . without a matter-of-fact history of the circumstances to which it relates", and it is as well to take this warning seriously. It is certainly a "biographical" poem, but its significance as such is much more internal than external.

The starting point, as the "Advertisement" informs us, was the poet's imminent retirement to an island, "one of the wildest of the Sporades . . . where it was his hope to have realised a scheme of life, suited perhaps to that better world of which he is now [being dead] an inhabitant, but hardly practicable in this". That Shelley was dreaming of such a retreat at the time we know from a letter to Mary: "My greatest content would be utterly to desert all human society. I would retire with you and our child to a solitary island in the sea, would build a boat, and shut upon my retreat the floodgates of the world . . . If I dared trust my imagination, it would tell me that there are one or two chosen companions besides yourself whom I should desire. But to this I would not listen—where two or three are gathered together, the devil is among them."[10]

It seems reasonable to assume a connection between the wish expressed in this letter and the hope of the unnamed poet of *Epipsychidion*, and the same train of thought follows both. Isolation, even though with ideal companions, is no refuge from the Devil, indeed it invites him; it is on an island, as we have seen, that Caliban makes his intolerable presence felt. The devil is certainly at work in *Epipsychidion*; most obviously in the ghastly attributes of the She early encountered in the poet's search for his "veiled Divinity"—

> . . . One, whose voice was venomed melody
> Sate by a well, under blue nightshade bowers;
> The breath of her false mouth was like faint flowers,
> Her touch was as electric poison, flame
> Out of her looks into my vitals came,
> And from her living cheeks and bosom flew
> A killing air, which pierced like honey-dew
> Into the core of my green heart. . . .

Who this evil enchantress was, if based on any real person, has puzzled many, but is not to the present purpose to inquire. It may be pointed out, however, that she has many relatives, and that the elements of her description, and setting—poisonous flowers, deadly sweetness—occur all through Shelley's poetry, from the wild arum verse already quoted onwards.

The mental origins of this electric ghost need not be further off, indeed, than the passage some eighty lines earlier, in which an incomplete thought—and an unfinished sentence—struggles with the "difference" between "mind and its object" and the powers of mind to divide evil from good. In Shelley the consequence of eating the apple of knowledge is not so much to distinguish evil from good as simply to deny its presence within the mind. Good, he is saying, is not just the opposite of evil, but different in quality; positive and therefore capable of infinite growth—"If you divide pleasure and love and thought,/ Each part exceeds the whole"—while evil, "suffering and dross", is a deprivation only, which by the process of division is whittled away to nothing. It is true : good is more than the reverse of evil, and whoever says like Antigone (whose great declaration Shelley had perhaps in mind) "I was born to share in love, not share in hate", enlarges its sum among mankind. But in this difficult passage, where Shelley is visibly struggling with unacceptable ideas, the attachment to good is somehow made to exclude altogether the possibility of evil : for "thought" itself, by which good is apprehended, is identified with it. "Pleasure and love and thought" are placed without differentiation in the same category. Thus by a kind of sleight of hand the meaning is slipped in that evil, the negative, has no part in "mind" at all, and the process of exclusion and denial begins which brings disaster. It is all very well, one may say, not to be attached to that great sect whose doctrine is that each one should select only one mistress or friend; to be liberal of love to many. But in the same breath it is suggested that love's inclusiveness is also exclusion of all that is not lovely : if those who in error

> With one chained friend, perhaps a jealous foe,
> The dreariest and the longest journey go—

then those who know better, loving all worthy of love, will break the chain and reject the unlovely.

When Love, which "to divide is not to take away" can tolerate, whether in few or many objects, only "loveliness", that is, its own reflection, then phantoms crowd in, ugly and revengeful. They are co-inhabitants of the island; at every attempt to go further off and find a more perfect island they already stand in the way. It is true that in *Epipsychidion* an attempt is made to get beyond or behind them, to get *back* to Eden, the "isle 'twixt Heaven, Air, Earth, and Sea" where are heard "echoes of an antenatal dream", but it is too difficult. Exhaustion sets in. The sould wearing chains of lead suggests something more than a poet's usual feeling, a certain pitch of intensity, that words—even winged words—are inadequate. In fact it is the intensity of feeling that is failing here, and it is no surprise to find the poet giving up the struggle : "I pant, I sink, I tremble, I expire !"

Gardens of Eden played a large part in Shelley's fantasy. A development might be traced from the actual "secret garden" which, according to Hogg, the two young men found when out walking near Oxford in the winter of 1810, and for which Shelley imagined the ideal Eve : fixing, after going over the possibilities and rejecting all with any trace of "grossness", upon a double occupancy by sister-gardeners, because "the love a sister bears a sister is unexceptionable". The last example of this garden so jealously protected from taint is perhaps in *The Zucca*, written in 1822, in which the poet is reduced to making a miniature Eden out of a single pumpkin plant, rescued from December frost and watered with his own tears while listening to the guitar played by the latest and most inaccessible object of his "soul's idolatry" (Jane Williams).

Midway there is the garden of *The Sensitive Plant* (1820), which provides a notable example of the sudden transformation of good into evil. The plant, that is the poet (an identification confirmed in a letter to Claire some time later)[11] is one, and the only one—it is "companionless"—growing in a garden tended by a female "power", described as Eve but specifically without Adam, perfectly pure, loving, and gentle. She actually does apologise to the ground for treading on it, "Her step seemed to pity the grass it pressed", and, like a Jain, she is careful only to "banish", not destroy, noxious grubs and insects. To the plants she is almost literally a mother ("If the flowers had been her own infants she/ Could never have nursed them more tenderly"), with the Sensitive Plant, unique, flowerless, shrinking and "feeble", yet a favoured child, "cradled within the embrace of night".

Part III of the poem brings an abrupt change. The lady dies (and lest any suppose this to be because some prototype actually did die one must point out that insofar as she "was" an identifiable person she was according to Shelley "a pure anticipated cognition" of Jane Williams, who survived them all)[12] and immediately the garden is blighted. Not simply suffering the effects of frost, though that is a contributory exterior cause, but by a dreadful interior change, so that the whole garden becomes "cold and foul/ Like the corpse of her who had been its soul", and a place of terror, enough "to make men tremble who never weep". Poisonous plants "at whose names the verse feels loath", and fungi, "Pale, fleshy, as if the decaying dead/ With a spirit of growth had been animated", spring up in the place of flowers. The garden is haunted by autumn leaves which "Like troops of ghosts on the dry winds passed" (the same wind, one must remember, which is the breath of autumn's being), and from another quarter comes "a northern whirlwind, wandering about/ Like a wolf that had smelt a dead child out". The winter comes and spring is not far behind; but the Sensitive Plant is

> . . . a lifeless wreck;
> But the mandrakes, and toadstools, and docks, and darnels,
> Rose like the dead from their ruined charnels.

Things gross and rank in nature possess it utterly; and though in the Conclusion an attempt is made to rescue the poem by the "modest creed" that all is a dream, and that "death itself must be,/ Like all the rest, a mockery", it cannot remove the effect of what is indeed quite horrific.

Plant-life, elaborately drawn upon by Hogg in the passage already quoted, is however only one, and not the most common source of similes for Shelley; it is too static, and also it is inconveniently attached to the earth. The usual way of thinking about him is of couse airy, either as a winged creature or in that condition to which flying things may be said to aspire, of being part of the air. Even Hogg's "elegant odoriferous parasitical plant" is soon etherealised to a volatile essence, or a picture painted in "flying colours". To be in flight is, as has been said, the typical Shelleyan mode of existence, nearly or completely "up in the air" as skylark, or cloud, or, most characteristically, as rushing wind. But, flying and drinking the wind, he did not escape the ghosts and demons, they simply came after him the faster.

Probably the best place to observe this is in *Alastor,* which (together with the unfinished poem *Prince Athanase,* a second go at very much the same thing) also shows very well the striking thing about Shelley's often frantic restlessness, that it was simultaneously flight and pursuit, the two being often hard to distinguish from each other. Of all Shelley's long poems, *Alastor* is possibly the one in which he made the most determined effort to find out what he was at in his perpetual psychic chases, the extreme withdrawal it represents providing both motive and opportunity for his mind to "visit its own habitations". It was written in 1815, at a time, as Mary described it, of comparative tranquillity and rural seclusion, staying near Windsor and exploring by boat the upper reaches of the Thames.

Shelley was in good physical health and happy with friends; but the mere act of retirement and self-exploration produced extraordinary disturbance. In a letter to Hogg written at the time of this water-expedition, or shortly before it, he said, "It excites my wonder to consider the perverted energies of the human mind . . . who is there that will not pursue phantoms, spend his choicest hours in hunting after dreams, and wake only to perceive his error and regret that death is near?"[13] The immediate subject of this remark was evidently a missionary Hogg had told him about, who wasted "benevolence and talent" in "profitless endeavours"; but the sentence quoted concerning "hunting after dreams" is so exactly a summary of *Alastor* that we cannot help seeing a reference, and perhaps an association in Shelley's mind between himself and the "benevolent" but perpetually disappointed missionary. *Alastor* may also be thought, as a poem published only six months earlier, to have been fresh in Mary's mind when she began, in 1816, to write Frankenstein.

Like Victor Frankenstein, its poet-hero is (as Shelley explains in his Preface) "a youth of uncorrupted feelings and adventurous genius led forth by an imagination inflamed and purified with all that is excellent and majestic, to the contemplation of the universe. He drinks deep of the fountains of knowledge, and is still insatiate." Like Frankenstein, he seeks knowledge in solitude; Alastor is the Spirit of Solitude (and in its Aeschylean origins also a spirit of vengeance). "The Poet's self-centred seclusion", says the Preface, "was avenged by the furies of an irresistible passion pursuing him to speedy ruin", and Shelley's gloss on his own creation goes on with a most curious ambiguity to explain that while the "luminaries of this world" in their quest for "doubtful knowledge" are thus struck with "sudden darkness and extinction", yet those who have no such ambitions and still withhold sympathy from their fellows are even worse off, "morally dead". The implication appears to be that the Poet of the story, again like Frankenstein in his turn, is one whose lofty search, though disastrous, is a self-justification.

As has been described already, the narrator of the poem speaks of his pursuit of knowledge "in charnels and coffins", hoping to force "some lone ghost" "to render up the tale/ Of what we are". His own search blends almost immediately into that of the Poet, with no material distinction except the alteration from the first to the second person. Seeking "strange truths in undiscovered lands", and following "Nature's most secret steps", he meditates "The thrilling secrets of the birth of time"; he has a dream in which the Ideal speaks to him (in the form of a "veiled maid"), with a voice "like the voice of his own soul", of "knowledge and truth and virtue . . ./ And lofty hopes of divine liberty". Dream intercourse follows, and the Poet, wakening, sets off in pursuit "Beyond the realms of dream . . ./ He overleaps the bounds". By day he thinks and puzzles about death, and by night the "passion" returns, now "Like the fierce fiend of a distempered dream", and *leads* him; but six lines later he is *"driven* o'er the wide aëry wilderness" by "the bright shadow of that lovely dream": it now seems that he is pursuing the fiend and flying from the beatific vision. This confusion is represented by the image of the mid-air struggle between an eagle and a snake, the bird (a female in this case) "precipitating"

Through night and day, tempest, and calm and cloud
Frantic with dizzying anguish, her blind flight.

The eagle-serpent combat, taken by Shelley from Zoroastrian
mythology, is a potent component of his imaginative drama,
reappearing in several other places, most elaborately as an omen
in the opening of *The Revolt of Islam*, and again, as a kite and
crane above the battlefield, "locked in inextricable flight", in
Hellas. In these struggles there is no strong moral differentiation between the combatants (it is remarkable indeed that for
Shelley snakes seldom had the usual association with evil),[14]
and it may be thought that in them he came his nearest to con-
taining and accepting moral opposition. At the same time they
are from their very nature intensely violent and unstable conflicts. The struggle can never, so to speak, come down to earth.
Such a solution is impossible for the poet of *Alastor*, who
touches earth little more than the eagle. His travels, over large
tracts of wild and desert territory, are virtually airborne, and he
himself has become a ghost : a "spectral form" which, seen on
"some dizzy precipice", is taken for "the Spirit of Wind/ With
lightning eyes, and eager breath, and feet/ Disturbing not the
drifted snow . . ." : very much a Prince of Air.

The violently agitated pursuit and flight is continued in one
of the entirely unseaworthy and insubstantial boats—whose
sides in this case "Gaped wide with many a rift, and its frail
joints/ Swayed with the undulations of the tide"—that repro-
duce the condition of the passenger here and elsewhere (one
may compare this one with the boat given to the Witch of Atlas
as being too "feeble" to bear Venus). Driven by storm, the
waves themselves now "like serpents struggling in a vulture's
grasp", boat and passenger pass through caverns and labyrinthine forests, carried on a stream. ("Rivers are not like roads",
wrote Shelley to Peacock from Switzerland in 1816, ". . . they
imitate mind, which meanders at will over pathless deserts, and
flows through nature's loveliest recesses, which are inaccessible
to anything besides."[15])

The wanderer's journey ends at last, but does not, one may
say, reach any conclusion. The Poet dies, or rather fades out,

having reached the realm of the "colossal Skeleton" and complete exhaustion of feeling. No real discoveries are made, despite or rather because of the intense self-absorption of the whole process : narcissus flowers grow beside the stream, and the Poet too looks at himself in a forest pool, "as the human heart,/ Gazing in dreams over the gloomy grave,/ Sees its own treacherous likeness there". The search-journey is, indeed, precisely *not* pressed to the farthest. The Poet reaches a point where the landscape becomes monstrous and menacing—rocks "in unimaginable forms", "black gulfs and yawning caves", a mountain which seems "to overhang the world"—and where the stream of his own mind, now gaining strength and turning into a river, falls into "the immeasurable void"; but in this terrific place he turns aside and finds a refuge "even in the lap of horror" where he perishes in languid tranquillity, and in the same atmosphere of luxuriant self-pity which, despite the assertion that the story is "not barren of instruction to ordinary men", is the most noticeable thing about the Preface.

It is a profoundly unsatisfactory ending, and Shelley must have felt it so, since he returned more than once to the scene of what, morally speaking, was unfinished business. Many of the elements of *Alastor* turn up again in the prose *Fable*, originally in Italian, which Shelley wrote five years later. In that piece a youth is led by Love into a labyrinthine forest and there left surrounded by veiled figures, attendants on Life, who unveil themselves and torment him : "And for many days those figures danced around him whithersoever he went, alternately mocking and threatening him; and in the night while he reposed they defiled in long and slow procession before his couch, each more hideous and terrible than the other."[16] The *Fable* is no more than a fragment, and breaks off leaving the youth and his newly acquired "compassionate lady" in a permanently suspended decision between Life and Death.

Prince Athanase (1817) is deliberately unfinished, and it is interesting to see why. The hero is by name explicitly immortal (it is amusing to contrast him with the profligate and constantly resurrected hero of Thomas Hope's novel *Anastasius*) and, as Mary observed in her Notes to the poem, is "a good deal

modelled" on the protagonist of *Alastor*. He is a youth of
"gentle yet aspiring mind;/ Just, innocent, with varied learning fed", wise, generous, frank, fearless, the target of hate, but
himself neither spurning nor hating "his weak foes", the
Shelleyan paragon; but, like the Poet in *Alastor*, is consumed
by "secret pain", so that his "vernal spirit" is turned prema-
turely "sere", the autumnal thinning and greying that afflicts
many similar figures in Shelley's *dramatis personae*. No one
knows what is the matter with Athanase, and he does not know
himself, having never found a "mirror" in other people. Others,
however, perceive in him the fatal split between thought and
feeling—the "adamantine veil/ Between his heart and mind"—
and make diagnostic suggestions, that "memories of an antenatal life/ Made this, where now he dwelt, a penal hell"; that,
like Ahasuerus, he was under "God's displeasure" but in his
case because he "owned no higher law/ Than love"; that he
was troubled by

> . . . the shadow of a dream
> Which the veiled eye of memory never saw,
> But through the soul's abyss, like some dark stream
> Through shattered mines and caverns underground
> Rolls, shaking its foundations . . .

These are the same products of introspection that Shelley
finds elsewhere; the dark underground stream is clearly the
same that carries the Poet of *Alastor* towards the abyss. But
here their inadequacy, or inconclusiveness is actually seen,
though characteristically projected onto others : it is "they"
who speak thus "idly", "babbling vain words and fond philosophy". Prince Athanase himself, it is said, "did not decline
this talk" but indulges in it with "subtlest wit" and also with
the detachment of self-alienation, "as if its theme might be/
Another, not himself". Only various "fragments" continue the
poem beyond this point (introducing, among other matter,
another example of the wise and benevolent ancient, "An old,
old man, with hair of silver white" whom we have met before);
and its unfinished state is explained in the poem itself. The

introspective quest pursued in dissociation, "vain and cold"
does Athanase no good:

> For like an eyeless nightmare grief did sit
> Upon his being; a snake which fold by fold
> Pressed out the life of life, a clinging fiend
> Which clenched him if he stirred with deadlier hold;
> And so his grief remained—let it remain—untold.

Shelley's own note to this abrupt breaking off says:

> The Author was pursuing a fuller development of the ideal
> character of Athanase, when it struck him that in an attempt
> at extreme refinement and analysis, his conception might be
> betrayed into the assuming a morbid character.

Certainly the "analysis" recounted in the poem is, as has
been said, of a kind which, with emotions dissociated or with-
drawn, never gets anywhere. That in itself, of course, is one of
the ways one can avoid getting somewhere or seeing something
intolerable. But it is safer to leave off altogether, leaving
obstinate questionings behind; when they in turn take up the
pursuit.

Examples can be multiplied, both in Shelley's short lyrics and
his long works. It is possibly worth noting that even in such a
poem as *The Revolt of Islam* in which—fortified by the love of
Mary, "Child of love and light", to whom it is dedicated, the
Shelleyan Idea is full of self-confidence and "will omnipotent"
—the shadows are not outdistanced. The story of the incestuous
alliance of Laon and Cythna which renovates the world (in the
original version, it will be remembered, they were brother and
sister; sibling incest, Shelley said, "is a most poetical notion")
is repetitiously filled with violence, carnage, pestilence, and
destruction, leading to the final redemptive martyrdom of hero
and heroine. But these are all the work of "tyrants", and thus
can be kept at a distance and looked in the face. Other threats
are there too, and less easily dealt with, though they do not
impede the frantic progress of the lovers to their posthumous
immortal haven; they do not impede, because they accompany

it. In Canto III Laon, newly parted from Cythna, dreams of
her and of their love, now even more ideally exalted ("nature
had a robe of glory on") until with nightfall sinister sounds rise
from the "cavern's secret depths" by which they are seated, and
they are seized by "a nameless sense of fear". The poem continues :

> The scene was changed and away, away, away!
> Through the air and over the sea we sped,
> And Cythna in my sheltering bosom lay,
> And the winds bore me; through the darkness spread
> Around, the gaping earth then vomited
> Legions of foul and ghastly shapes, which hung
> Upon my flight; and ever as we fled,
> They plucked at Cythna—soon to me then clung
> A sense of actual things those monstrous dreams among.

They wake, and find themselves in the hands of the
"degraded servants of tyranny." But the nameless fear comes
from within rather than without; the foul shapes, vomited from
caves of earth, are rather the progenitors of the ordinary flesh-
and-blood persecutors than the other way about. The whole
stanza, with its sudden scene-change and cry of "Away!"—
how many times is it heard in Shelley's verse!—describes again
very well the mental process we have been examining: the
abrupt onset of panic and immediate flight, the flight in itself
summoning the pursuing and vengeful shadows from their
secret caves. It adds to other examples, moreover, a vivid
suggestion of the borderline, even within the extravagantly
visionary scenery of the poem as a whole, between nightmare-
haunted sleep and a waking life which itself is not safe from
monstrous visitations.

For there were occasions, of course, when Shelley saw these
imagined terrors outside himself, or with waking existence.
"While yet a boy I sought for ghosts", he says in the *Hymn to
Intellectual Beauty*, and some of the incidents in the search
have already been mentioned. Throughout his life at times of
particular stress he was prone to see them; how far they were

deliberately summoned, how far they came unasked it is hardly possible or profitable to ask. The most famous incident was the mysterious affair at Tanyrallt in North Wales, where he was staying with his first wife Harriet and her sister in 1812. (It seems possible that he was already tiring of Harriet, and he was certainly heartily sick of Eliza Westbrook, whom he was later to describe as "a blind and loathsome worm" that awakened in him "an inexpressible sensation of disgust and horror" when he watched her caressing his baby daughter.[17]

The facts of this celebrated puzzle, whether Shelley actually was, as he maintained, the object of a murderous attack, or whether the man who came to "kill him and ravish his wife" was mere fabrication, seem impossible now to determine. To a sceptical mind like Peacock's the whole thing was an invention, a piece of play-acting of a kind he detected Shelley in on other occasions; but Peacock had little sympathy with people who saw visions of any sort. Certainly Shelley saw something at Tanyrallt that "objectively" was not there at all : an eyewitness afterwards related how, after the supposed encounter with the "assassin", Shelley bounced out upon the lawn and saw, or thought he saw the face of his enemy against the beech tree, "so hideous that he took it for a ghost or a devil". He later drew a picture of this devil on a firescreen and then tried to destroy it by burning; it was however copied by someone else in the house (a Miss Fanny Holland), whose sketch has been preserved. It shows the vague outline of a man's body, apparently naked, surmounted by a fiendish face drawn in some detail : with a mocking grin and a mouthful of fangs, topped by spiky horns and what appears to be a snake coiled on the top of the devil's head.

It certainly is, even at this remove, a remarkable and alarming apparition; and the whole incident may be called typical. Shelley summoned up or created a vision—that is to say, he found it in himself, whatever exterior circumstances may have provided the stimulus—which so frightened him that he tried to destroy it. His next move was flight : the Shelleys left Tanyrallt precipitately immediately after, leaving behind a mystery which has been a fruitful source of speculation ever since.

There were other occasions when Shelley was physically attacked, or thought he was attacked, or said he was; when closely examined the actuality of any incident is very hard to establish, and one definition shades into another. Peacock was doubtful of all of them, and claimed to have exorcised at least one "mysterious visitor" by refusing to credit Shelley's story about him (an episode in 1816). But his general scepticism was stated in an interesting way : "Whenever there are two evidences to one transaction, many of the recorded events of Shelley's life resolve themselves into the same mythical character".[18] It is the mythical rather than the historical character of these incidents that is our concern, and endows particular happenings with general significance. Shelley himself may have resented the imputation—on the occasion mentioned in 1816 his protest is recorded by Peacock that "It is very hard on a man who has devoted his life to the pursuit of the truth, who has made great sacrifices and incurred great sufferings for it, to be treated as a visionary". But it is precisely his visions that interest us.

One of special importance for this discussion was seen in 1816 at the Villa Diodati, when they were all telling or reading ghost stories and *Frankenstein* was in gestation. Byron was reading Coleridge's *Christabel*, as yet unpublished (Coleridge had sent him the poem in manuscript) and, when he reached the lines describing, in the original version, the disrobing of Geraldine, the snake-woman—

> . . . full in view,
> Behold ! her bosom and half her side,
> Are lean and old and foul of hue—

Shelley, who had been gazing at Mary, shrieked and ran from the room. He afterwards said that Mary had seemed to him to be half-naked and that instead of nipples her breasts had eyes. She appeared perhaps such a monster as is described in *The Witch of Atlas*, among other chimerical creatures drawn by the Witch's beauty—

> Centaurs and Satyrs, and such shapes as haunt
> Wet clefts, and lumps, neither alive nor dead,
> Dog-headed, bosom-eyed, and bird-footed—

a particularly frightening sort of harpy.

The sudden transformation into such a shape of Shelley's "best Mary", his "sweet friend", the woman who of all in whom he sought "the soul within his soul" filled the role most fully and longest, may well have produced panic. It stands as a powerful example of those sudden reversals, or revelations of something hidden in what has seemed familiar which is the most disconcerting trick of the unconscious. In the continual flux of Shelley's imagery things are always turning into other things or revealing new aspects of themselves, frequently of an alarming nature. Such metamorphoses are doubtless among the manifestations of the Mutability which, in the first of Shelley's poems of that title refers chiefly to interior alteration or even caprice—

> We rest—a dream has power to poison sleep;
> We rise—one wandering thought pollutes the day;
> We feel, conceive or reason, laugh or weep;
> Embrace fond woe, or cast our cares away.

The frightening thing about changes within rather than without is, apparently, that you can't control them, or even know when to expect them. The alterations of exterior nature at least are regular, may be understood and brought under control, but when the mind takes over as Omnipotent, you've no control over it whatever—

> It is the same!—For, be it joy or sorrow,
> The path of its departure still is free.

Thus the leaves of autumn may be thoughts which, though dead, are capable of nourishing new birth, or may, in *Alastor* be driven to make a kind of eternal hibernation place for the equally dead and withered Poet; or they may (in *The Revolt of Islam*) be

> . . . Death, Decay,
> Earthquake, and Blight, and Want, and Madness pale,
> Winged and wan diseases, an array
> Numerous as leaves that strew the autumn gale.

In the same place the name of the Spirit of Evil, the Fiend, is in a quite orthodox fashion Legion; in the verse *Letter to Maria Gisborne* it is the voice of revolution, which

> Flits round the tyrant's sceptre like a cloud,
> And bursts the peopled prisons, and cries aloud
> "My Name is Legion!" . . .

Here the change seems to be for the better, or at any rate to something more acceptable by Shelley. On the other hand a mountain, a sublime Titanic majesty such as Mont Blanc, a "still and solemn power", habitation of "the secret strength of things", may in the *Passage of the Apennines* (1818) become, as giants are liable to, an ogre :

> . . . when night comes, and chaos dread
> On the dim starlight then is spread,
> And the Apennine walks abroad with the storm.

A walking mountain is a terrifying way for Mind Omnipotent to show itself.

The transformations that may take place in birds are of particular interest, since flying is the typical activity of Ariel, the one in which he is so to speak in his element, but out of his bodily existence ("Now, alas! the poor sprite is/ Imprisoned for some fault of his/ In a body like a grave".[19]) Birds, of course, occur with great frequency in Shelley's poetry : someone who recently took the trouble to make a tally of avian references there counted 189 to particular kinds of birds, and 54 to birds unspecified, not to mention such associated epithets as winged, plumed, and so forth. The species totalled 31, the most commonly mentioned being the eagle, dove, nightingale, and (the emotional opposite of these) the vulture.[20] The same writer observes that "there is no real evidence that Shelley read a single specialised work on birds", and that "it must be admitted that most of his avian images do not strike us as the notes of a naturalist", neither of which, perhaps, is surprising. It should hardly be necessary to say that Shelley's birds—as indeed all the fauna and flora of his poetry—illustrate the natural history of the mind, and no other. Their forms and transformings, the origin, and evolution of their species are those of dreams, not Darwinism; it may be said that their changes are adaptive in the same way, but to an environment of the emotions. Metamorphosis and hybridisation are instantaneous and unrestricted; eagles can turn into vultures, birds combine with mammals, wings mutate into claws.

Claws, both bird-like attributes and belonging to many beasts, equipped very many of the creatures of Shelley's imagination. They, rather than hooves or a tail, are the mark of the Devil in the imitation of Coleridge, *The Devil's Walk*, that Shelley sent to Elizabeth Hitchener with the jocular confession "I was once rather fond of the Devil".[21] They can belong to a man, too, but only in jest. Shelley, writing to Fanny Imlay some months later, and trying to chaff her into response, says ". . . who and what am I? I am one of those formidable and long-clawed animals called a *man*, and it is not until I have assured you that I am one of the most inoffensive of my species, that I live on vegetable food, and never bit since I was born, that I venture to obtrude myself on your attention".[22] Like the Devil, he "just shows his claws", and quickly retracts them. It may be that the claws of a pard-like spirit are especially of this kind : a leopard's talons are formidable weapons, used for tearing flesh, but they can be retracted or concealed. The feline habit of play with soft paws was a metaphor for Shelley of the play of his own fancy, again in *The Witch of Atlas* : in the dedication or apologia "To Mary", introducing the poem and answering her objection that it was too exclusively "visionary", or devoid of "human interest" he asks :

> What, though no mice are caught by a young kitten,
>   May it not leap and play as grown cats do,
> Till its claws come? . . .

It seems odd that anyone who ever handled a kitten should suppose that it actually has no claws till it is grown; what is implied here is rather the idea of harmlessness and playfulness, with the real function of claws, which is for scratching and tearing and holding onto what is trying to get away, still no more than potential.

What claws are for appears most clearly not in any poem of Shelley's but in a drawing, a rough doodle scrawled on a page of the *"Epipsychidion* Notebook". It may be supposed to have some direct connection with that poem, since it represents extremely vividly the process of flight and pursuit through which *Epipsychidion* moves, like many others, and from which it is indeed an effort to escape. The haven sought, the blessed place to be shared in complete interpenetration and union of the poet and his lode-star, the "soul within his soul", is the Eden-island already mentioned, the "favoured place" untouched by ill and mutability. Change by-passes it: ". . . Night, /And Day, and Storm, and Calm, pursue their flight" round about, "Treading each other's heels, unheededly"; "Famine or Blight,/ Pestilence, War, and Earthquake" miss it, as "blind vultures, they/ Sail onward far upon their fatal way". But the escape to this pre-lapsarian isle is itself a flight, to be accomplished in one of Shelley's bird-boats, an albatross bark to which time and change are themselves "ministers". And even the island is caught up in the same process. It is a dawn-place, a "far Eden of the purple East"; therefore a beginning; therefore, if not fallen, falling, "Beautiful as a wreck of Paradise"; like the day-star apparently fixed, "Cradled, and hung in clear tranquillity", but in fact moving, "Bright as that wandering Eden Lucifer".

Chasing rest and flying from flight, a *perpetuum mobile* which has no end unless in utter exhaustion, find powerfully condensed expression in the drawing alluded to. Two naked figures are sketchily but vigorously shown running, apparently over mountain tops or through clouds; a horned moon[23] is below their feet. They are in identical attitudes of furious, or desperate speed, their arms outstretched in front of them. It has been suggested in a recent study of Shelley[24] that the slightly larger figure in front, the pursued, is hermaphroditic, and perhaps it is—it seems to have both breasts and a vague suggestion of male genitals. What there is no doubt about is the formidable claws, veritable talons, with which the pursuer is trying to catch it. The pursuing figure is indeed all arms and claws—the head is so faintly drawn as to be almost invisible, and the arms are so large that they are almost wings.

Wings and claws and women's breasts together make one think of a harpy; and there suddenly flies into one's mind the most arresting of all stage directions in Shakespeare, "Enter Ariel, like a Harpy". All the winged species that fly through the air of myth are related, as has been said, and can interbreed and change into each other with lightning ease, but it may be that between Ariel and a harpy there is a special affinity: between the most harmless, innocent and, though sometimes complaining and capricious, gentle thing that flies, and the most rapacious, whose name means snatcher. Ariel scarcely has a body, lives on nectar and among flowers; the harpy stinks of blood and corruption, is a devourer of flesh, and defiles what she does not snatch for herself. She is not Ariel's true opposite (that, of course, is Caliban's place) but his horrible sister, who can change places with him, and who indeed naturally inhabits the same place, the island of imaginary perfections and delicious, magically provided, and wholly innocent repasts.

Such an island is conjured up, a mirage-oasis in the wilderness, by the still persistent Tempter in *Paradise Regain'd*, where he shows to Christ

> In ample space beneath the broadest shade
> A Table richly spred, in regal mode,
> With dishes pil'd, and meats of noblest sort—

the feast being, moreover (according to the Devil) of a guaranteed good and lawful sort, kosher as it were—

> These are not Fruits forbidd'n, no interdict
> Defends the touching of these viands pure;
> Thir taste no knowledge works, at least of evil,
> But life preserves, destroys life's enemy,

Hunger, with sweet restorative delight.
All these are Spirits of Air, and Woods, and Springs,
Thy gentle Ministers, who come to pay
Thee homage, and acknowledge thee thir Lord :
What doubt'st thou Son of God ? sit down and eat.

And when Christ still refuses to accept the deceit the despoilers come—

> . . . With that
> Both Table and Provisions vanish'd quite
> With sound of Harpies wings and talons heard.

Milton's echo of *The Tempest* seems likely to have been direct, but that is not the point here; it is rather that harpies appear in one place as in the other as destroyers of illusion. The harpy is a terrible creature, but she has an important, even a necessary task. When Ariel enters like a harpy he comes both to make the banquet vanish and to expose treachery, to remind men who they really are and what they have actually done or (it is the same thing in this region) have secretly thought of doing. Of all the tasks he performs what he now does is by far the weightiest, as he interrupts and reveals murderous conspiracy and puts an end to unreal dreams of which each man has been making his own. Above the harpy's full breasts, the longed for haven of sweet nourishment, is her hooked vulture's bill, below are her clutching claws : they tear away pretence and catch at the fugitive. She brings men to their senses. There can be little doubt that Shelley had a harpy, his harpy, at his back. But he never let himself be caught. Or, to put it another way, Ariel never acknowledged his harpy-likeness, and so the potent recognition scene in which there is a "grace" even in "devouring" was impossible for him.

SEVEN

THE PURSUING SHADOW

THOSE WHO FLEE from shadows dare not stop to look back. As such a one hastens after the light—whether of Intellectual Beauty or simply of an *ignis fatuus*, one of those "midnight meteors" so common in Shelley, and in Romantic imagery generally—the shadow, which is his own shadow, is always behind him. One way to free oneself of it is to leave the ground : to the Skylark, as long as he stays aloft, it is possible to say "Shadow of annoyance/ Never come near thee". But even in the air one is not really safe; in the brief dialogue of *The Two Spirits* (written in 1820, the same year as the *Ode to a Skylark*) the one who, "plumed with strong desire/ Wouldst float above the earth", is warned that "A shadow tracks thy flight of fire"; above "the Alpine mountains" the pursuit of the "winged shape" goes on for ever. Another way to escape is to become a shadow oneself; spirits or ghosts don't cast shadows. But to do so does not really exorcise the terror, on the contrary it brings it so close that one is actually living in it, though it may be at the most exalted level : the worshipper in the *Hymn to Intellectual Beauty* is spellbound by the Spirit's own shadow "To fear himself, and love all humankind".

All humankind, the living and the dead, are assembled in the last long poem Shelley wrote, worked upon at Lerici during the months of sailing in the *Ariel–Don Juan*, of worrying about Mary and paying poetic court to Jane Williams, trying to help Leigh Hunt and not to hate Byron, a time of fleeting and uncomfortable pleasures and contagious hysteria (not Shelley alone but others in the party began to see phantoms at Lerici). Shelley mentions in his letters at this time an improvement in health, but also speaks of being in some general way at a complete impasse. He writes to Trelawney asking him to procure prussic acid ("that golden key to the chamber of perpetual rest"[1]), although he has "no intention of suicide at present"; on the same day in another letter he says : "I stand, as it were, on a precipice, which I have ascended with great, and cannot descend with [out?] greater peril, and am content if the heaven above is calm for the passing moment."[2] Such a situation, familiar in dreams, must have referred to many different things at the time in his exterior circumstances and in his mental life, always on the edge of crisis. The specific reference here is to his writing : "I feel too little certainty of the future, and too little satisfaction with regard to the past to undertake any subject seriously and deeply". Nevertheless he was writing (doing much of it, according to tradition, actually in his boat) the last and most profoundly agitated of all his poems, the unfinished *Triumph of Life*.

This triumph is not the victory of life but celebration of a conquest imposed upon it, a Juggernaut triumph in which a huge crowd rushes along in a perpetual motion of self-immolation. The poem is fragmentary, not only in its unfinished state, but in its essence : the endless flight-and-pursuit becomes here so universal that any directed movement seems impossible, and thought itself appears to be suffering the fragmentation of extreme anxiety. The multitude of mankind are reduced not merely to autumn leaves carried on the gale, "Some flying from the thing they feared, and some/ Seeking the object of another's fear", but to a cloud of gnats (an image that recurs) and presently to something even more shadowy. The "valley of perpetual dream" is full of shadows : some of the crowd "mournfully within the gloom/ Of their own shadow walked and called it death;/ And some fled from it as it were a ghost", while others "pursued or spurned the shadows" quite aimlessly. Later (as the poem has been arranged by its editors) there is a further vision, as the light wanes, of a grove which "Grew dense with shadows to its inmost covers,/ The earth was grey with phantoms . . ./ Phantoms diffused around; and some did fling/ Shadows of shadows, yet unlike themselves,/ Behind them . . ." They are like "a flock of vampire bats", pullulating and ubiquitous, breeding in skeletons, flying about the heads of men and perching on their hands.

Bats are flying shadows, animated fragments of darkness; the very conformation of their wings suggests tatters. The mind that sees such a cloud of them has reached a state of panic in which even flight becomes pointless and impossible. It is perhaps fear of this fear, of the complete disintegration that it brings, which drives on the earlier flight. The most dreadful thing would be to turn round and see, not a terrible shape pursuing, but no shape at all, the flying rags of darkness: nothing.

It was a risk that Shelley could not bring himself to take. For all the continual and subtle exploration of his own mind, the self-analysis described in *Prince Athanase* and exemplified throughout his writing, he could neither stop and look round nor reach the last or monster-inhabited region of the labyrinth. In his *Metaphysical Speculations* (written probably between 1812 and 1815) he expressed it exactly:

> Thought can with difficulty visit the intricate and winding chambers which it inhabits. It is like a river whose rapid and perpetual stream flows outwards—like one in dread who speeds through the recesses of some haunted pile and dares not look behind . . . If it were possible to be where we have been, vitally and indeed—if, at the moment of our presence there, we could define the results of our experience—if the passage from sensation to reflection—from a state of passive perception to voluntary contemplation were not so dizzying and so tumultuous, this attempt would be less difficult.

It is no wonder that, according to a well-known story, Shelley fainted with terror on first reading the lines from the *Ancient Mariner*,

> Like one who on a lonely road
> Doth walk in fear and dread,
> And having once turned round walks on,
> And turns no more his head;
> Because he knows a frightful fiend
> Doth close behind him tread.

The verse itself (the wording that of the original version in the *Lyrical Ballads*) is quoted in *Frankenstein*, as young Victor Frankenstein is walking the streets of Ingolstadt in terror and distraction the morning after the night in which he brought the Monster to life: "I . . . felt impelled to hurry on, although drenched by the rain which poured from a black and comfortless sky . . . I hurried on with irregular steps, not daring to look about me."

It is time to return to *Frankenstein* and to Mary Shelley, whose attitude to her own mind, so similar in many ways to Shelley's, was in this crucial matter different. She also was acquainted with the dark labyrinth of thought, but she did not despair of finding her way, nor was she deterred by fear of what she would meet. Introspection was for her the product of depression rather than an intellectual exercise, but she did not shrink from it. An entry in her *Journal* at a time of grief and dejection (in the early spring of her last year with Shelley) speaks of emotional outgoing without return—"Feelings, sentiments—more invaluable than gold or precious stones—are the coin, and what is bought? Contempt, discontent, and disappointment, if indeed the mind be not loaded with drearier memories", but she resolves to go on dealing with reality as best she may:

> . . . let me, in my fellow-creatures, love that which is, and not fix my affection on a fair form endued with imaginary attributes; where goodness, kindness and talent are, let me love and admire them at their just rate, neither adorning nor diminishing, and, above all, *let me fearlessly descend into the remotest caverns of my own mind, carry the torch of self-knowledge into its remotest recesses*: [my italics] but too happy if I dislodge any evil spirit or enshrine a new deity in some hitherto uninhabited nook.[3]

She had always been a determined and judicious young woman ("Judge: I know you like the job", said Shelley to her). When six years earlier and in the midst of the strange, exciting, and (as their troubled lives went) carefree summer in Switzerland something monstrous issued, uninvited, from those remotest caverns, she was ready to look it in the face. Ariel was, as usual, taking flight. It was left to Mary to grapple with Caliban. She, though not his creator, could actually acknowledge his existence : his right to exist.

The Monster, or fiend, as he is indifferently called in the novel—he has no name, and it is important that he should have none—is a frightening apparition; but right from the start, in which Mary saw that "what terrified me would terrify others", he is also a figure of pathos. When he comes on the first night to Frankenstein's bedside he is explicitly described as pitiful— "the wretch, the miserable monster whom I had created". The scene, in which he gazes at Frankenstein and tries to speak— "his jaws opened and he uttered some inarticulate sounds, while a grin wrinkled his cheeks. He might have spoken, but I did not hear; one hand was stretched out, seemingly to detain me"—is in truth one to arouse pity as much as fear, and certainly by the author's intention. But Frankenstein doesn't feel pity. The pathetic first attempt at a friendly expression is seen by him only as the ghastly smile that Milton's Death grinned horrible; the hand outstretched not to detain as one man will stop another for conversation, but to catch. He *escapes* and flies, to spend the rest of the night in a state of almost ludicrous terror and discomfort in the courtyard, "fearing each sound as if it were to announce the approach of the demoniacal corpse to which I had so miserably given life" : he himself, it will be noticed, rather than the Monster, is the object of his pity. Even at this early point the reader cannot help saying to himself : If only Frankenstein could have shown his creature some sign of recognition and affection, how differently it would all have turned out !

There is no doubt that the reader is meant to think something like that. Throughout the story the pitifulness of the Monster, his terrible loneliness and longing for affection or "sympathy" are made quite explicit; no doubt they drew strength from Mary's own feelings as a lonely child who longed for companionship and whose deepest fear—one which haunted her all her life—was to be rejected and unloved. The part of the Monster's own story in which he hides outside the cottage watching and listening for months to the family within and entering vicariously into their lives—"when they were unhappy, I felt depressed; when they rejoiced, I sympathised with their joys"—is of course a device, and no very plausible one, even granted his formidable intellectual powers, by which he can learn language and something of the social life of man.

He is the savage outside the stockade, looking wonderingly and longingly within; but he is not at this point predatory or envious. In fact he is actively, if clumsily benevolent, doing odd jobs for the cottagers by stealth, like a Robin Goodfellow. All that he wants is to share in the companionship and to learn more of the "overpowering" sensations with which he instinctively responds to the sight of human love; and the sojourn outside the cottage, the nearest he ever gets to breaking out of his utter loneliness, leads directly to the first big scene of rejection. Shelley himself, in his "Review" of *Frankenstein*, found this interview with the blind and venerable De Lacey "one of the most profound and extraordinary instances of pathos that we recollect". The Monster's scheme, to make himself agreeable first of all to a man who can't see how ugly he is, miscarries, and he is driven away, as already described. His fate is to be rejected, always to be on the outside of any wall, and that is clearly why Mary invented the education-by-eavesdropping, as a means whereby he could acquire a necessary share of human culture without any direct contact with human beings. (It is a form of education, one may observe, not without its instances today, and now not by necessity but as an aim, an admired accomplishment of technology.)

At every point of this stage in the story the Monster's claim for some consideration is rebuffed—and it is a reasonable claim, we must not forget, in Godwinian terms a claim for justice. The whole scheme of *Political Justice* is based on the assumption that the claim of need, for happiness or the means of happiness, is reasonable and therefore irresistible : it doesn't require to be argued, it only needs to be recognised. Unfortunately—and here Mary made her first deep undermining of her father's position—the most important claim is not for food and shelter, of which, as Godwin was fond of pointing out, and as the

Monster's way of life showed, one can really do with very little, but for gifts which are neither to be measured as material benefits may be—although material benefits flow from them— nor to be enforced. Godwin's system envisaged the absolute, automatic reign of "Justice" operating the moment the eyes of all human beings were opened to reason, but it was to operate and its claims were, naturally enough, to be effective between human beings only. What happens to those not recognised as human it did not occur to him to inquire, any more than it did to doubt that reason would always be in command of the affections.

The Monster himself, a better Godwinian than his creator, does begin to think in terms of justice and turns, again very reasonably, to Frankenstein for satisfaction: "on you only had I any claim for pity and redress, and from you I determined to seek that justice which I vainly attempted to gain from any other being that wore the human form". True, Godwin's doctrine (eagerly embraced by Shelley) denies that a parent has any particular claims on his children, or the other way about, but if one is the only individual of one's kind (and after all the existence of other individuals can only be inferred at the best of times, it can never be proved) to whom else can one turn than the author of one's being? Surely the plea for justice will be heard there, as Adam thought when he asked God, "Did I request thee, Maker, from my clay/ To mould me man?"

The Monster asks no more, makes no defiant or outrageous demands:

> I will not be tempted to set myself in opposition to thee. I am thy creature, and will be even mild and docile to my natural lord and king, if thou wilt also perform thy part, the which thou owest me. Oh, Frankenstein, be not equitable to every other, and trample upon me alone, to whom thy justice, and even thy clemency and affection, is most due. Remember, I am thy creature; I ought to be thy Adam; but I am rather the fallen angel, whom thou drivest from joy for no misdeed. Everywhere I see bliss, from which I alone am irrevocably excluded. I was benevolent and good; misery made me a fiend. Make me happy, and I shall again be virtuous.

The kernel of the problem is here, of which Shelley, as we have already seen, grasped only the more obvious half. He was much too close to Frankenstein himself to see why, being "equitable to every other", he denied the most obvious and pressing claim upon him. He did not understand why Frankenstein did not do as clearly he ought—he did not even ask the question—and Frankenstein could not see even that he ought. Truly, as Godwin himself was fond of saying in other contexts, "self-deception is of all things most easy".

It is self-deception, as he says, that allows a man to "impute his action to honourable motives, when it is nearly demonstrable that they flowed from some corrupt and contemptible source".[4] What is there corrupt or contemptible in Frankenstein, that noble young man of exalted spirit, whom only to meet is to admire and love? Nothing, of course: for the very act of self-separation which makes the Monster monstrous, evil, malicious and revengeful ensures that his own motives are irreproachable. It is not a question of hypocrisy, Frankenstein has gone far beyond that; his conduct is transparently sincere, with that indefatigable impartial candour which, again, was so important a part of Godwin's system, and which was exemplified so remarkably in Shelley. The only thing Frankenstein conceals from his family and friends is the existence of the Monster, and that he must do to preserve his own unblemished integrity: how can he be candid and own to having created a deceiver?

For it is the Monster who at the end is accused of hypocrisy; he comes to mourn his "last victim" and to own to a mixture of motives, assuming, indeed, within himself some of the conflict which, while Frankenstein was alive, was between them: "I was the slave, not the master, of an impulse, which I detested, yet could not disobey." Frankenstein himself could never have been forced to admit as much: his conflicts have all been merely in a choice between courses of action which may have different consequences but for which the motive of benevolence has been uniformly the same. The Monster has been cunning, cruel, and filled with hatred, and has the effrontery, outrageous to Walton, to confess it. Frankenstein would never have had so to abase himself; he, "the select specimen of all that is worthy of love and admiration among men", was above even thinking himself capable of such wickedness.

He is far above his miserable and nameless creature (actually "unnameable", as Mary Shelley noted years later), although he is of course joined to him in the peculiar symbiosis of flight and pursuit, pursuer and pursued frequently changing places, which has been noted in Shelley's imaginative chases and which in the novel reveals to us the bond between them. Like Falkland and Caleb Williams they may be far apart—Frankenstein never knows just where the Monster is, how nearly, as the saying goes, he is being shadowed—but they are continually and intensely aware of each other.

Unlike Godwin's pair, when they do meet face to face there is no question of reconciliation. At each of his direct encounters with the Monster, Frankenstein treats him with furious, indeed with growing hostility. First, when after all his labours he succeeds in bringing the Monster to life, he is immediately filled with "breathless horror and disgust". Secondly, after the first murder, when they meet on the glacier and the Monster makes his eloquent plea for sympathy, Frankenstein replies only "Begone! I will not hear you". He cannot even bear to see the Monster, who, with a touching simplicity, tries to "relieve" him by putting his hands over Frankenstein's eyes, making him like the monkey who will see no evil. Like everything else he does, it merely provokes rage in Frankenstein, who is far too effectively blindfolded already. He reluctantly listens to the Monster's history and his final poignant appeal for a female companion to be his mate and one "with whom I can live in the interchange of those sympathies necessary for my being". (It is noticeable that Frankenstein, here again less of a Godwinian than the Monster, seems himself to be unaware of the need for "sympathy"; he is more inclined to shut himself away from human intercourse like the poet in *Alastor*.)

At this point the argument of justice does make an impression, if a very small one, on Frankenstein, and though he continues to say "Begone!" (the equivalent, one may observe, of Shelley's "Away!") he is induced, as much by fear of the

Monster's power as anything else, to promise him a synthetic mate—"as hideous as myself", as the Monster says; it is the best he can expect. " 'It is true'," he adds, with bitter irony, " 'we shall be monsters, cut off from all the world; but on that account we shall be more attached to one another. Our lives will not be happy, but they will be harmless, and free from the misery I now feel.' " He goes on, Caliban-like, to envisage the life of not entirely ignoble savagery the two of them will lead, exiled to the primeval forest (" 'the vast wilds of South America' ") and living on fruit and nuts; he is, as he points out, vegetarian (" 'I do not destroy the lamb and the kid to glut my appetite' "), although the potential violence of his nature forcibly gives the lie to Shelley's expectation of pacific improvement on the adoption of a "natural diet".

As he listens to this, and can visualise the Monster living far away and almost in a state of innocence, Frankenstein's compassion is aroused; though as soon as he looks at him again and sees the Monster's actuality, "the filthy mass that moved and talked", he is disgusted and his feelings change back to "horror and disgust". Nevertheless, he agrees grudgingly, and the bargain is struck, with a significant difference in the manner of agreement between one party and the other. Frankenstein demands that the Monster should give his "solemn oath" to observe his side of it to live in perpetual exile and far from all neighbourhood of man with the female companion to be provided. The Monster readily complies, in eloquent and moving terms " 'I swear, by the sun, and by the blue sky of Heaven, and by the fire of love that burns my heart, that if you grant my prayer, while they exist you shall never behold me again.' "

Frankenstein for his part does not swear at all, he merely "consents". The Monster, especially in that aspect of him which shows most at this point, of savage or wild man, is able to make an affirmation, calling to witness the splendours of nature and the strength of his own feelings; he is even able to pray, or to think of his desires as prayer. But Frankenstein, though he has raised himself intellectually to the point where he himself can be the object of prayer, has nobody to pray to or swear by. He, even more than his creature, is utterly alone.

It is interesting to see how, when the interview is over and he leaves, gazing at the mountain scenery about him (the same that Mary and Shelley saw together), he feels none of the Monster's kinship with sun and sky, but is wholly alienated even from the "wonderful solemnity" : " 'Oh! stars and clouds, and winds', " he exclaims, " 'ye are all about to mock me : if ye really pity me, crush sensation and memory; let me become as nought; but if not, depart, depart, and leave me in darkness.' "

This is the real crisis of the story, though as commonly happens when motives are disguised or unacknowledged, the breaking point is postponed. Frankenstein departs to lay his plans for a second creation, incidentally putting off his proposed marriage to his "cousin" Elizabeth; there is a direct link between the wedding of monsters and his own—"I must perform my engagement, and let the monster depart with his mate, before I allowed myself to enjoy the delight of a union from which I expected peace." He chooses an island in the Orkneys as suitably barren and lonely; islands are, as it appears, the most favourable places for such work, from Prospero's to the *Island of Dr Moreau*. But it is already clear that what he has engaged to do is, from his point of view, "unthinkable", and he has only embarked upon it by not thinking about it. Prometheus is represented, as we saw earlier, as the maker of man but not of woman (who could only be made by God); whether or not the "modern Prometheus" knew this detail of his ancestral legend, he certainly suffered the same inhibition.

As the work progresses his fears and disgust grow, and he reflects that just as he had no notion, when making him, of the character of the original Monster, so he knows even less of the "disposition" of a female, more mysterious and more dangerous than the male. The Monster may have sworn to live in the desert, but not she, "who in all probability was to become a thinking and reasoning animal", and she might refuse. (Is there a distant echo here of Shelley's dismay when his first wife, "a splendid animal" as he called her, turned out to be not exactly what he expected?) She might become "ten thousand times more malignant than her mate, and delight, for its own

sake, in murder and wretchedness". The thought of the copula-
tion of the monsters, and their progeny, strikes Frankenstein
next, possibly with a memory of that overwhelming image of
sexual disgust, the figure of Sin in *Paradise Lost*, whose incestuous mother-son union with Death breeds the pack of "yelling
Monsters" who issue from and take refuge in her horribly
fertile womb. He reflects that "a race of devils would be propa-
gated upon the earth, who might make the very existence of
the species of man a condition precarious and full of terror.
Had I the right, for my own benefit, to inflict this curse upon
everlasting generations?"

We can already see the way things are going; and it is no
surprise when, self-persuaded by these arguments of expediency
—after all, what dishonour or crime is not justifiable if upon it
may be represented to depend "the existence of the whole
human race?"—he decides to break his promise. A glimpse of
the Monster looking in at the window merely moves him to
fury as he sees on the Monster's face an expression of "the
utmost extent of malice and treachery". It is he himself, of
course, who is contemplating treachery, and he proceeds immediately to tear the half-made female monster to pieces. The act
does not relieve his mind, on the contrary it produces "the most
terrible reveries"; later on he partially admits to himself what
he has done in destroying the "half-finished creature": "I
almost felt as if I had mangled the living flesh of a human
being." To bring forth a child, a new creation, and for it then
to die, was something Mary knew about; she also realised that
the mind can have its miscarriages and abortions, and that in
some ways they are worse.

By this time, however, the Monster has discovered how he
has been cheated, and denounces Frankenstein in memorable
terms: "Slave, I before reasoned with you, but you have
proved yourself unworthy of my condescension. Remember
that I have power; you believe yourself miserable, but I can
make you so wretched that the light of day will be hateful to
you. You are my creator, but I am your master.' It is a
striking, though as we can see an inevitable reversal of positions,
and even Frankenstein can see it himself: " 'The hour of *my*

irresolution is past, and the period of *your* power is arrived' "
(my italics). He continues to be "firm" and "inexorable", and
to exclaim "Begone!", but these assertions of unalterable purpose have a notably ineffectual ring. Despite the counter-
threats he utters on this and other occasions, he is completely
unable, even when armed, to overcome the Monster or to carry
out his declared intention of killing him. It is a remarkable
evidence of Mary's insight into the workings of alienation, that
this step should be felt as "resolution". Frankenstein's real
resolution, clearly, is to deliver himself entirely into the hands
of the Monster: it is an act of will by which the will is
abandoned.

The Monster departs, with a final menace—justly balancing
what Frankenstein has been doing to womankind in his destruction or abortion of the female monster—"I shall be with you on
your wedding-night." It is necessary for the plot, but it is also
perfectly fitting, that Frankenstein should mistake this obvious
threat to his bride as being directed against himself; he has a
natural predisposition to think of himself before anyone else as
the subject of misfortune and the object of malignity. Moreover, it is in the essence of their relationship that while the
Monster understands him very well, knows his thoughts, and
can anticipate his actions, Frankenstein has no idea what goes
on inside the Monster's head and always, if he thinks about his
intentions at all, gets them wrong. Thus the rational intellect
naturally, indeed almost necessarily, denies the possibility of
unconscious thought, which is inconceivable in its own terms;
and thus the unconscious is, as it has been expressed, "wiser"
than consciousness.

From now on, in any case, Frankenstein is completely in the
Monster's control. His friend Clerval is strangled, the circumstances pointing directly to him as murderer, but he is of course
proved "innocent" by an alibi; his "innocence" is a necessary
part of his relationship with the Monster. The wedding with his
foster-sister "cousin" is arranged, and Frankenstein remembers
the Monster's threat, but with infatuate egocentricity continues
to think of it only as directed against his own life; he even looks
forward with something like complacency to sacrificing himself

for his bride—"I would die to make her happy." He arms himself with pistols (we remember Shelley's fondness for pistol-shooting) and mounts guard *outside* the marriage-chamber; when the Monster has strangled his Elizabeth he rushes in and gets a chance, of course ineffectually, to shoot at the Monster through the window.

It is impossible not to recall the incident at Tanyrallt, when Shelley's "assailant" came at him through the window, declaiming like a villain in melodrama, "By God I will be revenged! I will murder your wife and ravish your sister", and Shelley's ready-loaded pistol "misfired". As Frankenstein describes it, this violent encounter with the Monster exactly parallels Shelley's account of what happened at Tanyrallt (retailed by Harriet); in the same way Frankenstein, "with a sensation of horror not to be described" sees at the open window "a figure the most hideous and abhorred"; the Monster, a "grin" on his face and seeming to "jeer", sounds very like the apparition drawn afterwards by Shelley, also looking back with a fiendish grin. The reaction of bystanders, too, is the same : as Frankenstein says, there is a search for the assailant, but "After passing several hours, we returned hopeless, most of my companions believing it to have been a form conjured up by my fancy".

The difference is that a murder has been actually done. Frankenstein's brush with the Monster is a much grimmer business; and it is tempting not only to look back to Tanyrallt but forward to the much more dreadful and ominous night at Lerici, during the extraordinary time of dreams and visions shortly before Shelley was drowned. Then Shelley, walking and screaming in his sleep, saw (as he afterwards told Mary) first the Williamses like corpses, Edward Williams saying "Get up, Shelley, the sea is flooding the house and it is all coming down", and then "the figure of himself strangling me" (i.e. Mary herself).[5]

After the final murder the chase is resumed, but with Frankenstein now pursuing the Monster, "Hurried away by fury" and, indeed, mad; there is an interval during which he is confined as a lunatic and when he is released and attempts to enlist the help of the magistrates—the only time, apart from his dying narrative to Walton, that he tells another human being of the Monster's existence—he is disbelieved. He sets off alone to find the Monster, in a condition approaching delirium : "all voluntary thought was swallowed up and lost."

Volition, in fact, has passed to the Monster, who in this strange pursuit controls and guides the pursuer. He waits to see if Frankenstein is alive and fit to follow, deliberately lingering to make contact again; as the chase moves away, through Europe and northwards further into desolation, he leaves clues for Frankenstein to pick up and help him on his way. Franken-stein, finding food mysteriously left for him or "insurmountable obstacles" overcome, does not appear to recognise these as the Monster's work or, if he does so, describes it in an odd way, believing that a "spirit of good followed and directed my foot-steps". It is a curious phrase altogether, for it is difficult at first to see how one's footsteps can be guided by a follower; it is in fact the Monster, leaving footprints in the snow or messages written on trees, who is directing and leading him. But it is natural that Frankenstein should put it in such a way. It is impossible for him to accept any help from the Monster or acknowledge him in any way as a "spirit of good", although by seeking him instead of fleeing him he has already reversed their relationship. As previously he fled towards "the light", the exalted goodness, knowledge, and altruism to which he was devoted, and his shadow followed, so now in his abandonment the light is behind him and his shadow goes before, like the Spectre of the Brocken.

EIGHT

INNOCENCE AND GUILT

IT IS AS useless to pursue shadows, of course, as it is to fly from them. The only way to come to terms with a shadow is to stand still, which may give one a chance to look at it and recognise it as joined to oneself. But Frankenstein is no more capable of that than was Shelley.

It is impossible that he should catch up with the Monster, or sit still and wait for the Monster to return to him. In the final stage of his flight and pursuit all he can do is suffer and die, thus escaping in the only way open to him; and the Monster, who leads him deliberately to regions of the most extreme harshness and loneliness, is ready to co-operate, urging him indeed to take just such precautions as will prolong his agonies as long as may be: "Wrap yourself in furs and provide food", reads one of the messages he leaves behind, "for we shall soon enter upon a journey where your sufferings will satisfy my everlasting hatred." They arrive, seriatim, on the shores of the Arctic, and a delicate irony shows Frankenstein kneeling down and thanking "my guiding spirit"—that "spirit of good" which he discerns at work, though blind to its identity with the Monster himself—"for conducting me in safety to the place where I hoped, notwithstanding my adversary's gibe, to meet and grapple with him". The Monster, too, looks forward to a last meeting; in an earlier guide-note he has already urged Frankenstein, "Come on, my enemy; we have yet to wrestle for our lives".

But there is no Peniel in the Arctic sea; this Jacob can never catch up or be caught by his angel, nor can there be even the sort of dying reconciliation that ends the pursuit of Caleb Williams. That there should not be anything of the kind, despite the obvious temptations in the way of a grand Miltonic encounter and expostulation, argues an extraordinarily fine instinct in Mary Shelley; indeed it shows her obedient to forces shaping her work of art beyond her conscious will. That there should be no final encounter and consequently no resolution of the antagonists is essential, as we shall see, to the story's effect upon us. It is, so to speak, unfinished, but that does not mean it is imperfect. What happens in the final scene of the novel, though quite different from such a consummating set-to as might be envisaged—a trial-scene of the kind Godwin was so fond of staging—initiates a trial more searching and prolonged.

For Frankenstein himself the story ends, in frozen exhaustion. He has lived only long enough to tell Walton his history, a device which not only provides the mechanism of the novel as a retrospective narrative, but places it as a whole against the background of its beginning and ending. Nothing is said about this in the course of the story, there are none of the realistic asides which another writer might have been tempted to insert for the sake of verisimilitude, to remind us where and when the story-within-a-story is being told. Such interruptions would be quite inappropriate. But at the end all is brought into focus again, within its actual scene of Arctic desolation; where the whole may be seen, if not as a formal trial, as the presentation of evidence.

By the time it is complete—by the time, that is to say, Frankenstein has brought his history up to the present—the action, and his life, are over. There is neither summing up nor verdict; there is no judge, nor is there a jury in the ordinary sense—though perhaps what happens in these last pages of *Frankenstein* is something of the kind that William Godwin envisaged when society should have become perfectly just and equitable, and the only governing bodies should be juries, assemblies of equals in which all should consider the conduct of all. Everything now, as first Frankenstein and after him the Monster make their final pleas in the presence of Walton, is called in question, and accuser and accused constantly change places. Nor, indeed, is Walton himself unaffected. There are no detached observers, none with the "angelic impartiality" that Godwin required in moral discussion. All are personally involved in the case; and we ourselves, hearing it long afterwards, are not, perhaps, more disinterested.

In the last hours of his life Frankenstein revolves again, inconclusively but revealingly, the question of his own responsibility, of guilt or innocence. He arrives at no new discoveries about himself; but the very fact that he does not makes the nature of his innocence—or it would be less misleading to say his guiltlessness—more apparent. It is emphasised, of course, throughout the story. He suffers agonies of conscience, it is true, he is hagridden by remorse, but it is always made perfectly clear, using the central device of the whole story as means, that he is not personally to blame for the disasters that overtake him and his family. The crimes of which the novel is a catalogue are committed not by him but by the Monster, and even when he is inclined to name himself as their author by proxy, there are others to dissuade and reassure him.

He is accused of one murder (of Clerval) and even imprisoned, but soon cleared and released with apologies and expressions of sympathy. From time to time he accuses himself, asserting that all the victims "died by my hands", but it is taken, and meant to be taken, as the extravagant self-reproach of an over-sensitive soul. He is unable to explain what he means by these self-reproaches because, of course, the very existence of the Monster is a secret, a truly guilty secret, which he cannot share. From the very start, before any crime has been committed, the close secrecy in which Frankenstein sets about his work and, having accomplished it, his extreme anxiety lest its result should become known point to the strongest feelings of guilt. His immediate repulsion and rejection of the Monster have already been noted, but even these are not so strong as his desire for concealment; when, the day after the Monster has been brought to life Frankenstein's friend Clerval turns up, there is no question of unburdening himself; on the contrary, Frankenstein is terrified lest Clerval should find out what has happened. When the two return to his room, where the newly living creature may yet be, "I dreaded", he says, "to behold this monster; but I feared still more that Henry should see him."

That, of course, is before the Monster has revealed—or has
developed—his "malignity". After the first murder, with Frankenstein's immediate certainty that the Monster is the murderer,
his absolute inability to reveal his knowledge is even more
striking. The servant-girl, Justine, is accused of the crime and
her life is at stake; Frankenstein, knowing the truth and even
promising beforehand that he will be able to save her, is quite
unable to declare it. He even reaches the absurd position of
contemplating a bogus confession: "A thousand times rather
would I have confessed myself guilty of the crime ascribed to
Justine; but I was absent when it was committed . . ."; he cannot, however, tell the truth. We are reminded, throughout the
story of Justine's wrongful conviction and execution, of the
murder in *Caleb Williams* to which Falkland *cannot* confess,
although two innocent men are hanged for it; but the effect is
hugely enhanced here, is indeed removed to another level of
expression, by changing Falkland's overriding regard for his
"reputation", which makes it impossible for him to acknowledge his crime, to the actual innocence, in literal terms, of
Frankenstein. In this he never alters, though continuing to
express it ambiguously: after the murder of Clerval has been
added to the list, he may say that he has been the cause of all
these deaths and exclaim that "they all died by my hands", but
he says it, of course, in such a way that no one believes him,
and even in the same breath (speaking here of Justine) describes
her as being "*as innocent as I*".

Even at the last when, as has already been described, he
resolves to make a clean breast of it and formally lay accusation
against the Monster before a magistrate, he is disbelieved, and
is bound to be: for just as he is literally innocent, so is the
existence of the Monster literally incredible, and the region
where the contradiction may be resolved is only understood as
"delirium". Faced with the magistrates' rational scepticism
(which mirrors his own) he makes no further attempt at self-
revelation, but departs with what is the only possible comment
on such eminently reasonable incredulity: " 'Man', I cried,
'how ignorant art thou in thy pride of wisdom!' " He speaks
not only to the magistrate, but to himself.

Frankenstein's innocence, the unsullied and conscious up-rightness of his motives, is no less than Shelley's: who was, of course, in his own eyes and the eyes of all but his enemies, the most blameless of men, actually incapable of doing wrong. "You know Shelley, you saw his face," wrote Mary indignantly to a retailer of scandalous stories about him, "and could you believe them? . . . none who had ever seen my husband could ever credit them . . . Shelley is as incapable of cruelty as the softest woman."[1] It was Byron's opinion, it was Trelawny's, it was Shelley's himself; it had to be. A good conscience was necessary to him in a degree hard for those to imagine who can conceive of such a thing as a bad conscience, which Shelley could not. A bad conscience is an unreasonable state of mind: the pure doctrine of Godwinism, codifying and making rigid, literal, and devoid of irony the Socratic saying that all sin is ignorance, laid it down that, as it is only necessary for an action to be demonstrated as good or just for it to be adopted, so it is needful only for evil to be recognised for it to be abandoned. That "That which gives the last zest to our enjoyment, is the approbation of our own minds" is a fundamental precept of *Political Justice*. In Shelley's own *Proposals for an Association of Philanthropists*, written when he was twenty, he laid it down that "Conscience is a Government before which all others sink into nothingness"—a gloss upon Godwin, but with a binding force upon himself throughout the whole of his life. It enabled him to stand up to mere terrestrial governments, and heavenly ones as well, with extraordinary courage and constancy. But in elevating something within himself to such absolute, or tyrannical power he invited its deception: the first thing that happens to tyrants is that they are told lies.

In the dedicatory verses of *The Revolt of Islam*, addressed to Mary, Shelley recorded his resolution in childhood, "I will be wise,/ And just, and free, and mild", and there is no question that this resolve, which immediately produced calm ("I then controlled/ My tears, my heart grew calm, and I was meek and bold") remained with him, and that he kept it: in his own sight, that is to say, and under the command of his conscience. It was therefore impossible for him to do wrong, though he might be in error, or be deceived; indeed he went through life being grievously deceived by others.

The principle that all evil-doing is error did not necessarily extend to other people. The consequences could have elements of farce, as in the affair of Elizabeth Hitchener, the free-thinking schoolmistress to whom in 1811 and 1812 Shelley wrote a series of exalted letters, full of the most extravagant expressions of love and esteem, and who, when finally induced to join the Shelley menage, degenerated so rapidly in his eyes to "the Brown Demon". There is something humorous perhaps, about the spectacle of Shelley darting from extreme to extreme : writing, for instance, to Miss Hitchener his absolute conviction of her "taintlessness and sincerity" ("But wherefore do I talk thus, when we know, feel, each other; when every sentiment is reciprocal; when congeniality, so often laughed at, both have found proof strong as internal evidence can afford?") and going on in the next sentence to speak of another, presumably Hogg, in whom he had been "fearfully deceived" ("It is not the degradation of imposition that I lament, but that a character moulded, as I imagined, in all the symmetry of Virtue, should exhibit the loathsome deformity of Vice—that a saviour should change to a destroyer.")[2] The farce may be heightened if we move on a year and find Shelley writing this time to Hogg about Miss Hitchener : "She is an artful, superficial, ugly, hermaphroditical beast of a woman, and my astonishment at my fatuity, inconsistency, and bad taste was never so great, as after living four months with her as an inmate. What would Hell be, were such a woman in Heaven?"[3]

Such reversals are ludicrous enough (though less funny for the unfortunate Miss Hitchener at the time); indeed one may almost see in them a self-mockery very near the surface, the jeering grin of the demon whom a short while later Shelley saw and drew at Tanyrallt. It is interesting, also, to see the mechanism at work by which as one person appears a paragon (or, in the case of Hogg, is reinstated as such) another becomes, apparently by necessity, a beast : like the Fair and Foul weather figures of a toy barometer popping in and out, being in fact (though the works are not visible) joined together.

Shelley's life continued to be full of people who suddenly revealed the loathsome deformity of being less than perfect, and in time he came almost to expect it. To some extent the oscillations of Fair and Foul became, with experience, stabilised : the opposition was not so much between the angels and demons of new acquaintance as between his own virtue, of which he was sure, and the world's turpitude, of which he became (and not without good reason) convinced. In the affair of the slander already mentioned, the story repeated by the Hoppners to Byron that Shelley had had a child by Claire Clairmont, and had abandoned it in a Neapolitan foundling hospital—which was possibly the most vicious of many malicious tales told about him—he could be calmer than Mary. His calm rested on the unshakable consciousness of his virtue in a wicked world; he was however anxious that Mary should take action to clear his name, and the letter in which he urged her to this expresses his idea of himself very clearly :

> . . . when persons who have known me are capable of conceiving me—not that I have fallen into a great error, as would have been the living with Claire as my mistress—but that I have committed such unutterable crimes as destroying or abandoning a child, and that my own ! Imagine my despair of good, imagine how it is possible that one of so weak and sensitive a nature as mine can run further the gauntlet of this hellish society of men. You should write to the Hoppners a letter refuting the charge . . .[4]

It may be noted that as Shelley conceived himself, what he was capable of (as he was certainly capable, even in his own eyes, of taking a mistress) was to be thought of as error; anything else, including something so "monstrous and incredible" as the crime, which he was prepared to call a crime, that the Hoppners believed of him, was completely out of the question. Yet such crimes are committed by men.

A day later he wrote to Mary again, exhorting her further to refute the calumny : "A certain degree and a certain kind of infamy is to be borne, and, in fact is the best compliment which an exalted nature can receive from the filthy world, of which it is hell to be a part; but this sort of thing exceeds the measure." Indeed it did, it was revengeful malice and black-mail; and indeed, again, it is obviously true that Shelley was much slandered and ill-used by an obtuse and censorious world, eager to believe the worst of him. It is not his resentment that is surprising, or his feeling of being an outcast and suffering undeserved injury, but the manner of expressing it. Under attack anyone tends to exaggerate; but it is not many who feel able to say, as Shelley did, in his first exchange of letters with Leigh Hunt:

> . . . I do not seek to conceal from myself, that I am an outcast from human society; my name is execrated by all who under-stand its entire import—by those very beings whose happiness I most ardently desire. I am an object of compassion to a few more benevolent than the rest, all else abhor and avoid me. With you, and perhaps some others . . . my gentleness and sincerity find favour, because they are themselves gentle and sincere . . .[5]

Within a few days of writing thus, in the December of 1816, Shelley's consciousness of gentleness, sincerity, and just dealing was put to a severe test, with the news that the body of his first wife, Harriet, had been taken from the Serpentine. It seems that she had drowned herself, in loneliness and despair, some weeks before; the exact circumstances of her suicide and of her life immediately beforehand, whether or not she was, as reported, pregnant, and by whom, will probably never be known, and are still the subject of lively partisanship, in which it is no part of the present purpose to enter. The point here is only to note Shelley's partisanship on his own behalf, his readi-ness to believe the worst of Harriet, and his absolute repudia-tion of any blame attaching to himself. To Mary he wrote:

> I have spent a day, my beloved, of somewhat agonising sensa-tions, such as the contemplation of vice and folly and hard-heartedness, exceeding all conception, must produce . . .
> It is through you that I can entertain without despair the recollection of the horrors of unutterable villainy that led to this dark, dreadful death . . .

Everything tends to prove, however, that beyond the shock of so hideous a catastrophe having fallen on a human being once so nearly connected with me, there would in any case have been little to regret . . . everyone does me full justice; bears testimony to the upright spirit and liberality of my conduct towards her [Harriet].[6]

It is a strange letter, or it would seem so if it were not perfectly consistent with Shelley's general idea of himself : the immediate conclusion that the "unutterable villainy" of other persons must have been at work in a wretched business in which, as usual, no one of those concerned seems to have been much more or less to blame than another, is an interesting example of the way this mental mechanism works. According to Leigh Hunt, whose "delicate and tender attentions" helped him to bear "the horror of this event", he never forgot it, and well might he not. Indeed he knew that "the curse of this life is, that whatever is once known, can never be unknown"[7]; however much one cries "Away !", knowledge comes along too. But the memory remained as it were encapsulated, neither changing nor bringing about change. Four years later (in replying to the accusations of Southey) it still seemed to Shelley that the fate of Harriet was no more than "a single passage out of a life otherwise not only spotless, but spent in an impassioned pursuit of virtue, which looks like a blot". Before God, supposing him to exist, Shelley is ready to affirm, "I am innocent of ill, either done or intended."[8]

It is a declaration that might stand for the whole of Shelley's life. It was Mary who long after remembered things differently, across more than twenty sufficiently grievous years : "Poor Harriet, to whose sad fate I attribute so many of my heavy sorrows, as the atonement claimed by fate for her death."[9]

The different operations of guilt in Shelley's and Mary's imaginations are well illustrated in works written by them almost at the same time, Shelley's drama *The Cenci* (completed in May, 1819) and the unpublished novella by Mary, *Mathilda*, written in the late summer and autumn of the same year; both, moreover, deal with the same subject, of father-daughter incest.

The Cenci is the one long work of Shelley's which concerns not the grand undifferentiated misdeeds of God, kings, and other tyrants, but an identifiable human crime; its theme, as he said in his dedicatory letter to Leigh Hunt, was not "dreams of what ought to be or may be", but "a sad reality". He enlarged in his preface upon this promise to show the real rather than the ideal, to cast light into "some of the most dark and secret caverns of the human heart"; and very justly maintained that only by appearing herself a creature of passion, swayed by motives of revenge and retaliation, could his heroine Beatrice be a genuinely tragic character.

But this promise he was in practice quite unable to fulfil. His Beatrice Cenci, though based on an historical personage, documented and contemporarily portrayed (her portrait by Guido powerfully affected Shelley as "one of the loveliest specimens of the workmanship of Nature") becomes in the play another embodiment of the Shelleyan Idea. She bears wrongs like Prometheus, entangled in the appalling ambiguities of life—

> Horrible things have been in this wide world,
> Prodigious mixtures, and confusions strange
> Of good and ill—

but remains herself pure, unmixed or unsullied, in fact innocent. She is also, of course, a murderess, the instigator of her father's murder in revenge and atonement for her rape; and though parricide was of all violent crimes the one least likely to have Shelley's disapprobation, yet crime it was even in his eyes, incompatible with absolute virtue and mildness, the qualities of "one of those rare persons in whom energy and gentleness dwell together without destroying one another".

The solution to this contradiction in the emotional substructure of the drama is simple denial. Beatrice denies the murder and maintains her innocence before her judges and torturers with exemplary fortitude; she herself, her family, and, one feels, her author maintain her guiltlessness alone amidst all the rest—

> . . . the one thing innocent and pure
> In this black guilty world —

with a vehemence that almost—although we have actually seen Beatrice urging on and paying the murderers—seems to make the murder disappear. When she is condemned it somehow appears that the sentence is unjust, not merely in the sense of being harsh and cruel punishment for an act to which she was overpoweringly provoked, but as passed on one who has done no ill whatever. She herself by this time has, one may say, quite forgotten the murder; she goes to her death exhorting her brother to be constant

> . . . to the faith that I,
> Though wrapped in a strange cloud of crime and shame,
> Lived ever holy and unstained.

There is no doubt that herein lies the one serious flaw in *The Cenci* as a work of art. That the historical Beatrice denied the murder is, in this context, neither here nor there; Shelley did not so represent her for the sake of verisimilitude but because in obedience to his own emotional needs and prohibitions he had to; to have acknowledged it would have involved exploring "the dark and secret caverns of the human heart", further and deeper than he could tolerate. Beatrice, the noblest of heroines, of unblemished purity, tenderness of heart, dauntless courage, goes to her death, therefore, in the name of a lie; which may very well happen in ordinary human terms, but those are not the terms in which the play is written or her character conceived. She defies the rack in the name of truth while actually perjuring herself and urging others to perjury; and though she convinces one witness at least (one of the assassins who killed her father at her bidding) of the "higher truth" that "she is most innocent" she cannot convince the reader or close the gap between the Shelleyan Ideal which she represents and the actual human evil done both upon and by her. To be convinced, indeed, an act of dissociation was necessary; which Shelley performed not only in the play but (with a direct echo of lines already quoted) in the preface where he was speaking of the historical Beatrice, of "simple and profound" nature so like his image of his own : "The crimes and miseries in which she

was an actor and a sufferer are as the mask and the mantle in
which circumstances clothed her for her impersonation on the
scene of the world." She and her life, as victim of incestuous
rape and suborner of murder, were disconnected; almost they
were different persons.

The heroine of *Mathilda*[10] tells her history and looks on her
part in it in a different way. The story is of great biographical
interest : Mary wrote it at a time of deep depression after the
deaths first of her baby daughter Clara and (in June 1819)
of little William Shelley; in her grief she appears to have
become estranged from Shelley, or at least to have treated him
with "coldness" for which she afterwards reproached herself.
Mathilda was an attempt to come to terms with her desolation,
to look it in the face and understand it. Death itself, she says,
with the knowledge of experience, is "too terrible an object for
the living", it is "one of those adversities which hurt instead of
purifying the heart; for it is so intense a misery that it hardens
and dulls the feelings". But the death of her children led her
to think back to her own lonely childhood, and to write about
it under a thin disguise with a candour she allowed herself
nowhere else.

Mathilda, like Mary, loses her mother in infancy; her
emotional life is entirely focussed on her father; later she meets
a young poet and, philanthropist, Woodville, whose life is
dedicated to the good of others. Mary, Godwin, and Shelley
are easily to be seen here; but the story is rather of their place
in Mary's inner life than their external relationships, with the
overpowering, and mutual, attachment of father and daughter
as central theme. There is little reason to suppose that Godwin
ever showed—or felt—such a passion for Mary;[11] the incestuous
love of Mathilda's father may be taken, however, as a true
representation of her fantasy. Mathilda, a solitary child in the
care of an aunt (who, "without the slightest tinge of a bad
heart . . . had the coldest that ever filled a human breast" :
Mary's view of her stepmother?) fills her thoughts with dreams
of her absent father and at the age of sixteen is blissfully
reunited with him : "And now I began to live. All around me
was changed from a dull uniformity to the brightest scene of

joy and delight." The aunt dies, father and daughter are together in exclusive and intense affection, until he suddenly changes to a "heart-breaking coldness"; in despair Mathilda at length forces him to acknowledge what by shunning her he has tried to hide, his incestuous passion for her.

The revelation is equally shattering to both : it is made quite clear that her father's love, though striking Mathilda with horror, is reciprocated. She alternates between repulsion and love : ". . . at one moment in pity for his sufferings I would have clasped my father in my arms; and then starting back in horror I spurned him with my foot." She runs away and locks herself in her room; the sound of his footsteps outside excites "the most painful reflections; nor do I now dare express the emotions I felt". Her father disappears, leaving a long letter in which he declares that he cannot eradicate " 'this guilty love more unnatural than hate, that withers your hopes and destroys me for ever' " and that consequently she must never hope to see him again.

Forwarned by a dream, she follows him to the sea-coast, where she learns that he has drowned himself. Prostrated by grief, she seeks absolute solitude and, deliberately leading her relatives to suppose her dead, retires to a lonely cottage where, in fact, she waits to die. She makes the acquaintance of the poet, Woodville, also mourning, in his case the loss of his bride; he exhorts her to hope on grounds of general philanthropy, and dissuades her from the joint suicide she proposes, but her "old habits of feeling" return, "for I was doomed in life to grieve, and to the natural sorrow of my father's death and its most terrific cause, imagination added a tenfold weight of woe. I believe myself polluted by the unnatural love I had inspired, and that I was a creature cursed and set apart by nature." She contracts consumption and writes the last of her history expecting death.

The story, couched in the ordinary manner of Gothic romance,[12] shows extraordinary insight, not least into Mary's feelings for Shelley himself. For Woodville, the poet-paragon, "glorious from his youth", "as one the peculiar delight of the Gods, railed and fenced in by his own divinity, so that naught but love and admiration could approach him"—the ideal shell of Shelley, so to speak—Mathilda has esteem but not love. For this she reproaches but cannot help herself, "the spirit of existence was dead within me"; solitary grief had, she says, made her stony-hearted, "arrogant, peevish, and, above all, suspicious". Mary appears here to be expressing remorse for her coldness to Shelley at this time; but also, though discounted as "peevishness", there may be discerned in Mathilda's complaints of the all-too perfect Woodville Mary's reproach to the unalterable benevolence of the Shelleyan exterior and lack of real feeling. "I . . . thought that if his gentle soul were more gentle, if his intense sympathy were more intense, he could drive the fiend from my soul and make me more human. I am, I thought, a tragedy; a character that he comes to see act : now and then he gives me my cue that I may make a speech more to his purpose; perhaps he is already planning a poem in which I am to figure. I am a farce and I play to him, but to me this is all dreary reality . . ."

The actual mutual passion of Mary and Shelley, their reckless abandonment to each other in 1814, is here most interestingly transferred to Mathilda's love for her father when she is reunited with him at sixteen (Mary's age when Shelley and she eloped). It is emphasised that he is young to be her father, and the effect is enhanced by saying that the interim of his absence has passed for him "as a dream", i.e., unreal : he has become a young man again. He is already an amalgam of Godwin and Shelley, a "man of rank", "sent to Eton and afterwards to College", of extravagant generosity "earnestly occupied about the wants of others"; when he returns and falls in love with his daughter he speaks to Mathilda of her dead mother exactly as Shelley did to Mary of Mary Wollstonecraft. He speaks with "the imagination of a poet"; and his feelings are volcanic; "so tremendous were the ideas which he conveyed that it appeared as if the human heart were far too bounded for their conception". This, we may say, was far more nearly the Shelley Mary fell in love with in 1814 than the wooden compendium of virtue Woodville; and Mathilda's description of her feelings—"O, hours of intense delight !", "there was a new sun and a

new earth created for me; the waters of existence sparkled:
joy! joy!"—must surely hark back to the marvellous early
summer (Mathilda's father returns in the same season) of their
meeting in London.

Even more strikingly, and in ordinary terms, it may be
thought inexplicably—since in this case it harks *forward* three
years—Mathilda's account of her father's drowning, and of her
agonised search for him, driving to the sea and praying only
that she should find him alive—"Let him be alive! It is all
dark; in my abject misery I demand no more: no hope, no
good: only passion, and guilt, and horror; but alive!"—pre-
sages Shelley's death and her desperate drive along the shores
of the Gulf of Spezzia with Jane Williams, seeking for news.
Storm, rain, the roaring of the sea—a sound which after the
catastrophe of 1822 she could never bear to listen to—were all
present in her imagination when she was writing *Mathilda*.
Mary herself drew the parallel, remarking that "Mathilda fore-
tells many small circumstances most truly—and the whole of it
is a monument of what now is".[13]

The impressive thing is that Mary could herself see and
represent in *Mathilda* the connection between her love for her
father and her love for Shelley; it entered indeed into all her
emotional relationships, so that in the story of Mathilda's love
and loss, all her own, her mourning for her little boy and her
prophetic fears for her husband, had a share. She was thus
able, perhaps, to help herself in the depths of her depression;
she was certainly able to deal more justly with the theme of
incest than could Shelley in *The Cenci*, where it becomes in
effect no more than another crime chalked up against the
tyranny of fathers. That Mary, a woman, should view the
matter differently was perhaps natural; but what makes the
difference between Beatrice and Mathilda is not only, nor even
so much that Mathilda loves her father and pities him while
Beatrice makes a "religion" of her hatred[14] but that the love
and guilt are equally real emotions, and are felt by both father
and daughter. There is no question about the guilt; both are
shattered by it, and to this extent *Mathilda* may perhaps
properly be described as a "morbid tale".[15] But the guilt is not

all fastened upon one person, leaving the other spotless; it is not even fastened exclusively upon fate (though Mathilda, dying, does liken herself to Oedipus at Colonus, entering the "sacred horror" of her history as he walked into the grove of Eumenides). It is not, in a word, depersonalised; therefore it can co-exist with and even arise from the same human sources as love. "I had no idea", says Mathilda, "that misery could arise from love, and this lesson that all at last must learn was taught me in a manner few are obliged to receive it" : in the same manner, one may say, it was taught to Beatrice Cenci, but she was unable to receive it.

The love of Mathilda and her father (who is never given a name) is felt to be monstrous. She describes herself as "this monster with whom none might mingle in converse and love"; her father, having admitted his passion, feels himself to have become a "monster" or fiend : "perhaps I am changed in mien as the fallen archangel." It may well be conjectured that the Monster himself who stepped out of Mary's unconscious and came to Frankenstein's bedside had some of his origins in the same place. (There is evidence that *Frankenstein* was a good deal in Mary's thoughts when she was writing *Mathilda*.) But the monster of incestuous desire is not separated, in the second, from human subjects; precisely, in fact, Mary was saying that you can't deal with the "inextricably intwined" good and evil in the world by making one person an angel and writing off another as a monster.

In *Frankenstein* she said the same thing, but in another, vastly more powerful and far-reaching way. For the Monster is separate, and necessarily separate from his maker, the separation being simultaneously the consequence of Frankenstein's absolute virtue and the means of continuing it, a device for committing murder at a distance while remaining innocent one-self, far more effective than Beatrice's bribed assassins and denial of complicity. But the Monster is not merely a device or, one may say, a machine; he is a living creature, and that is the whole point about him. If he is metaphorical he is a living metaphor, and has a life, and desires, and a will of his own quite beyond his maker's control. Indeed, as we have seen, he increasingly assumes control of Frankenstein himself: if he, like the "crimes and miseries" which were only the "mask" of Beatrice, is a life from which Frankenstein is voluntarily divorced, he more and more takes command: he lives Frankenstein's life for him.

To return: Frankenstein, after he has told his whole story to Walton, speaks of his expected death and his fears that he will leave his mission unfulfilled; he still dreams of catching up with the Monster and destroying him—although nature itself, by splitting the ice between them at the climax of the chase, clearly forbids it. He tries to engage Walton as his deputy—" 'swear to me, Walton, that he shall not escape; that you will seek him, and satisfy my vengeance in his death.' " In the same breath he half withdraws lest such a demand seem "selfish", and pins his hopes on his "guiding spirit", the unseen "ministers of vengeance" who may bring the Monster conveniently to hand so that Walton can perform the "task" without putting himself out. He even expects to join these disembodied ministers himself: "call on the *manes* of William, Justine, Clerval, Elizabeth, my father, and of the wretched Victor, and thrust your sword into his heart. I will hover near and direct the steel aright."

The situation in the meantime is complicated by the fact that Walton, in pressing on to the North Pole, has run his ship into danger, thus further exposing Frankenstein's ambivalence towards his "task". It was acquaintance with Walton's perilous ambition as an explorer that induced Frankenstein in the first place to tell his story, as a cautionary tale; now, however, he himself urges Walton on, and even employs his own eloquence (he has just told Walton to beware of the Monster's persuasive and treacherous eloquence) to whip up enthusiasm in the reluctant crew. He delivers a line-of-battle speech of the most hollow kind—" 'Oh! be men, or be more than men. Be steady to your purposes, as firm as a rock. This ice is not made of such stuff as your hearts may be; it is mutable, and cannot withstand you, if you say it shall not. Do not return to your families with the stigma of disgrace marked on your brows. Return as heroes who have fought and conquered . . .' " After such an effort, not surprisingly, he is "sunk in languor, and almost deprived of life". The crew, however—or again perhaps we should say Nature—are not so easily talked into being "more than men", with hearts harder than ice. Walton agrees to retreat, "blasted by cowardice and indecision", if the surrounding ice allows; and at once, as in the *Ancient Mariner*, and possibly with a memory of it, "The ice did split with a thunder fit;/ The helmsman steered us through", and they set course homewards, the crew shouting with "tumultuous joy".

The effect of this renunciation upon Frankenstein, who had urged it in the first place, is fatal: he cannot return to life as nothing more than man. He cannot go back, he cannot go on, he is now like one who stands on a precipice which he has ascended with great peril and cannot descend without greater. He must die, and does so, with a last speech which leaves everything unresolved, elucidating nothing but the contradictions of his own state. That, however, it does brilliantly. He now, as a dying man, repudiates revenge and "burning hatred", but still feels himself "justified in desiring the death of my enemy"; in fact, having spent his last days examining his conduct, he exonerates himself from all blame, and exhorts Walton purely in the name of "reason and virtue".

On the one hand he owns that, having made the Monster, he was "bound towards him, to assure, as far as was in my power, his happiness and well-being" (we remember that he did nothing whatever to promote either). But on the other, " 'My duties towards the beings of my own species had greater claims to my attention, because they included a greater proportion of happiness and misery' ": on such explicitly utilitarian grounds (not to mention those of overriding loyalty to his "own species", or race) he concludes that the Monster deserved and still deserves death as a measure of social hygiene: " 'Miserable himself, that he may render no other wretched, he ought to die.' " He renews his request that Walton should take on the job, now in the name of "reason and virtue", which are of course irresistible. Nevertheless he recognises that he cannot really ask Walton to give up everything for the sake of pursuing and destroying the Monster, which is unlikely to seem a rational employment to anyone else; and being now in some doubts about his own rationality (" 'my judgment and ideas are already disturbed by the near approach of death' ") ends by throwing the whole responsibility back on to Walton and, we may say, on to his larger audience: " '. . . the consideration of these points, and the well-balancing of what you may esteem your duties, I leave to you . . . I dare not ask you to do what I think right, for I may still be misled by passion.' "

In his last words Frankenstein returns, with a truly fascinating ambiguity, to the great question he has hitherto only mentioned incidentally, his own responsibility for creating the Monster in the first place. He seems at first to be repeating what he urged on Walton at the beginning, that he should "dash the cup" of scientific and exploratory ambition from his lips: " 'Farewell, Walton! Seek happiness in tranquillity, and avoid ambition, even if it be only the apparently innocent one of distinguishing yourself in science and discoveries.' " And then he turns again and looks at himself with a flash of real honesty, the first genuine, and genuinely detached piece of self-observation he has shown: " 'Yet why do I say this? I myself have been blasted in these hopes, *yet another may succeed*' " (my italics). He has no real regrets for his discovery, nor does he seriously expect successors to be deterred by his catastrophic example.

"Yet another may succeed" is his last utterance; he dies soon afterwards. His death, and the return of the ship southwards, Walton mourning both "the untimely extinction of this glorious spirit" and the disappointment of his own ambitions, immediately brings the Monster, and a Monster significantly changed. He is as monstrous as ever, "of such loathsome yet appalling hideousness" that Walton, who surprises him contemplating Frankenstein's body, cannot bear to look at him; but, freed from his creator's hatred, he has himself lost his bitterness towards Frankenstein. He does not come to triumph, as Frankenstein expected, but to mourn. He is repentant and full of remorse: " 'Oh, Frankenstein! generous and self-devoted being!' " (what a strange and doubtful epithet, *self-devoted*) " 'what does it avail that I now ask thee to pardon me? I, who destroyed thee by destroying all thou lovedst.' " He tells Walton

—whose first notion, to obey Frankenstein's dying wish and destroy the Monster if he gets a chance, is now turned to "a mixture of curiosity and compassion"—that he used to pity Frankenstein, who never pitied him, even while committing crimes against him. He could not, he says, help himself : " 'A frightful selfishness hurried me on, while my heart was poisoned by remorse.' " He describes himself, preparing the last stroke of his revenge upon Frankenstein in the murder of his bride, as helpless in the grip of his own impulses, even though knowing " 'that I was preparing for myself a deadly torture' ". So he reached the point at which he could repeat the words of Milton's Satan, "Evil be thou my good".

That is, of course, a very odd expression, which linguistic analysis would doubtless cause to vanish into nothing, an equation in which, since the terms define each other, they cancel out. It does not follow that it is devoid of meaning; and perhaps the Monster gets as near to showing us its meaning, not by analysis but more effectively by setting its component and contradictory parts in action before us, as anyone who ever used it. " 'I was the slave' ", he says, " 'of an impulse, which I detested, yet could not disobey :' " an exact echo of his last threatening words to Frankenstein in Orkney, but now applying the master-slave image to himself. He now contains and acknowledges within himself the dichotomy that Frankenstein never recognised.

But it is not simply a question of being split, which, alone, merely produces impasse; there is a deliberate choice, in which whatever chooses consciously opts for despair and destruction, including self-destruction. " 'Urged thus far, I had no choice but to adapt my nature to an element which I had willingly chosen.' " "Willingly chosen", "I had no choice" : isn't this nonsense ? By no means : the act of self-deception by which the absurd formula is accepted, that evil may be good, is an act of will; an act, it may be said, of *pure will*, that is to say of the will as far as it may possibly be divorced from the other elements of mind which now become its dupes. The instincts, or whatever you like to call them, poor devils, are tricked into lending their energies for a false end : thus evil can actually be made to feel like a satisfaction, a good, and provide corroboration of the original lie. When embarked on this disaster course, and the last murder committed, " 'then' ", the Monster says, " 'I was not miserable. I had cast off all feeling, subdued all anguish, to riot in the excess of my despair . . . The completion of my demoniacal design became an insatiable passion.' "

So exactly might Frankenstein have said of himself at the beginning of his enterprise, and so indeed he then implied, describing how, starting his work, his feelings "bore me onwards like a hurricane" (O wild West Wind), and how he became indifferent to everything else, including his own human nature, which often turned "with loathing" from what he was doing. It is not accidental that the summer of the Monster's making "was a most beautiful season : never did the fields bestow a more plentiful harvest or the vines yield a more luxuriant vintage", to all of which he is oblivious. Nor is it accident that in his terrible uneasy sleep between the first animation of the Monster and its appearance at his bedside he is troubled by fearful dreams, in which he embraces his betrothed, his cousin-sister, who turns into a corpse in his arms, and then changes into the putrefying body of his mother. For it is "nature", and especially female or maternal nature, that his work insults.

Frankenstein's dream no doubt reflects the fact that Mary was herself a woman, that in her identification with Shelley-Frankenstein she was in part denying her womanhood; and also that, insofar as the Monster is a creation of incestuous wishes, his emergence must have been so to speak from her mother's grave. It cannot escape notice that Frankenstein, the "modern Prometheus", is in one respect a very odd one, in that his deed of rebellion, whether in stealing fire from Heaven or in the impious act of imitating the Creator, is not in *defiance* of anybody. The contrast has already been remarked between Frankenstein-Prometheus and the Prometheus of Goethe, the robustly down-to-earth Heaven-stormer, who addresses the Father of the Gods, "Dem Schlafenden da droben" (that Sleeper up there) with cheerful contempt, not unlike Blake's manner towards old Nobodaddy up aloft :

Cover your sky, Zeus, with vaporous clouds, and try out, like a boy knocking the heads off thistles, your strength against oak-trees and mountain-tops : you must still leave me my earth standing, and my hut which you did not build, and my hearth for whose warm glow you envy me.

Indeed, the striking thing about this superbly self-reliant Prometheus is that he much more resembles the Monster than Frankenstein; when he speaks of his faith in himself and his "holy glowing heart" ("Hast du nicht alles selbst vollendet,/ Heilig glühend Herz"), so close is the echo in the Monster's oath on the Mer du Glace, "by the fire of love that burns in my heart", that one can't help wondering if Mary knew Goethe's poem at the time. The last two verses certainly seem to picture, not Frankenstein's fears, but the Monster's hopes at that time, when he thought of living with his mate, "linked to the chain of existence" but remote from the sight of man :

Perhaps you thought I should find life hateful, and run away into the wilderness, because not all my dreams blossomed to maturity? Here I sit, making man in my own image, a race that shall resemble me, a race that shall suffer and weep, and know joy and delight, and be heedless of you, as I am.[16]

Two observations must be made at this point. First, the significant difference between Frankenstein and the Monster that the latter—even as, by his own development, he becomes more like his creator—does actually change and develop. To a limited, indeed crippled extent, he "grows up", he passes through the stages, savagely compressed, of innocence and experience. That Frankenstein never does, for all the harrowing things that happen to him; he remains what he was at the beginning, the favourite child of loving parents, bestowed on them by Heaven, "whom to bring up to good, and whose future lot it was in their hands to direct to happiness or misery, according as they fulfilled their duties towards me". They certainly have not failed in their duty, as Frankenstein under-stands it; having been brought up to good, therefore, he must *be* good : the break-out from the position of good and loving child is never accomplished.

Secondly, that Frankenstein, though Mary's creation, and reflecting as has been suggested her attitude towards her own father, is no different in this respect from Shelley. Shelley can hardly be said on the face of it to have lacked awareness of conflict between father and son; and yet the very extreme to which it went in him brings him very near Frankenstein, who never shows anything for his father but pious regard. The resemblance of his revered, benevolent and silver-haired parent to Shelley's ideal old man has already been noted; he is completely different from the vigorous, youthful, and passionate father of Mathilda. As a father, indeed, he scarcely exists; and in the same way Shelley, in the complete irreconcilability of his quarrel with his father, didn't so much defy as abolish him. As Peacock said of him, "he never came under any authority, public or private, for which he entertained, or had cause to entertain, any degree of respect".[17] As a father Timothy Shelley, not evil-intentioned but blundering and self-absorbed, seems rather to have abdicated than have been worsted by his enigma of a son; in the same way that Lord God the Father Almighty in *Prometheus Unbound*, though toppled, topples himself.

The situation there, and in *Frankenstein*, is quite different, therefore, from that of Goethe's Prometheus. His noble, heartening, healthy utterance is in a sense pre-lapsarian; he has not been bound, nor has God been dethroned; they co-exist in a state which, if not altogether peaceful, has not yet led to the annihilation of either. Prometheus, himself young, addresses God as a "boy"; the poem clearly belongs to the Goethe who was (in Schiller's sense) "naive". It has a place in the development of the Prometheus myth; but it shows nothing like the profound and sombre insight of Mary's into the condition of "the modern Prometheus".

All three of the survivors at the end of *Frankenstein* are orphans. Walton's father, as we learn at the beginning, died long since, with the injunction that his son is not to go to sea; his mother is never mentioned. He eventually becomes a sailor and navigator as he has always wished, but again with little sense of defying his father, or in connection with him in any way: he inherits a fortune from a cousin, and devotes it to a career of exploration. Frankenstein's father has died of grief, old age, and sheer ineffectiveness soon after the last of the murders; he counts as one of the Monster's "victims", and his death among those for which Frankenstein can blame himself, but only in the histrionic way already described. His mother has died before his departure for Ingolstadt to learn science and embark on Monster-manufacture. The Monster himself never had either father or mother, and his maker abandoned him, so to speak, at birth.

All three in the final scene are on their own, lost, and without roots of any kind—Walton, it is true, writes letters home, but only to a sister, the nearest thing, in this symbolic structure of relationships, to writing to oneself. Roots indeed are impossible, for who could put them down in the Arctic ice?—Intentionally or not, their situation contributes powerfully to the intense loneliness at the end of the story; and especially to the condition of the Monster, on whom at last, after the death of Frankenstein, all attention is concentrated.

The Monster, it has been suggested, takes on at the end more and more of his maker's characteristics: as Frankenstein becomes progressively de-natured (he has not very far to go) so the Monster acquires more of nature's complexities. But if he has a share of human nature, it only makes more clear, to him and to us, that it is a nature men have repudiated. To Walton he is, literally, too hideous to look at; to himself he is beyond hope of contact with any living creature: " 'No sympathy may I ever find . . . now that virtue has become to me a shadow, and that happiness and affection are turned into bitter and loathing despair, in what should I seek for sympathy? I am content to suffer alone . . .' "

He enlarges terrifyingly before our eyes; for if, specifically, he was Frankenstein's nature that Frankenstein would have nothing to do with, Frankenstein is now dead and he remains as all that part of nature with which men in general, except insofar as they try to control it, have lost touch. The Monster is manifestly out of control, indeed he always has been; Frankenstein, though he had originally dreamed of a new species "blessing" him and obedient to him, abandoned all such possibility and the right to seek it at the beginning. Lost, dangerous, unpredictable—for clearly now he has a will of his own—the Monster departs again, borne away on his ice-floe. He leaves with a promise of self-immolation; no one else, it is implied, has power to destroy him. At the Pole itself, the most extreme point of frozen isolation, " 'I shall collect my funeral pile, and consume to ashes this miserable frame' " and " 'Soon these burning miseries will be extinct' ".

But the last scene, when "the light of that conflagration will fade away" and the Monster's ashes will be "swept into the sea by the winds", though vividly envisaged in advance, is not reached in the book and, we suspect, has not yet been enacted. We cannot but think that the Monster, like Ahasuerus, is not able to perish so easily. We know in fact that he is still alive. The novel ends there, "lost in darkness and distance"; where, waiting for the final bonfire, we still are.

NINE

PROPHECY AND PROJECTION

IT IS DIFFICULT to think of Mary's prophetic vision and the flash of insight that produced it as accidental. To speak in Shelleyan terms, the association of Mary and Shelley, and the strange company they made a part of at Diodati, and the feelings, literary fashions, and common aspirations of the age made a "cloud of mind" whose "uncommunicated lightning" was discharged through Mary; the image of lightning, fire from heaven, instantaneously revealing and blinding, destructive and vivifying, being itself used by Shelley, Mary, and Byron over and over again, and flickering continually throughout Romantic literature in general. Up to now we have been considering some of the influences and connections behind Mary's invention, or what was conceived in her. Now we may turn to look at its implications, which are not less extensive. For it is not simply a question of literary descendants; *Frankenstein* belongs to the literature (and so of course does any work worth talking about in some degree) which has progeny not only in other writing but in ways of thought and consequently in acts : bringing not only other books but worlds into sight.

The purpose of much that has been said so far has been to try and show the extent to which the drama and metaphorical components of *Frankenstein* were *personal* : that is to say how closely and directly they were related to Mary's own situation, and in particular how they sprang from her insight into the character of her extraordinary lover : into the effects of the Shelleyan Idea, the consequences of being Shelley and of being connected with him.

How close was the connection is worth emphasising again. The mutual attraction and attachment of Shelley and Mary was of like to like, and perhaps it may be said that it had to be;

the very temperament they had in common and the attitudes and opinions they adopted favoured such a union, the merging of things akin to one another rather than the fitness of things complementary. "We are born into the world, and there is something within us which, from the instant that we live, more and more thirsts after its likeness", said Shelley in his fragment of an *Essay on Love* (c. 1814). That such a Platonic love, when it came to actual relationships between persons, was incestuous, did not affect its intensity. (In Shelley, brother-sister incest at least, "a most poetical conception" as he called it, was consciously approved: as we have already noted, *The Revolt of Islam,* written out of and to some extent about his love for Mary, was of course originally, as *Laon and Cythna,* an open celebration of it.)

A letter from Shelley to Hogg in the autumn of the year in which he and Mary eloped makes retrospectively some revealing comments both on his disenchantment with Harriet and his feelings about Mary. "Love", he says, "makes men quick-sighted, and is only called blind . . . because he perceives the existence of relations invisible to grosser spirits";[1] but the first use of this quick-sightedness seems to have been in the service of dislike, or hate, rather than love, for he goes on in the next sentence, "I saw the full extent of the calamity which my rash and heartless union with Harriet . . . had produced. *I felt as if a dead and living body had been haled together in loathsome and horrible communion*" (my italics). He proceeded to describe his further reactions "in the subduing voluptuousness of spring" —these thoughts apparently went back to the previous May— and the change in his feelings *before* his introduction to Mary:

A train of visionary events arranged themselves in my imagination until ideas almost acquired the intensity of sensation. Already I had met the female, who was destined to be mine, already she had replied to my exulting recognition, already were the difficulties surmounted that opposed an entire union. I had even proceeded so far as to compose a letter to Harriet on the subject of my passion for another.

He concludes by describing the fulfilment in Mary of this

pre-ordained event—pre-ordained, that is, by himself—saying, "so intimately are our natures now united that I feel whilst I describe her excellencies as if I were an egoist expatiating upon his own perfections".

To Mary herself, in one of the few letters they exchanged at the height of their mutual passion, Shelley told what she was to him in words which strikingly display part of the process of "falling in love", the vesting of all value in another person; and which describe perhaps more clearly than he did anywhere else the sense of inter-animation, the dialogue in which each speaks with the voice of the other's soul. He did not mention that he had, so to speak, resolved to love her before he met her; but he did say what his love for her meant.

It is not only that, as he said to Mary, she should "shield" him from "impurity and vice", though that in itself was a remarkable thing for one to say who generally denied completely the possibility of being touched or tempted by either. Mary was more than a shield, Shelley said, she was the regulator, in her "originality and simplicity of mind", of his own : "If I were absent from you long, I should shudder with horror at myself; my understanding becomes undisciplined"; and, even as we see here again Shelley's inability to stand still and look steadily at himself, he invites and expects Mary to do what he cannot. Each will see the other and, being one, will thus see themselves. Together, they are

> each moment to become wiser in this surpassing love so that, constituting but one being, all knowledge may be comprised with the maxim γνωθι σεαυτον (know thyself), with infinitely more justice than its narrow and common application ![2]

It was not hyperbole but recognition that Mary did indeed enter into him in a way he could not himself; the most emphatic tribute one can pay to his powers of mind is that here he realised that someone could know more about himself than he himself could; that there were things inside himself that he could not see but another might.

On Mary's side it was her "sympathy" with Shelley, in the

sense in which they both used the word—that's to say as denot-
ing *fellow*-feeling, raised to its highest pitch—that enabled her
in an almost literal sense to enter into his feelings and ideas.
Such identification can be traced in everything she wrote (we
don't possess anything she wrote before she met Shelley). But it
went much further than imitation. Not simply his ideas but he
himself appears in all her imaginings; and not merely the
exterior or common notion of the man (which was also her
own), the man with the "genius for goodness"[3], but in other
forms the shadow behind him; not only his life, but his fate.

That he was fated was something felt by Mary throughout
their life together, and there is nothing particularly surprising
about that: Shelley's own conviction that he was persecuted
and doomed to an early death must, actual circumstances apart,
have been hard to resist. But her forebodings (which she took a
certain sombre satisfaction in remembering after his death) were
often rather different from those that might reasonably have
sprung from the anxieties of one person about another. They
were combined with her own personal fears in a way common
enough, perhaps, but unusual by reason of the wider knowledge
Shelley spoke of in the letter quoted: having intuitive access
(in the "originality and simplicity" of her mind) to what in him
and in her lay beyond the exterior, she drew her presagings
from the place where the unrealised fears and wishes of both
were intermingled. The way that in *Mathilda* Mary saw
Shelley's death by drowning in the person of the heroine's
father—her own loss foreseen as punishment for incestuous
desire—has already been mentioned. Another instance may be
added from her full-length historical novel *Valperga*, written
after *Mathilda* and not published till 1823, but completed
before the summer at Lerici.

The heroine of *Valperga*[4] (the story taken from Machiavelli)
has the remarkable name of Euthanasia. She is a curious blend
of Shelley and Mary. In many ways, clearly, she is a self-
portrait, a motherless girl, the "favourite daughter of a father
she adored", learned and even wise, with looks "in which deep
sensibility and lively thought were pictured, and judgment and
reason beyond her years". On the other hand her physical

description—golden-haired and blue-eyed—is nearer Shelley;
and the same passage in which it is given continues in a moral
picture of an idealised Shelley: "the very soul of open-hearted
Charity dwelt on her brow, and her lips expressed the softest
sensibility; there was in her countenance, beyond all of kind
and good that you could there discover, an expression that
seemed to require ages to read and understand; a wisdom
exalted by enthusiasm, a wildness tempered by self-command,
that filled every look and every motion with eternal change."
There is no need to go into the plot of this long novel; but the
end, which is also the end of the heroine, is worth noting.
Euthanasia, betrayed on all sides and taking flight by sea to
Sicily, is lost in a storm which is rising as they embark :

> Presently they saw huge, dark columns, descending from
> heaven, and meeting the sea, which boiled beneath : they were
> borne on by the storm, and scattered by the wind. The rain
> came down in sheets; and the hail clattered as it fell to its grave
> in the ocean; and the ocean was lashed into such waves that,
> many miles inland, during the pauses of the wind, the hoarse
> and constant murmur of the far-off sea made the well-housed
> landsman mutter one more prayer for those exposed to its fury.
> Such was the storm, as it was seen from the shore.
> [We may remember Trelawny's account of the day Shelley
> sailed from Leghorn, when the storm blew up suddenly and the
> mate of Byron's yacht, watching from the harbour, said "look
> at the smoke on the water; the devil is brewing mischief". The
> novel continues].
> Nothing more was ever seen of the vessel which bore Euthanasia.
> It never reached its destined port, nor were those on board ever
> seen.
> She was never heard of more; even her name perished. She
> slept in the oozy cavern of ocean; the seaweed was tangled in
> her shining hair; and the spirits of the deep wondered that
> earth had ever trusted so lovely a creature to the barren bosom
> of the sea, which, as an evil step-mother, deceives and betrays
> all committed to her care.

It is not a question of fortune-telling, but of entering the
thoughts and emotions of another person and following where

they pointed: Shelley's love of the sea and reckless confidence in it—the "fascination which so forcibly attracted him without fear or caution to trust an element which almost all others hold in superstitious dread" noted by Trelawny—combined with her own fear and dislike of it, and her general inclination to look on the dark or underside of all things.

Shelley, though finally caught in them, did not speak of the oozy caverns of ocean. The sea-voyagers in his poems, though frequently storm-tossed, swept onwards by whirlwinds and overhung by mountainous waves, never actually come to grief. The Poet in *Alastor* remains

> Calm and rejoicing in the fearful war
> Of wave running on wave, and blast on blast
> Descending, and black flood on whirlpool driven—

perfectly safe, indeed invulnerable, as if he "Had been an elemental god". His invulnerability and indifference exactly mirror Shelley's extraordinary calm which so impressed Byron when, during their long boating trip in the summer of 1816, they were caught in a sudden squall on Lake Geneva and were in real danger: when Byron prepared to swim for his life and to save his companion, but Shelley announced "with the greatest coolness", as Byron remembered it, that "he had no notion of being saved, and that I would have enough to do to save myself, and begged not to trouble me". It was almost as though (although he could not swim and never learnt, his response to sinking in water appearing to others as suicidally passive) he could not imagine drowning.

For him the sea even in its fury was, we may say, a dream of containment, the all-embracing mother of life and love, the Ocean of sweet oblivion in which to be submerged might well be called euthanasia, good or easy death. For Mary, seasick and terrified, the sea was a sunderer, full of treachery; one which, with the impressions of her childhood upon her, might be expected to turn from loving mother to cruel step-mother, choking the breath with bitter water and tangling the hair of abandoned children in the ooze. For both, no doubt, the sea was a powerful symbol of emotions in which an individual can be carried away and lost; but Mary, understanding such "storms of passion" more fully, or treating them with more respect, had a visionary grasp of internal realities which also gave her glimpses of their merely literal consequences.

The physical or actual consequences of moral causes may be certainly known but not thereby avoided. At another point in *Valperga* Euthanasia reflects, "Is there not a principle in the human mind that foresees the change about to occur to it? Is there not a feeling which would warn the soul of peril, were it not at the same time a sure prophecy that that peril is not to be avoided?" It is the burden, even the curse, laid upon those who have "the sight", as we know, that, foreknowing consequences and giving warning of them, they also know that their warnings, whether directed inward to themselves or outward to others, will be ineffectual. It may almost be concluded, and it has of course been proverbially laid down, that it is a test of the true prophet that he should not be heard. Cassandra knows what is going to happen, and also knows that when she tells of it no one will pay attention; an insensate indifference which is at once confirmation of her role as the mouthpiece of divinity and a torment to her as a human being. It is what drives her mad.

But the part of Cassandra, the dishonoured prophetess, does not exhaust the clairvoyance of those who, like Mary, are able to "descend the remotest caverns" of the mind. In *Valperga* there is a second heroine, Beatrice, who is actually an acknowledged seer, a sort of Renaissance pythoness. Her powers are greater than Euthanasia's, and she has a clearer sight of the fate of the hero, Castruccio, whose desires "outleap possibility and bring ruin on his head". But what she sees is not limited to such definite forecasts of calamity; it goes further, indeed, than she can explain. At a turning point of the story she has an interview with a witch, herself a fortune-teller of the ordinary hubble-bubble-toil-and-trouble kind, who tells her not to ask others but to "Consult your own heart, prophetess; and that will teach you far more than I can do. Does it not contain strange secrets known only to yourself? Have you never owned a power which dwelt within you : so wise that you confessed, but could not comprehend its wisdom?" And what this internal but independent power, wiser than the conscious mind, is capable of knowing, is unlimited, because the object of its contemplation is itself. It cannot be explained or even fully expressed within the scope of conscious or rational thought, but it may emerge in the forms of art.

There is a figurative representation of this process in the introduction to a later novel of Mary's, *The Last Man*, written after Shelley's death. It is a long and rambling story, full of incidental biographical interest as it projects into the future the people and circumstances of her own life. From the main element of the narrative—the devastation and depopulation of the earth by pestilence and war, and the literally absolute loneliness of "the last man" alive—much is to be learnt of the widowed Mary's own feelings. It is not a cheerful view of futurity; in taking as epigraph yet another tag from *Paradise Lost*, "Let no man seek/ Henceforth to be foretold what shall befall/ Him or his children", the emphasis is all on the grim prospect before the sons of Adam—"evil he may be sure,/ Which neither his foreknowing can prevent".

When the book ends there is no possibility, in the situation of the solitary survivor, of any regeneration. The empty sea he sets sail upon is no longer hostile but completely indifferent, and he reflects its indifference in a state of emotional insensibility looking only for something to fill his vacancy : "Neither hope nor joy are my pilots—restless despair and fierce desire for change lead me on. I long to grapple with danger, to be excited by fear, to have some task, however slight or voluntary, for each day's fulfilment . . . Thus around the shores of the deserted earth, while the sun is high and the moon waxes or wanes, angels, the spirits of the dead, the ever-open eye of the Supreme, will behold the tiny bark, freighted with Verney— THE LAST MAN." It is a picture of utter desolation that obviously reflects backwards on the final scene of *Frankenstein*; but before we return there it is interesting to see Mary's imaginary account of its source, and the symbolism it employs.

In her introduction to the novel Mary describes a visit to
Naples in 1818, the year in which she and Shelley did in fact
go there; they saw all the sights, including—as Shelley told
Peacock in a letter—"the cavern of the Sybil (not Virgil's Sybil)
which pierces one of the hills which circumscribe the lake [of
Avernus]."[6] Both he and Mary in her *Journal* recorded some
disappointment in their sight-seeing. But in her imaginative
return it was different. The narrator and her "friend" go into
the "Sybil's Cave" a little way and are then left by their
Italian guide who refuses to go further; they persist, through
narrow and low passages, until their torch (the torch of conscious self-knowledge) is extinguished and they have to grope
in the dark. They go on, until through "a very doubtful
twilight" they emerge into a succession of gradually lightening
caves and passages leading to a larger space open, though
remotely, to the sky : an "aperture let in the light of heaven"
dimly, obscured by an overgrowth of brambles and bushes.

The floor of the place is littered with dried leaves and other
fragments which the "friend" picks up, exclaiming, " 'This *is*
the Sybil's cave; these are Sybilline leaves' ". They are covered
with writings in various languages, both ancient and modern,
"prophecies, detailed relation of events but lately passed;
names, now well known, but of modern date; and often
exclamations of exultation or woe, of victory or defeat". The
two companions pick up some of the leaves and make their way
out of "the dim labyrinthine cavern", but return "often" and
collect more; since then the narrator, now left alone—"the
selected and matchless companion of my toils" being dead—has
been deciphering them. She now presents them, adding links
and form herself, "but the main substance rests on the truths
contained in those poetic rhapsodies, and the divine intuition
which the Cumaean damsel obtained from heaven". "Sometimes", she reflects, "I have thought that, obscure and chaotic
as they are, they owe their presence to me, their decipherer."

Mary concludes, speaking undisguisedly as herself :

How could I find solace from the narration of misery and
woeful change? . . . Such is human nature, that the excitement

of mind was dear to me, and that the imagination, painter of tempest and earthquake, or worse, the stormy and ruin-fraught passions of men, softened my real sorrow and endless regrets, by clothing these fictitious ones in that ideality which takes the mortal sting from pain.

The whole introductory story is a very remarkable account, as condensed as a dream, of the original process of artistic creation, couched in the same terms as Mary's resolution to explore to the uttermost the "remotest caverns" of her own mind. On this occasion "the torch of self-knowledge" goes out, which does in fact happen in the course of such an inward journey: it commonly enters darkness through which it is only possible to grope in blind trust and no guarantee of emergence at all. If the explorer does emerge it is into an unfamiliar place, or, more characteristically, into one that seems both strange and familiar, recognised in a sensation of *déjà vu*. In this case it is into a place both sacred and secret, open to heaven and once known to men, but long unvisited and neglected; now recognised immediately by the explorer's "companion", her psychopomp.

The "leaves" found there are not read on the spot but brought out for study and interpretation in the light of common day; they are the raw material, as yet unshaped, of artistic vision. But even while "deciphering" these materials and giving them form, the artist removes himself from them so as to create "fictions": metaphors, imitations, not "the real thing" but the only means by which the real thing in its hidden cave can be contemplated. The artist is thus seen, not as the original creator of this reality, but the medium by which it is brought into visible life; the tokens of reality "owe their presence" in the daylight of consciousness to him. The "reality" or otherwise of works of art is bound to be constantly in doubt, in the artist's mind as much as among those he is addressing, his audience; since it depends on his view of what was in the cave. And the only evidence he possesses that he was ever in the cave is the fiction in his hand: a self-perpetuating puzzle represented by Coleridge's parable that a man might dream he was in Paradise and pick a flower, and when he wakes find the flower in his hand—"Aye, and what then?"[7]

But there is another response to what is in the cave and the fear of it—for it is frightening, and becomes more so as this way is chosen. That is, to cease to look for, still less at, the object of fear, and to take refuge in action; especially in flight. We have glanced at three examples of such flight. That Shelley's poetry is in full flight is the first association most people make when they think of it. It is also, as our second example, the first thing they think of in his life. Hogg's character of him, "fugitive, volatile", has stuck, and not without reason, being corroborated by almost everything his other contemporaries said about him, and also by what he said about himself; there is perhaps no need to labour the point further. The third flight is Frankenstein's, reflecting the other two, that is to say repeating the pattern of flight and pursuit to be found both in Shelley's art and his life. It is itself a work of art, an invention making comment from a third position on both the others; and enabled in this detachment to describe events no more than implied in one place before they emerged in the other.

Some instances of Mary's capacity to see and foresee such implications have been taken from her later novels; but it is when we return to her first that we see it at its most startling. *Frankenstein* was begun in the summer of 1816, when the destruction that (shall we say) dogged Shelley, or that he spread about him, had scarcely started; and it foreshadows step by step, as the Monster kills off Frankenstein's family and friends, the fate of those who were close to Shelley. The suicides, first of Fanny Imlay, Mary's half-sister (who was supposed, at any rate by her step-mother, to have loved Shelley) and then of his first wife Harriet, took place in the autumn and winter of 1816. After their marriage and removal to Italy, there followed the deaths of Mary's first surviving children by Shelley, in 1818 and 1819. In 1822 Shelley himself, Edward Williams, and the sailor-boy Charles Vivian were drowned together on the last voyage of the Ariel.

The most poignant of these deaths before Shelley's own is

perhaps that of little William Shelley, in Rome, at the age of three. Of all Shelley's children William, "Willmouse", "Willman", "Blue Eyes", seems to have been the one he and Mary loved most, and his death—like that of his baby sister Clara not long before, of "a disorder peculiar to the climate of Italy"—was a blow from which Mary took a long time to recover, if she ever did. References to him, to his infant beauty and development, are frequent in both Shelley's and Mary's letters and her *Journal*, from the summer of 1816 (when, an infant in arms, he was with them in Switzerland), all through the period in which she was writing and revising *Frankenstein*. It can hardly be accident that when naming the favourite small brother of Victor Frankenstein, the "darling and pride" of the family, Mary should have called him William too. And whether or not one calls it accident that the William in the story is the Monster's first victim, killed in childhood as William Shelley was to die, three years *after Frankenstein* was written, depends on the meaning one attaches to the word.

For the deaths of his first wife, his children, his friends, Shelley was blameless, in his own eyes and most other people's. That the Shelleys went to live in Italy, with its climate so deadly to small children, for the sake of his health ("you will never be quite happy till I am well", he told Mary in arguing for the move,[8]) and that their restless mode of life contributed to Clara's and William's fatal illnesses Mary may privately have laid upon him; her grief after his own death seems to have included remorse for feelings of this kind. But that is not the point. Nor is it the point that Mary was gifted with second sight, whatever that may mean, or that the deaths in *Frankenstein* are to be chalked up in the same bizarre category as Mary's forecast in *The Last Man* of royal abdication in the House of Windsor.

The point is rather to emphasise the connection between the life and the work of art, the metaphor and the act. Shelley was driven, and not without good reason, to think of himself as peculiarly hounded by disaster—"it seems to me", he wrote to Peacock after little William's death, "as if, hunted by calamity as I have been, that I should never recover any cheerfulness again"[9]—and before the end of his life he came to expect it. The daemon that followed him is usually thought of simply as misfortune, for which blame should be attached to nobody, or at any rate certainly not to the sufferers. But Frankenstein also was blameless in his own eyes and the world's, even if he felt himself accursed : "I was guiltless", he says, after the Monster's penultimate murder, of his friend Clerval, "but I had indeed drawn down a terrible curse upon my head, as mortal as that of crime." The difference between the two is only that Mary, writing her story, showed a direct link between the man and the daemon, his own creation.

Mary's great talent was to grasp the relationship between inner and outer events, to show the consequences in what happens to us of being what we are or, in the deepest sense, of what we think. It was one she inherited, or learnt from her father, whose insistence in political doctrine on "opinion" as the final and all-powerful arbiter of public affairs was a rationalised statement of the same thing, and whose works of imaginative fiction, as we have seen, made a symbolic drama of components in the human psyche in the same way. It was one that she shared in an eminent degree with Shelley, though his use of it was very different; it was indeed the opposite to hers. Shelley's mind moved from within to without; he fled through the cave and away again, outwards and upwards, away from the shadow. His whole life, even if considered purely in exterior terms, was a continual movement of this kind; it could be described, at least during certain critical periods, as a state of fugue.

To speak of his terribly short career as a "whole life" sounds inappropriate, and yet it did seem such to him, and more. Just before he was drowned he said he had already lived to be "older than his father"—he was, he said, already ninety years of age. In part no doubt that was simply an expression of fatigue; but it seems likely also to have been connected in his mind with the idea of living for ever, like the Wandering Jew who haunts his writings. The condition of Ahasuerus, the accursed, is at once cause and consequence of his unreality, his status as an immortal ghost. He must always be on the move, to keep ahead of mortality; and in the hurry of experience, involved in perpetual motion, events may be sharply enough felt, but they have no weight, it is possible to pack an infinite number of them into the smallest space : ninety, or a thousand years may well be contained in thirty.

Mary (although she also felt the shortness of Shelley's life to be its "sole imperfection") came to the same conclusion later, though by a different process, when she declared that her eight years with Shelley encompassed a lifetime. The events of his life, and even especially the events of their short time together, have in retrospect a recognisable order, which certainly cannot be called harmonious, but was in a sense complete : in the same sense as is used of a work of art. Shelley's life seems to an uncommon degree to have been *willed* : it may seem absurd to say so of one who was so notoriously the victim of fate, but it was a fate which followed in the wake, so to speak, of a course which the victim himself to an uncommon degree felt was chosen by himself. What it looks like depends on whether one looks forward or back. "I always go on until I am stopped", Shelley told Trelawny, "and I never am stopped."[10]

One chooses one's way ahead, and fate follows behind; and the fate that dogs one's steps cannot help but seem to do so by invitation. Its final stroke is a part of the play, even if the play is cut short thereby; being already older than one's father, one may not feel capable or obliged to last out the full five acts of *Lear*. There is no need to suggest that Shelley's death was even a disguised suicide (though his request to Trelawny for prussic acid shows that it was in his mind at this time). At the very most the last voyage of the Ariel cannot be called more than a suicidal risk. It was the kind of action known as tempting Providence, which is especially something those are driven to who feel a monstrous fate, or misshapen Providence, at their heels. For, frightful though it may be, it is still a necessary part of their lives, indeed it truly is their earthly life in hideous form; and the fugitive is continually compelled to reassure himself that it is still there, that he is still its quarry. Otherwise he would cease to exist. Frankenstein *without* the Monster is inconceivable, even by himself : he would indeed be a lost soul.

To tempt or test fate in this way is the behaviour known as "acting out"—turning outwards an internal unease : transforming it into action or, it may equally well be said, representing it by acting, as a player does on the stage. On a close personal scale it is possible to say that the life of Shelley and of those involved with him acted out an intra-psychic drama : it made actual what is shown in the metaphor of *Frankenstein*. But so, notoriously, history has continued to do, on the scale of worldwide social and technological development. Mankind has made monsters of all sorts, on all sides, and of all varieties of material, including human material; the distinguishing feature of all of them being just that they are material creations, the actual or embodied form of ideas.

To enumerate them in detail is unnecessary, indeed impossible, since the list is continually growing as this or that achievement of technique or organisation is felt to be and is called monstrous. The number of monstrosities made by men is now positively Miltonic, rivalling the inmates of Pandemonium in number, ingenuity and destructive power; not for nothing is *Paradise Lost* at the back of so much we are discussing. The structure and rise of modern civilisation can look very like the "Fabrick huge" which "Rose like an exhalation" at a single blast, unsurpassed in wealth and luxury and overpopulated by devils : getting our chronology straight, the model following the type, we may say that London is a city much like Hell. But Milton's swarm of demons are capable of shrinking back as suddenly as they arose from fantastic gigantism to miniature, a cloud of flying insects or "Faerie Elves"—reminding us that Milton's Hell, unlike our metropolis, does belong to fairy-tale, or myth.

And here may be seen the crucial difference between these imaginative forms and Mary's. For in *Frankenstein* the myth has already taken a decisive step towards the rigid fantasies of science which alter mythology as science has altered the world. The change has already been noted that was overtaking fantasy at the time, and the division between the fictions that were content to remain "inexplicable" or with implication of supernatural agency (*The Castle of Otranto* to the tales of "Monk"

Lewis) and those in which, more closely in tune with the needs of the age, the most bizarre events were required to have a "natural" explanation. Behind it can be seen the spread of a changed attitude to mental phenomena in general. The primitive state of mind, that in which fairy-tales and myths readily arise and are accepted, does not distinguish precisely between "inner" and "outer" events, and a ghost or spirit, known to be different from other beings—capable, that's to say, of performing acts which "real" creatures cannot, and therefore in this sense "supernatural"—can nevertheless be allowed to have "objective" existence. (All such terms are awkward in this context, since the whole point is that such distinctions were not felt to be absolute.) But to science, or to habits of thinking in which scientific knowledge and practice became a common property of society, the distinction between "inner" and "outer" and recognition that nothing in the phenomenal world could be both, are essential. It is not that mental phenomena such as visions were denied existence (even the crudest mechanist could hardly do that) but that their existence, if acknowledged, had to be of a different sort; it could not be "objective".

It is a question, at bottom, of control. The "objective" world is governed by "laws" which are not the arbitrary decisions of men's minds but operate outside human agency, can be "discovered", and then used to manipulate whatever is felt to be real. "Object", in fact, signifies that which is acted upon. "Subject", on the other hand, the "inner", has apparently no laws at all, or they are laws which, according to this way of thinking, the subject can make up as he goes along. Perception, the relation of subject to object, can be investigated, and a great deal of philosophical inquiry at this time revolves about it; but imagination, which appears to be arbitrary and beyond control—frequently described as "lawless"—can have nothing usefully said about it.

At the point where this fundamental shift in human thought was emerging into common attitudes, we find acknowledgment of anything that can be simultaneously "objective" and "subjective", "inner" and "outer", "real" or "natural" and "supernatural" confined more and more to a carefully enclosed area known as religious belief, in which "miracles", vulgarly thought of as supernatural events which had real or natural occurrence, could be accepted in theory, but in truth only by keeping the part of the mind in which such belief was supposed to reign carefully separate from the rest. Since consistency is always desired (at any rate in the kind of thinking encouraged by scientific inquiry and logical analysis alike) it was assumed that, though "miracles"—inner events happening naturally, or out-wardly—were no longer observed to take place, they were theoretically possible. Indeed those to whom religious faith was important were inclined to look for them, as confirmation that the inner world, or "world of the spirit" existed. And if miracles could still occur (though the "age of miracles" were past) then spirits and other manifestations of inner life could also, in theory, appear and have "actual" existence.

Such things were however impossible to the other part of the mind, and could therefore only occur by the direct sanction of God, for whom all things are by definition possible, and were consequently the concern not of ordinary discourse but of theology. Samuel Johnson would maintain his belief in the possible existence of ghosts because he was a religious man; the pious Mrs Radcliffe, though using fear of them as a cliff-hanger device—"mysterious terrors . . . continually creating in the mind the idea of a supernatural appearance, keeping us as it were upon the very edge and confine of the world of spirits"[11] —always came down on the other side, excluding the super-natural from her novels as improper in a work of fiction. Only those of a more cynical turn of mind, such as Horace Walpole or, a little later, "Monk" Lewis and his imitators, could allow themselves to use as the subject matter of profane fiction some-thing which either was nonsense or was sacred. And even Lewis, of course, upheld as necessary the connection between believing in ghosts and believing in God: as we have seen, there was an argument about it at Diodati, when Shelley maintained exactly the opposite point of view, that it was possible to believe in ghosts without holding any theistic beliefs whatever. The terms of the argument are not known, and all that is on record is

Shelley's scorn for the standpoint of Lewis and Byron, "in the very face of reason" that one kind of belief was necessarily dependent on the other. But Shelley's own attitude, as a professed atheist (this was the period when he openly gloried in the name, signing himself as such in the visitors' book of the Chamonix inn and elsewhere, to much public scandal) and actual visionary, is interesting and important. His notions of phenomenology, of "inner" and "outer", were, of course, of a subtlety not to be grasped by a mind so downright, though agile, as Byron's. It was also—or so one may surmise—a question of proprietorship: Byron might be unwilling to believe in spirits except as belonging to an entire supernatural order, belonging in a sense to God; Shelley was strongly impelled to believe in supernatural beings, but would not allow them a place in any hierarchy. If ghosts belonged to or were under the command of anyone, they belonged to him.

The question of attitudes to "the supernatural" has a close bearing on the writing of *Frankenstein*, which both in form and matter was heir to the changes thus very briefly outlined. The influence on Mary of Charles Brockden Brown, a notable pioneer on the frontier between the "imaginary", the "real", and the "unreal" in fiction, has already been touched on. Mary it is true made no very elaborate efforts to provide a "factual" framework for her story, her scientific-speculative background for Frankenstein's discovery is rudimentary, and, furthermore, she actually maintains with great skill a foot on each side of this shifting division: the supernatural, the "more than natural", or whatever is not subject to natural law, is never rigidly excluded. Rather it is that natural law is imbued or re-endowed with the incalculable qualities of the supernatural; within a formal framework of "natural" events the mysterious and unlooked for and, specifically, the uncontrollable do not, as in an ordinary ghost story, make single and discrete appearances on the calculable sublunary scene, but take possession of the whole.

But the distinction between the objectively possible and (in "natural" terms) the impossible is maintained. The opening of the original Preface, written by Shelley, is very definite on this point: "The event on which this fiction is founded, has been supposed, by Dr Darwin and some of the physiological writers of Germany, as not of impossible occurrence", and the Preface goes on, while describing the story as "a work of fancy", firmly to disclaim any intention of "merely weaving a series of supernatural terrors"; the novel is "exempt from the disadvantages of a mere tale of spectres and enchantment". What these disadvantages were has been indicated. The "merely supernatural" was disparaged as being outside general rules of thought, and therefore frivolous; indeed when one looks at the ghostly inventions of the time it is undeniable that they were for the most part quite contemptible, tolerable only (as were many of Lewis's) as more than half a joke. Both Mary and Shelley were admirers of Lewis, and Shelley certainly followed him in his Gothic juvenilia. But the drawback described by Coleridge in his attack on *The Monk* when it first appeared—that "all events are levelled into one common mass, and become almost equally probable, where the order of nature may be changed whenever the author's purposes demand it"[12]—was certainly apparent to Shelley by 1817.

The advantages of excluding the impossible were however much more than a matter of preserving the power to surprise. By claiming possibility for the ground idea of *Frankenstein* the Preface takes a decisive step, or rather underlines the step already taken by Mary in making the Monster the product not of "enchantment" but of science. The boldness of this step may be appreciated the more when it is remembered that what the members of the party at Diodati set themselves to do at Byron's suggestion was just to dabble in "supernatural terrors", each to write "a ghost story".

The Monster is not a ghost. He is not a genie or a spirit summoned by magic from the deep; at the same time he issues, like these, from the imagination. He is manifestly a product, or aspect, of his maker's psyche: *he is a psychic phenomenon given objective, or "actual" existence*. A Doppelganger of "real flesh and blood" is not unknown, of course, in other fictions, nor is the idea of a man created "by other means than Nature has hitherto provided", the creation of Prometheus being the

BY WAY OF SCIENTIFIC "EXCUSE"

archetype. But Frankenstein is "the modern Prometheus" : the profound effect achieved by Mary lay in showing the Monster as the product of modern science; made, not by enchantment, i.e., directly by the unconscious, an "imaginary" being, but through a process of scientific discovery, i.e., the imagination objectified. That the "science" involved is sketchy and improbable does not matter at all : science itself can with confidence (if not with safety) be left to look after that, and make the improbable commonplace. What is important is that the Monster is simultaneously an example of the way the scientific drive operates and a symbol of it in operation, at once illustration and metaphor. And what we can see in the light of this fictitious invention is a restoration of their metaphorical significance to actual scientific discoveries and technical inventions, the application of the "immutable" laws found by scientific inquiry to the mutable universe.

We are so used to speaking in metaphor that we hardly notice it : in the late eighteenth and early nineteenth centuries men could speak of "Promethean fire" without thinking what they were saying—or thinking merely that it was a "way of saying", a "so to speak". Nowadays men will speak of a "Frankenstein monster", of "creating a Frankenstein" in the same way, supposing that it is "only a metaphor", a picturesque way of talking; it cannot be an accurate description of an actual event. If you want to speak accurately and directly about real things, it is assumed, you must use the language of science; science has, indeed, rescued communication from metaphor. But when men "create a Frankenstein", when out of their instability, their ingenuity, curiosity, and ambition they make something—a new mechanical device, a weapon of new destructive power, a political party to harness social energies, or a whole culture in which all these things are collected and linked together—which goes beyond their control, they are expressing something already expressed, as we have seen, in the metaphor. Metaphorical expression in truth is not "merely a way of speaking", it is the description of real events in the soul in the only way available : and action is no more than another, but uncommunicative way of expressing the same thing.

In his sleep the dream of an angel or Titan stealing fire from heaven and using it to imitate the creations of heaven tells something to man of his own nature : he wakes to consciousness and proceeds to act out his dream, or make it actual. His work is a metaphor made literal. It thereby becomes opaque, or impossible to read as metaphor; for it is always *through* a metaphor, while it is living, that its significance can be seen. And at the same time the traditional language of metaphor becomes itself incomprehensible. To speak today of gods and angels, titans and devils, conveys no real meaning; in their place we have the contrivances of science fiction which, using the language of science (or a popular approximation to it) for expression and the possibilities of science for material, are a degree further removed from whatever metaphor can speak of.

The great bulk of SF, or at least of the more serious and carefully thought-out varieties of it, is manifestly concerned with moral or, more strictly, with ethical problems (being thereby clearly distinguished from the other large branch of popular writing, "crime fiction"). To some extent it is well adapted to treat of many pressing problems in contemporary ethics. Man in his environment, the moral responsibility of scientists in general, and even the disappearance of "spirit" from the world, the "death of God"—all of these have been touched on in "scientific" romances in the recent past. But, to the degree to which these works are fictions—creations, that's to say, not merely dramatised discussions—the forms of their fiction make it impossible for them to say anything real about their subject. The mechanised morality cannot speak about its own nature, which, by virtue of being made exterior, governable, "objective", ceases to be human nature. The kingdom of the robots, computers, and other manipulated marvels both of science fiction and of actual or applied science, is *without*, but the kingdom of metaphor, to speak metaphorically, is *within*.

It makes little difference, indeed, whether it is science in fact (that is, realised or performed) or science in fiction that we have to deal with; it is a commonplace that one shades into the other with accelerating speed, so that last night's science fiction is this morning's fact. But though, in both, possibilities continually expand, both fact and the fiction which takes its mode therefrom are restricted to the world of the possible, that is the measurable and controllable; and the ground of all possibility, which is interior and known only metaphorically, becomes impossible to reach or even to remember.

TEN

PROMETHEUS UNBOUND

IN *Frankenstein*, AS we have seen, the myth can be seen in transition, both in content and form of expression. In form the story is an early type of science fiction, insisting (though admittedly more explicitly in Shelley's Preface than anywhere else) on its credentials as dealing in "possible worlds", and with exterior reality. In practice, however, Mary's possession by the vision that came to her from within was such that her work takes its stand in two places at once, and from one is able to comment on the other.

The subject matter is in part, or from one aspect, the progress of science itself: the repudiation of magic and the embracing of empirical knowledge that "dabbles in dirt" and searches out secrets not in old books but with a new microscope—i.e., in observation and experiment—is a crucial stage in Frankenstein's personal history. His monstrous dreams, of raising ghosts and devils and finding the elixir of life, remain dreams ("chimeras") until the instrument of scientific knowledge is put into his hands. But when realised through science the Monster retains enough of his dream-quality, and the biographical significances of his creation are pressing enough to make it clear that his origins are not in the laboratory but the psyche, the "ground of all possibility". In exactly the same way the secondary, parallel ambitions of Walton, the explorer, are attributed by him, in confidence and as a "secret" of which he is slightly ashamed, to quite "unscientific" motives. His "passionate enthusiasm" for discovering "the dangerous mysteries of ocean" originated, he says, in his reading of *The Ancient Mariner*, by "the most imaginative of modern poets". He admits that he does not really know what his motives are:

"There is something at work in my soul which I do not understand."

It is curious, and an indication perhaps of the means by which he managed to avoid seeing what *Frankenstein* was really about, that Shelley in his Preface should have so emphasised the scientific plausibility of the story. It is all fancy, he says, the author must not be "supposed as according the remotest degree of serious faith to such an imagination"; nevertheless it "affords a point of view to the imagination for the delineation of human passions more comprehensive and commanding than any which the ordinary relations of existing events can yield", and it does so as something "not of impossible occurrence".

It is curious because his own method was quite different. In delineating human passions and their consequences on the largest scale and with the most comprehensive reference—with an eye to present and future, that is, not the past—he chose the means not of science fiction but of fairy-tale and myth. He very freely used components of existing mythology, classic and oriental, giving himself the liberty to alter, combine, and abstract elements as he pleased: the effect, in his superabundant flight of ideas and images, often approached the chaotic state from which, we assume, myths arise rather than so well formed a thing as a myth itself. His *Prometheus Unbound* is certainly not free from this confusion, but it has form and force that make it the most coherent as well as the most powerful of his "prophetic" utterances. Its presence, as Shelley's own explicit treatment of the Promethean theme, as the poem, of all his long works, in which he was playing for the highest stakes, and as the most complete expression in one place of the "Shelley Idea", has been at the back of much that has been said hitherto, and it is time to look at it more closely.

Prometheus Unbound, written in 1818–19 and published in 1820, has been the subject of copious commentary and interpretation ever since; in Shelley's own eyes it was the "favourite" among his works, in his "best style" and his most enduring claim to poetic immortality. As such it is almost idle to look for particular influences in it, since it may reasonably be assumed that Shelley put into it everything he knew; it can be regarded as an epitome of his thinking and indirectly at least of all the extraordinarily wide reading that nourished it. A number of specially influential sources or models have, however been named, Aeschylus apart; these include Milton, Calderon, Goethe, and Byron. Shelley's admiration for Calderon is known, and resemblances have been traced between his poem and the Faustian drama of the *Magico Prodigioso*. Goethe's *Faust* (of which he knew the first part only) excited even more enthusiasm in him. In the case of both these works, however, his reading as recorded in his letters was after the composition of at any rate the main part of *Prometheus Unbound*; they may perhaps show in the "afterthought" of Act IV. Goethe's own fragmentary Promethean drama cannot have been known to Shelley, and there is no direct evidence that he knew even the short lyric *Prometheus,* already referred to, which was the only part published before his death.

The connections with Byron are more direct, resemblances having been found between *Prometheus Unbound* and two at least of Byron's long poems, *Childe Harold* and *Manfred*; the last being regarded by some specifically as the challenge to which *Prometheus* was the "answer". The two poems share, literally, some of the same background, the Alpine scenery which Byron and Shelley discovered and admired together in the summer of 1816; in the first part of *Prometheus* especially there are direct echoes not so much of Byron's poems of that time as of Shelley's own, notably *Mont Blanc,* addressing the mountain-power which "dwells apart in tranquillity, / Remote, serene, and inaccessible" and which is in fact very like the chained Titan himself, racked with earthquakes and pierced with glaciers. The melodrama of *Manfred* uses the same paraphernalia—"Ye toppling crags of ice ! / Ye avalanches whom a breath draws down/ In mountainous overwhelming, come and crush me !"—but rather with the effect of stage backcloth; in *Prometheus Unbound,* as in *Mont Blanc,* mountains, glaciers, indeed all the gigantic forms and forces of nature are actors.

This apart, it is likely enough that Shelley, in his unacknowledged rivalry with Byron—to which, indeed, there seems to be

oblique reference in his insistence in the Preface on the inevitable appearance of "imitation" between contemporary poets—
should have realised at least that people might suppose he was
"answering" Byron or going one better. It is certainly possible
that the conscious gloom of *Manfred,* with its pleasure in contemplating "A noble wreck in ruinous perfection" may have
provoked Shelley; even, perhaps, that the extravagantly Gothic
catastrophe, the hero spurning an importunate crew of demons,
may have reminded him painfully of his own youthful excesses
in this line. Certainly the pessimistic conclusion, that "knowledge is not happiness, and science/ But an exchange of
ignorance for that/ Which is another kind of ignorance"
represents an attitude which *Prometheus Unbound* seems
designed to refute. Again, it is an "answer" to, or at any rate
a direct contradiction of the Byronic description of men, who,
"Half dust, half deity, alike unfit/ To sink or soar, with our
mix'd essence make/ A conflict of its elements". The same
sentiment is stated in Byron's own short poem *Prometheus,*
belonging to the same period, in which the Titan-hero is a
symbol less of man's aspiration than of "His own funereal
destiny".

But though these and other similar utterances of Byron may
well have been in Shelley's mind, it is of course greatly under-
rating his poem to think of it as more than incidentally referring
to them or challenging comparison with them. Yet the idea of
it as argument, or counter-statement, persists, if only because of
the peculiarly combative, even defensive tone of Shelley's Preface, in which, speaking of himself "with unaffected freedom",
he does indeed make clear his ambitions for the poem both as
poetry and prophecy, part of the "collected lightning" which
the contemporary "cloud of mind" is discharging. The Preface
disclaims direct didactic purpose for the poem, but, acknowledg-
ing the poet's "passion for reforming the world",[1] asserts for
poetry the complementary function of imaginative inspiration :

My purpose has hitherto been simply to familiarise the highly
refined imagination of the more select class of poetical readers
with beautiful idealisms of moral excellence; aware that until

the mind can love, and admire, and trust, and hope, and endure, reasoned principles of moral conduct are seeds cast upon the highway of life which the unconscious passenger tramples into dust, although they would bear the harvest of his happiness.

Prometheus Unbound is to prepare the imagination; and to prepare it to receive other seed than that sown by "Paley and Malthus", representing orthodox piety and anti-philanthropic reasoning. Such preparation is the work of poetry, where the greatest are not too exalted as models or rivals. Aeschylus himself is scratched from the contest, ostensibly as being too high, but in truth because his own conjectural *Prometheus Unbound,* in which Prometheus and Zeus are brought together offers so inadequate or (to Shelley) repugnant an example: "I was averse from a catastrophe so feeble as that of reconciling the Champion with the Oppressor of mankind." The Preface goes on at this point to consider Milton's Satan as, so to speak, a rival to Prometheus, "the only imaginary being . . . in any degree" resembling him as Champion-hero. Prometheus, says Shelley, is "a more poetical character"—a more suitable vehicle, that's to say, for the sublime and purified emotions in which poetry deals—because he is "exempt from the taints of ambition, envy, revenge, and a desire for personal aggrandisement, which, in the Hero of Paradise Lost, interfere with the interest". His meaning is of course not that Satan is a less "interesting" character in the modern sense, meaning an object of curiosity, but as engaging the interest or partisanship of the reader. With Prometheus, who is perfect, we can—Shelley says—be invited to identify without reservation; with Satan, who, for all his virtue as defier of All-Might, is undoubtedly flawed, we can only do so by "a pernicious casuistry which leads us to weigh his faults with his wrongs, and to excuse the former because the latter exceed all measure".

The heroes of Aeschylus and Milton are thus disposed of. But if, consciously, Shelley was either dismissing the example of one as too feeble or the other as morally too confusing, he had unconsciously a much more troublesome comparison to make and a much more formidable, if humbler, case to answer at home, in *Frankenstein*. It is difficult to believe that, as he wrote his own Promethean drama, "the modern Prometheus" never crossed his mind; but there is certainly no evidence, external or internal, that it did; unless the very absence of reference be taken as a sign of its having been blocked out.

If Shelley was able to do so, it must have been partly due to the difference of form : not so much that between poetry and prose as in the kind of imagery employed. *Frankenstein* is a novel, of a sort, it "tells a story" of a personal kind about men and women living, more or less, actual lives. One can hardly put it more strongly than that, but already one obvious difference is apparent from *Prometheus Unbound,* which does not pretend, of course, to deal with incarnations ("as to real flesh and blood, you know that I do not deal in those articles", said Shelley to the Gisbornes; "you might as well go to a gin-shop for a leg of mutton as expect anything human or earthly from me"[2]) but with ideal attributes, sometimes given personal names but scarcely anything imaginable as bodies.

"The imagery I have employed", he says in the Preface, "will be found, in many instances, to have been drawn from the operations of the human mind, or from those external actions by which they are expressed." What does this mean ? At first sight it appears to say nothing at all, since there doesn't seem to be anything in human experience not embraced by such a formula. But obviously Shelley does not intend such an empty generalisation; he goes on to say that what would appear on the face of it to include every possible kind of imagery is in fact "unusual in modern poetry", though common in Shakespeare and even more in Dante. It is clear, indeed, that "the operations of the human mind" here do not include perception of the external world, but thought itself as the object of thought; mind not as passive receptor but in active creation of "its own" forms, for which external objects are taken purely as symbols, not as description.

Now, if we may risk a gloss, such a view of "the operations of the human mind", distinguished from "those external actions by which they are expressed", seems to say very much what has been suggested concerning internal images and their "acting out", the impersonation of the internal drama of the psyche. And thus by this account Shelley's aim in *Prometheus Unbound* is, we may say, to present the metaphoric drama direct and self-consistent, a system of imagery which, of course, has reference to the external world—since images must be drawn from somewhere—but does not impinge upon it. Metaphors are still in their primary, "mental" stage, not solidified into act or fact.

To this extent the poem is a counterpart or parallel to *Frankenstein,* which specifically shows such incarnation of a metaphor, its rendering, by artifice, as external act and object; as a parallel it cannot meet or touch it. The "operations of the human mind" that both works deal with are indeed the same, but though they complement they cannot consciously comment upon each other: they stand back to back, as it were, and look in opposite directions.

Prometheus Unbound deals, exclusively, consistently, and relentlessly, and to an extent without equal in any other work of imaginative literature in English, with the capacity of human thought to transcend itself : to lift itself up by its boot-straps. Those for whom such a description is no more than a way of saying it is impossible and absurd have small patience with the poem or, usually, with Shelley in general. But any-one who recognises at least the reality of the urge to overcome gravity—and everything that we mean by gravity—must value it as an extraordinarily complete and eloquent (or, it would be better to say, true) account of the impulse.

If they also find it dizzying and intoxicating—both effects of exposure to high altitude—they will allow such sensations to be appropriate. The poem may be described as airy or even (and with no disparagement intended) gaseous; all the ethereal epithets ever applied to Shelley or his work in general belong here with peculiar force. But force is not a word to be used idly in this context. Shelley shows in *Prometheus Unbound* both at his most insubstantial and his most forceful, and it is difficult to reconcile the two adjectives; until one thinks of that force which, consisting in the expansion or gasification of material, is all exerted outwards. Explosive, or flying out, are terms that come to mind, in evident contradiction of the essence of the Shelleyan Idea as pacific and mild; indeed it is difficult to stick to the notion of Shelley as feeble or ineffectual in the presence of this giant centrifuge.[3]

The force is, perhaps, hard to recognise because it is not expressed in conflict. There is no struggle in *Prometheus Unbound*. Prometheus at the beginning of the drama, though uttering what one can only call formal cries of agony, does not fight against his bonds : he has endured his millennia of "sleep-unsheltered hours" and God-inflicted torment not as striving flesh and blood but as the earth itself, subject to the shaping forces of geology. He is, as has been noted, identical at one point with Mont Blanc, the calm enduring mountain giant ("The crawling glaciers pierce me with the spears/ Of their moon-freezing chrystals") : at another it is Shelley himself, contemplating Mont Blanc in the earlier poem, who foreshadows Prometheus :

> I seem as in a trance sublime and strange
> To muse on my own separate fantasy,
> My own, my human mind, which passively,
> Now renders and receives vast influencings
> Holding an unremitting interchange
> With the clear universe of things around.

Prometheus is also entirely passive, awaiting his inevitable release in the knowledge that it will require no effort on his part but is, literally, merely a question of time. It is this, the actual unbinding of Prometheus, which may be thought the weakest part of the poem, although it is also a crucial one; indeed it is not so much weak as absent. (Hercules, who unlooses the bonds, is degraded to a vestigial functionary, with four lines of verse only to explain that he, as "strength", ministers to Promethean virtues "like a slave".) The force that is supposed to bring the release about, by the preliminary dethronement of God, is simply Time. To elevate Time itself, the Hour, to an agency—like the Marxist's abstract deity History, even more abstracted—without any indication of what will use Time or how, is to say nothing at all: the whole paraphernalia of the charioted Hours flying through eternity, drinking "With eager lips the wind of their own speed", cannot disguise the inadequacy of foretelling that what is going to happen will happen. The Hours are, it is true, represented as agents; as the line quoted reminds us, they take to themselves the attributes of Ariel ("I drink the air before me") and even some of the added characteristics of Shelleyan flight as "Some look behind, as fiends pursued them there": the idea of Time the pursuer itself being pursued is so odd that it distracts attention from the fact that what we're offered here is a tautology.

Time is the only thing that *does* anything in *Prometheus Unbound,* even reversing itself for the purpose. Everything is flying into the future, and it is this headlong flight forward and outward which is the essence of the poem and constitutes its great claim to represent the spirit of the age. (The reiterated cry "Tomorrow comes!" already announces it in *Queen Mab*.) But the idea of the future contained in the past is also made use of, and necessarily, if anything is to be learned about direction; in such a flight there is no time, so to speak, to look anywhere but backwards. Prometheus, the Forethinker, cannot do that of course, and it is interesting that his brother Epimetheus, who can, has no place in the poem nor anywhere else in Shelley's writings.

Nevertheless Prometheus seeks reassurance from memory at the beginning of the poem, and in a very curious way. The past, it has already been hinted, is inhabited by fiends; Prometheus can have no dealings with them, he cannot even acknowledge their erstwhile existence; he must employ an interpreter, an intermediary, between himself and the ghosts of the past. When he was originally bound, Prometheus cursed God, and now both wants and doesn't want to recollect it (exactly as Shelley, newly arrived at Oxford, was half-reluctant, half-pleased to recall how at Eton he had "cursed his father and the king" and repeated an elaborate anathema, though it was something he "had left off", with accurate memory).[4]

Prometheus also has "left off" cursing God, because he is now entirely without hatred; nevertheless Jupiter is hateful

and worthy to be cursed. (We remember Shelley's question to
the hateful, though unhated reviewer, "what profit can you
see/ In hating such a hateless thing as me?", ending by not-
hating, not-cursing the wretched man into nothingness, "to pine
into a sound with hating me". And also his lines to the Lord
Chancellor, "I curse thee, though I hate thee not, O slave".)
The very thought of hating is instantly rejected : if Prometheus
looks forward to the time when God shall be overthrown and
trampled underfoot, the idea is at once dismissed, since he
would disdain to spurn "such a prostrate slave"; and disdain
is immediately renounced in turn, to be replaced by pity,
joined with satisfaction at God's just fate.

The rapid succession of reactions, and the combination of
"pity" with something quite its opposite have a very strange
effect, and the lines should perhaps be quoted in full :

> The wingless, crawling hours, one among whom
> —As some dark Priest hales the reluctant victim—
> Shall drag thee, cruel King, to kiss the blood
> From these pale feet, when they might trample thee
> If they disdained not such a prostrate slave.
> Disdain ! Ah no ! I pity thee. What ruin
> Will hunt thee undefended thro' the wide Heaven !
> How will thy soul, cloven to its depth with terror,
> Gape like a hell within ! I speak in grief,
> Not exultation, for I hate no more,
> As then ere misery made me wise. The curse
> Once breathed on thee I would recall . . .

To recall a curse can mean two things, simply to remember
it or to call it back, to renounce it; and the ambiguity here
again allows Prometheus to have it both ways. The elements
have received his curse and store it up, so that even though he
no longer means it or would repeat it, it remains operative :

> . . . If then my words had power,
> Though I am changed so that aught evil wish
> Is dead within; although no memory be
> Of what is hate, let them not lose it now !
> What was that curse? for ye all heard me speak.

He is answered by his mother, Earth, who informs him that what he himself has forgotten and no living thing dare speak nevertheless exists elsewhere in the shades and can be summoned thence. The meaning of this celebrated passage—

> For know there are two worlds of life and death :
> One that which thou beholdest; but the other
> Is underneath the grave, where do inhabit
> The shadows of all forms that think and live
> Till death unite them and they part no more—

has been much debated, with varying speculation on derivations from Platonic, Zoroastrian, or Paracelsan doctrine. Without disputing these, it is clear that the region of shadows where the curse still dwells can also be described as the unconscious mind of Prometheus himself, where everything he knows or knew, present or past, is stored. He has himself already acknowledged it, in speaking of evil wishes that are "dead within" (no very healthful state of affairs); and from such entombed dead or shadow selves ghosts will readily arise, with or without bidding. In this case the apparition is carefully controlled; the Phantasm of Jupiter is summoned to recite the curse directed originally against himself. The memory remains thus wholly dissociated : even in recollection Prometheus cannot contemplate *himself* cursing, but re-learns it at second hand, its dangerous charge absorbed by the person on whom it was first projected. (Thus the accursed becomes a curse, a fate usually reserved for the scapegoat.)

In this way Prometheus is enabled to await the preordained future with perfect calm, since the act which is to bring it into being has already been performed; the problem of overcoming the Omnipotent is by-passed, as well the more perilous difficulty of foreseeing eternal torment ("thine Infinity shall be/ A robe of envenomed agony") for an enemy while wishing no evil to befall any being, even the all-highest.

In a word, Prometheus has been unbound already, and the unbinding, with the question of how and by whom, is somehow elided. It has been the work of Time, but the living acts of those who work in Time (that is, men) have been abolished. It only remains to remove from the scene Shelley's Jupiter, a figure from the melodrama of Shelley's early Gothic stories, indeed almost from pantomime—swigging nectar like Claudius at the court of Denmark and gloating over his fatal rape of Thetis —and that is accomplished easily and perfunctorily, like the disappearance of a painted stage villain down the demon-trap. His fall is indeed described in terms of a demoniac overthrow, a condensed version of the fall of Satan. His own vision of it, embroiled with Demogorgon—

> Even as a vulture and snake outspent
> Drop, twisted in inextricable fight,
> Into a shoreless sea—

repeats the image of vulture or eagle in mid-air fight with a snake which, as we have seen, occurs in many of Shelley's poems, and in which symbols of good and evil are in truth "inextricable" from each other and frequently change place— it is not easy to say whether bird or snake is the evil principle.

Indeed what happens here is that the struggle itself is ended, which is of course logical enough; if Jupiter, in whom all evil is concentrated, is thrown down, then good has nothing thereafter to strive against, the natural consequence of victory in the dualist Zoroastrian battle from which the eagle-serpent fight is taken. The fall is more conclusive than Satan's, but otherwise exactly corresponds to it; by the end of the poem God the Father and tyrant has completely filled the place of the fallen Lucifer, the vanquished Son of the Morning, his conquest "dragged captive" and himself turned into the very same old serpent, cast down, chained, humiliated, though never completely destroyed, whom Eternity keeps up her capacious sleeve. Jupiter falls "Dizzily down, ever, for ever, down" while Prometheus "like a cloud" rises up; thus do things turn into their opposites, and thus is there no movement up or down without a corresponding one in the opposite direction.

It has just been suggested, however, that the opposing elements have been left behind, or rather that the fact of their opposition has been done away with; and the idea of the abolition or shedding of evil is at the heart of the poem. It is an attempt to be free altogether from the seesaw, the fundamental principle of compensatory justice, that animates *Prometheus Unbound;* the unbinding loosens the very idea of equilibrium in the universe. The attempt is made elsewhere in Shelley's work, of course, but nowhere else in so sustained and coherent a way, nor so nearly successful. For *Prometheus Unbound,* especially in the later added Act IV, does set the entire cosmos going up and out, and with an extraordinarily convincing effect : convincing, that is, as the description of a mental event, something observable in "the operations of the human mind". The question whether it also describes an exterior process, the "expansion of the universe" as an astronomical postulate, is not the present point (and may be left perhaps to those who, like A. N. Whitehead, see Shelley as "a Newton among poets")[4]. As a psychological event, at any rate, it is persuasively demonstrated; and in these terms as much as those of physics it must be asked where the energy for this huge expansion is to be sought. Gravity, or Force, has bound Prometheus; Force briefly reappears in the person of Hercules to unbind him, but thereafter is spoken of no more, for gravity has been overcome. Indeed even to use the word "overcome" suggests too much the exertion of force against Force; it is rather that the universe of *Prometheus Unbound escapes* from gravitation.

It is interesting at this point to make a comparison with what Simone Weil says about gravity. Her thinking in many striking ways resembles Shelley's, sharing the same influences in Plato and Greek thought generally. For her too the Prometheus of Aeschylus was the supreme hero of ancient mythology, specifically in her view a prefiguration of Christ, an incarnation of divine love and wisdom and, though bound, a liberator ("All is freedom in this drama built of chains and nails"[5]). But she moved apparently to an opposite conclusion.

For her, gravity, virtually identical with causation, rules all phenomena without exception, mental as well as physical : the only counter is grace. (E.g., "All the natural movements of the soul are controlled by laws analogous to those of physical gravity. Grace is the only exception.")[6]. We may ask whether the movements in *Prometheus Unbound* come within this description. Jupiter, subject to gravity, or Necessity (who is in *Queen Mab* "mother of the world") falls, Prometheus rises, and there is an obvious, though unacknowledged connection between the two motions. But the rise of Prometheus (or mankind) continues independently and indefinitely: the dethronement of Jupiter is less like a descent producing ascent than a trigger which releases a force vaster than itself, and again it must be asked what this force may be. The "supernatural grace" invoked by Simone Weil, and all that is given in her terms from "above", is excluded by Shelley; it may however be urged that he has the true equivalent of it in love.

Love is—or can be claimed to be—the true animating principle of *Prometheus Unbound*. It is love that endures all vicissitudes, the only thing not subject to "Fate, Time, Occasion, Chance and Change", the various aspects of necessity, and it is love that "from its awful throne of patient power" reigns over all at the end. Like Simone Weil's grace it is the equivalent of light ("Two forces rule the universe: light and gravity")[7], intangible but, unless excluded by the interposition of something grosser, universally diffused. Though itself immaterial, it can shine through material bodies; it is an internal fire which sheds an external illumination, "like the atmosphere / Of the sun's fire filling the living world".

It shines through the whole poem; yet it must be doubted whether love is indeed the power that imparts to the universe of Prometheus its headlong outward motion. Rather it seems itself to be in the grip of this motion, and subject to the same expansion and evaporation. It is a fire that shines like light through material bodies and transforms them, making them translucent to themselves. Filled with their own light, Shelley's embodiments of love also become light in another sense, airy, even dispersed in the atmosphere. The beautiful speech of Asia, "Common as light is love, / And its familiar voice wearies not ever" is answered by a voice "in the air", identified as that of Prometheus himself, replying to Asia as the representative of love, Shelley's Aphrodite: "Child of light! thy limbs are burning/ Through the vest which seems to hide them"—an image used in other places by Shelley, notably in the dedication of *The Revolt of Islam* to Mary, "thou Child of Love and Light". The voice, already disembodied, becomes in contemplation ecstatic:

> Lamp of Earth! where'er thou movest
> Its dim shapes are clad with brightness,
> And the souls of those thou lovest
> Walk upon the wind with lightness,
> Till they fail, as I am failing,
> Dizzy, lost, yet unbewailing!

It is like the lines at the end of *Epipsychidion* which, it has been suggested, express rather exhaustion than enduring intensity of feeling. To be "unbewailing", moreover, seems an oddly negative description of an extremity of joy. The effect is general. If the "Voice in the Air" is that of Prometheus, enamoured of Asia, so Panthea earlier in the poem speaks as a kind of proxy for Asia, and relates a dream of her love for and with Prometheus in the same terms:

> . . . the overpowering light
> Of that immortal shape was shadowed o'er
> By love; which, from his soft and flowing limbs,
> And passion-parted lips, and keen, faint eyes,
> Steamed forth like vaporous fire; an atmosphere
> Which wrapped me in its all-dissolving power,
> As the warm ether of the morning sun
> Wraps ere it drinks some cloud of wandering dew.

What seems to be happening here, as elsewhere in Shelley's dealings with an idealised sexual love, but more crucially than in any other poem, is a contest between the urge towards flight and the longing for containment; between the onrush of the Hours with "burning eyes", drinking "with eager lips the wind of their own speed"—presenting in fact the same appearance as the vision of Prometheus in the lines just quoted—and the enduring love which springs "from the last giddy hour", "And folds over the world its healing wings". The embodiments of both, it will be noted, are creatures of the air.

The contest is not brought to any conclusion, and perhaps it cannot be. But what does happen in the course of it is that love itself is scattered or dissipated. That seems to denote its omnipresence and universal exchange—the "love to and from all" which, in Shelley's magnificent formula, ought to be "a superscription over the gate of life"[8]. But it also results in an extreme tenuousness; that love is like "the all-sustaining air", lovely indeed though the simile is as a way of describing that in which all live and move and have their being, also renders it vague and insubstantial. That a spiritual quality should be insubstantial may be thought obvious, even necessary; it may be that Shelley's imagery here is, so to speak, more accurate, nearer to actual description of the indescribable, than the solid forms of other attempts to symbolise the idea of universal love. Yet, if we are to speak in such terms, we cannot forget that substance, or essential nature, is exactly what imagery here is trying to make visible; it is not merely a play on words to say that a satisfactory image of the underlying essence of love must be substantial. To refer again to Simone Weil, it may be seen that for her grace, a spiritual substance as ineffable as love, had in a manner of speaking to *acquire weight;* the dove descends, that is why it has wings: "Gravity makes things come down, wings make them rise: what wings raised to the second power can make things come down without weight?"[9]

Weightless things that acquire weight have exactly the opposite significance for Shelley: they are evil. It was a "solid cloud", a strikingly paradoxical instrument, that Jupiter in the bad old days sent to punish Earth and the children of Earth with "hot thunder-stones". Freed from these, and the evil power that used them disposed of, the Earth itself becomes airy. In Act IV the triumphant amours of Earth and Moon (the former transformed, in one of the protean changes frequent in Shelley, from the mother of Prometheus to a male, consort and brother of the female Moon) are similarly a business of dissolving dews, dawn-mists, and vapours. His "granite mass" interpenetrated by love, the Earth indeed evaporates, like a dew-drop that becomes a "winged mist" and lingering sunset-cloud. It is Prospero's insubstantial pageant but from a wholly different point of view: the difference between one who watches a departure and one who is departing.

It is man himself who departs, or sets off ("Shall we set off?" asked Shelley of Jane Williams, casually proposing a joint suicide; another variant of the cry "Away!"). Man ("oh, not men!" exclaims Earth in disgust, not individuals but collective Man, "a chain of linkéd thought") actually takes over some of the function of gravity,

> Compelling the elements with adamantine stress
> As the sun rules, even with a tyrant's gaze,
> The unquiet republic of the maze
> Of planets, struggling fierce towards heaven's free wilderness.

and since gravity is subject to his will alone it ceases to be a restraining force at all. Nothing will impede the voyage to "life's wildest shores" which, though endlessly receding, will own his dominion.

The dominion is explicitly of love, which now guides and "rules"; again we can see an attempt to reconcile the ideas of ceaseless outward movement and containment, but now love, steering the tempest-winged ship of man "through waves which dare not overwhelm" seems to have turned altogether into a figure of flight itself, omnipotent and invulnerable by its own speed, like the Poet of *Alastor* steering his frail boat unharmed through the storm.

Man and the world take off together, and the movement of both is brilliantly maintained and combined, Earth being by now so entirely identified with man as "one harmonious soul of many a soul" as to alternate with him as subject. It is an extraordinary achievement; nowhere else in Shelley, and perhaps nowhere else at all is the sense of getting away into outer space so strong. In *Queen Mab,* in this respect as in many others a trial run, there is what may be called a single space mission: the journey taken by the spirit of Ianthe, in the

Fairy's charge, reaches a point of vantage from which "Earth's distant orb appeared/ The smallest light that twinkled in the heaven", and "Innumerable systems", the alternative worlds of "this interminable wilderness", show themselves for the edification before her return to her body and terra firma. In *Prometheus Unbound* the Earth itself is launched and lost in space and time, and for lack of gravitation begins to disintegrate or dissolve :

> The joy, the triumph, the delight, the madness !
> The boundless, overflowing, bursting gladness,
> The vaporous exultation not to be confined !

sings the Earth, set free.

This is no longer an Earth to which man is or can be bound; and man whether leaving Earth or identified with it, is on the outer edge of the explosion. His condition has already been described in resounding terms by the Spirit of the Hour at the end of Act III :

> Sceptreless, free, uncircumscribed, but man
> Equal, unclassed, tribeless, and nationless,
> Exempt from awe, worship, degree, the king
> Over himself; just, gentle, wise : but man
> Passionless?—no, yet free from guilt or pain,
> Which were, for his will made or suffered them,
> Nor yet exempt, though ruling them like slaves,
> From chance, and death, and mutability . . .

The history outlined here—a history which, in Marxist phrase, is to "begin" when Prometheus is unbound—is recognisable, if sometimes with difficulty, as human : that is to say as capable of accomplishment in human terms. To say so may seem a quibble, since man's capabilities are thought of as without limit. The point is certainly a nice one, reflected in the curiously ambiguous formula by which man, though not exempt from chance, should nevertheless rule it : chance which can be ruled ceases to be chance. That it should be stated thus is, however, not mere carelessness; in these two lines one can see

Shelley standing as it were with a foot on each side of an invisible line—the frontier of human will and the non-human —of crucial importance for his whole outlook.

Man is not to be imagined as doing the impossible— *Prometheus Unbound* in other words is not to be thought of as "a mere tale of enchantment"—but at the same time he is not to accept the possible as in any way confining him. He may not overleap, but continually pushes in front of him the bounds of possibility. It is, of course, the formula of modern science and technology. The dynamism thus released far outstrips Shelley's mentors in contemplation of human affairs : men and women have become the repositories of all virtue which Godwin before, as others since, have looked to follow the establishment of political justice, but the perfection thus attained is not static. Their lives, in Shelley's prospect, are more imaginatively active; the intellectual pursuits which Godwin supposed would occupy his limited population of perfectly virtuous elders have become a kind of Bacchic dance; language, the "father of thought", already taught to mankind by Prometheus, becomes "a perpetual Orphic song", a mediator of "Daedal" or shaping harmony; as science the gifts of Daedalus—which had formerly shaken but not brought down "the thrones of earth and heaven"—show man at once how to measure and control all the forces of nature :

> The lightning is his slave; heaven's utmost deep
> Gives up her stars, and like a flock of sheep
> They pass before his eyes, are numbered, and roll on !
> The tempest is his steed, he strides the air;
> And the abyss shouts from her depth laid bare,
> Heaven, hast thou secrets? Man unveils me; I have none.

Man does not merely understand but steps out into the universe : as the Chorus of Spirits sing who in Act IV "come from the mind/ Of human kind",

> We'll pass the eyes
> Of the starry skies
> Into the hoar deep to colonise;

Death, Chaos, and Night,
From the sound of our flight,
Shall flee, like mist from a tempest's might.

In the cosmos thus humanised, or made subject to human will, heavenly bodies, the works of man, and man himself are no longer clearly distinguished. The very orbit of the earth about the sun is a mixture of human and planetary history, a representation of Earth's course and of the Moon's spiral about it simultaneously as a dance of courtship (in which Shelley was in a strong sense subliming his current relations with Mary) and a projection of that distant view from a vantage point beyond it that the astronauts travelling to the moon could enjoy, looking back at the "green and azure sphere" from outside, as the "Brightest world of many a one".

This is undeniably a glorious and intoxicating vision : the best of Shelley whether considered as his own favourite poem or (what in his way of thinking would be the same thing) the most successful expression of what we have called the Shelleyan Idea, a complex of attitudes and tendencies which can be found elsewhere, but nowhere else so complete. Nowhere else is the idea of man's self-elevation and self-sufficiency so *winning* : so persuasive by its sweetness, and the beautiful influence of love, so compelling by the force of its own conviction, so victorious over doubt.

The victory is achieved, however, not by any process of reason, but a *coup-de-main*. That it should be so, that the transformation is brought about in the twinkling of an eye and at the sound, if not of the trumpet, of the conch-shell blown by the Spirit of the Hour, may be explained as merely allegorical, representative of whatever long evolution the social forecaster pleases. Nevertheless there is a real difference, within the terms of allegory, between the act—the unbinding of Prometheus—which thus brings a new mankind into being and the more laborious work of Prometheus Plasticator, making men from clay. It is, as the Spirit of the Hour explains, an inward change, not "expressed in outward things", but it is comprehensive : all Shelley's common emblems of evil, "toads, and snakes, and loathly worms,/ And venomous and malicious beasts, and boughs/ That bore ill berries in the woods . . . Hard-featured men, or with proud, angry looks,/ Or cold, staid gait, or false and hollow smiles,/ Or the dull sneer of self-loved ignorance" and "women too, ugliest of all things evil" suddenly show themselves changed into the "mild and lovely forms" of their moral opposites.

Their evil natures are shown to have been no more than disguise, "foul masks", and what this masquerade has been hiding the beautiful and true—a little later it appears to be equated with the "painted veil called life"—is uncertain, and has been much discussed. Whatever it is, is cast aside, to pass like a company of ghosts "floating through the air, and fading still/ Into the winds that scattered them". Such a way of disposing of evil seems rather dangerous; it reminds us less of the Ancient Mariner's blessed water-snakes (though these may be guessed at in the background) than of the terrifying cloud of bat-shadows that pollute the air of *The Triumph of Life*. But in *Prometheus Unbound* these shadows are not given a chance to return, or to catch up; the break with the past is complete.

It is even a break in the operation of cause and effect: an equally sudden transformation converts "the links of the great chain of things" (i.e., of causation) that hitherto have weighed upon "every thought within the mind of man" to a completely different "chain of linkèd thought", the combined free wills and intellectual capacities of man which, with "love and might to be divided not", enables him to break out into a non-gravitational universe. That chains binding and chains linking may be the same thing does not occur to Shelley, though he (as others of the time) used both as a common figure of speech. There is to be no restraint. Only for an instant, at the end of this great rhapsody of overcoming and release spoken by the Spirit of the Hour at the end of Act III, is there the hesitation already noted, the reflection that man is not "yet exempt" from death and change. It is even at this stage brushed aside with the paradox that they are ruled like slaves; and, since they are the only remaining impediment, there is no doubt where man is heading. They are only the "clogs", and those no more than temporary,

> . . . of that which else might oversoar
> The loftiest star of unascended heaven,
> Pinnacled dim in the intense inane.

The inane : nothingness; the void. For an instant the goal of all this Promethean endeavour looks quite different, and more perhaps as Mary saw it, in the dreadful isolation of the Monster when we had our last glimpse of him, borne away on his ice-raft into darkness and distance. In Mary's vision the shadow, abandoning and even surviving man—for Frankenstein is dead—moves on and away into emptiness. In *Prometheus Unbound* there is no shadow; God the Father, transmogrified into Satan, that old serpent, is the nearest approximation, and he, by the inevitable work of time, has been cast down and away. His fall is unending, "ever, for ever down", the equivalent of man's rise; they move perpetually away from each other. The "immortal day" into which man enters has got beyond darkness and night; he has outdistanced the pursuer. His flight has now, literally, no object; in truth it never had a goal, it was always rather a flight from than a journey to. Now the motive itself, the blackness at his back, has dropped away; man is outside the "dim night", his motion has no counter-force against which to exert itself but like a rocket-ship requiring no atmosphere, self-reacting, completely self-contained, moves outward through and to vacancy.

Whether his progress is to be considered as soaring flight or bottomless fall can't be said, since gravity has been abolished. Or rather it has been replaced by a different pull, one that was felt before as he got off the ground but now has man completely in its grip. In terms of space it is the pull of the void itself, in terms of time it is the future, which is also an absolute emptiness, waiting for man to "invent" it. There is perhaps nothing new in this situation, it has been implicit from the beginning in the idea of progress, but now it is unconcealed as man moves out from the shadow of the past and all restraining influence into completely free space. The new day that has dawned is one that, like the Marxist's "beginning of true history", abandons or makes a *tabula rasa* of the past. In it, man is possessed only by the future : and is drawn into it at an ever-accelerating speed, hurtling towards nothing.

To recapitulate : though so different in form and manner, *Frankenstein* and *Prometheus Unbound* are alternative ways of telling the same story, alternative life-histories of the same metaphor. Since one Promethean story follows the other it is tempting to think of the second as "answering" the first, but in fact, though so closely related, it ignores it, and was indeed bound to : any accuser or negative that requires an answer is left behind together with all other darkness. If there is no dialogue between them, however, there is the kind of commentary that two monologues can make upon each other. To what extent one or other gets the better of this dislocated argument is less important than that both statements should be taken into account : if a choice must be made between them, it is probably a matter of temperament which is thought more powerful or persuasive. But in truth it shouldn't be made, for neither is to be dismissed. Both are opposing faces of the same question, and though neither is looking at the other, both are looking at us.

ELEVEN

SCIENCE AND POETRY

THE STATEMENT MADE in *Prometheus Unbound* is not a scientific one. To say so would appear to be needless, since at first sight it is hard to imagine anything less like scientific discourse than the insubstantial, evanescent, and shifting scenery of the poem and its exalted language. However, it has been pointed out that Shelley's interest in and knowledge of the science of his day, traceable in much of his poetry, shows most extensively here, in his greatest poem. References to scientific discovery and theory have been identified (notably by Carl Grabo)[1] in much of the imagery of *Prometheus Unbound,* and many of its obscurities of detail thus elucidated; it is certainly helpful to understanding of the poem to think of it in relation to an age of rapidly expanding theoretical knowledge and practical application in the sciences.

But it would be quite mistaken to take Shelley's poetry, here and elsewhere, as a kind of disguised scientific communication, capable of being deciphered, or translated, into the terminology of science. Shelley may have learned much in fact and speculation from an Erasmus Darwin, decorously wrapped up in metre, but he certainly didn't wish to write like him; didactic poetry, as he explains in the Preface to *Prometheus Unbound,* was his "abhorrence". Anything that can as well be said in prose, he insisted, should be left in prose; poetry has other functions. They were not incompatible with scientific knowledge and might well draw inspiration from it : in such a sense the claim of Shelley's most eminent admirer among scientists, A. N. Whitehead, that "What the hills were to the youth of Wordsworth a chemical laboratory was to Shelley"[2] may be true enough.

But it cannot mean more than that each found in these

different places the appropriate stimulus to his developing thought; and even then it must be observed that Shelley never worked in a laboratory as Wordsworth lived among his hills. From his boyhood Shelley had a random passion for scientific experiment, but in practical terms it never got beyond a boy's interest in tricks and gadgets. In later life he could indeed become deeply involved in a technical project, the steam-boat which, with his money and drive behind it, was to have been built in Italy; but the engineering, though it provided him with imagery, he left to someone else. It is a long way from there, or from the fire-balloons and explosive concoctions of his youth, to Whitehead's inference that "if Shelley had been born 100 years later the twentieth century would have seen a Newton among chemists".

The formulation that Shelley was "a Newton among poets" is easier to accept. He would surely have been ready to accept it himself, unless he felt it to be unnecessary: for as he claimed that "Lord Bacon was a poet"[3] he might have said the same of Newton himself. It was not, for him, that poetry may be scientific, but that science might be poetic, not in its mode of expression, but in its essence. We have no need to think of him therefore as scientist manqué; but his poetry does have a real and direct relation to scientific thought. One will look in vain for accurate observation of the natural world in *Prometheus Unbound*; at any rate one won't find the epiphenomenal world of every-day experience there. It is just the exact Wordsworthian description of nature in concrete and vivid terms that is missing. But then, of course, Wordsworth's account, though it may be reckoned that of a good field naturalist, is not scientific precisely because it is concrete; and the very insubstantiality of Shelley's imagery can be seen to bear a relation to the abstract descriptions of chemistry and physics. We can understand Whitehead's respect for Shelley as a scientific thinker; but, again, it is not so much a matter of detailed correspondences (the earth's "pyramid of night", for example, which for Whitehead "could only have been written by someone with a definite geometrical diagram before his inward eye".) as of something underlying them.

When, again, Whitehead takes Shelley's opening lines in the *Ode to the West Wind,* "from whose unseen presence the leaves dead/ Are driven, like ghosts from an enchanter fleeing", or *The Cloud* saying "I change but cannot die" and finds in them reference to the nature of matter, the perpetual agitation of particles and mutation of form, we are inclined to retort that the nature Shelley saw in these images was his own nature, the vaporous, elusive, ever-flying-and-pursuing character and course in life of which we have perhaps already said enough. But we are pulled up short by the consideration that, whether he saw such a personal connection or not, Whitehead probably and Shelley certainly would have regarded it as no obstacle at all. Great poets, says Whitehead, "express deep intuitions of mankind penetrating into what is universal in concrete fact", and these intuitions they find within themselves. Shelley, a more thorough-going Platonist, says in the *Defence of Poetry*: "A poem is the very image of life expressed in its eternal truth . . . [it] is the creation of actions according to the unchangeable forms of human nature, as existing in the mind of the Creator, which is itself the mirror of all other minds."

The huge claims made for poetry (and by implication for art in general) in the *Defence of Poetry* are often thought of as hyperbole and pardonable exaggeration, a reply in appropriately high style to Peacock's exaggerated and mocking derogation in *The Four Ages of Poetry.* Shelley's answer has outlasted Peacock's attack, which was indeed forgotten soon after it was made, and only remembered now for the sake of what it provoked. But it is worth recalling at least Peacock's peroration which, if he did make it with his tongue half in his cheek, still expressed accurately a view of poetry common at the time and commoner since. It has a direct bearing on the present theme.

> . . . when we consider [said Peacock] that the great and per-
> manent interests of society become more and more the main-
> spring of intellectual pursuit; that, in proportion as they become
> so, the subordinacy of the ornamental to the useful will be more
> and more seen and acknowledged; and that therefore the

243

progress of useful art and science, and of moral and political knowledge, will continue more and more to withdraw attention from frivolous and unconducive, to solid and conducive studies; that therefore the poetical audience will not only continually diminish in the proportion of its number to that of the rest of the reading public, but will sink lower and lower in the comparison of intellectual requirement; when we consider that the poet must please his audience, and must therefore continue to sink to their level, while the rest of the community is rising above it : we may easily conceive that the day is not far distant when the degraded state of every species of poetry will be as generally recognised as that of dramatic poetry has long been; and this not from any decrease of intellectual power, or intellectual acquisition, but because intellectual power and intellectual acquisition have turned themselves into other and better channels, and have abandoned the cultivation and the fate of poetry to the degenerate fry of modern rhymesters, and their olympic judges, the magazine critics, who continue to debate and promulgate oracles about poetry, as if it were still what it was in the Homeric age, the all-in-all of intellectual progression, and as if there were no such things in existence as mathematicians, astronomers, chemists, moralists, metaphysicians, historians, politicians, and political economists, who have built into the upper air of intelligence a pyramid, from the summit of which they see the modern Parnassus far beneath them, and, knowing how small a place it occupies in the comprehensiveness of their prospect, smile at the little ambition and circumscribed perception with which the drivellers and mountebanks upon it are contending for the poetical palm and the critical chair.[4]

The provocation to Shelley (or any poet) is gross and obvious; what is interesting is that the claims made for "intellect" are quite as high as his for poetry, and that Peacock's own image of its stupendous pyramid also soars, in a most Promethean manner, into the upper air. In abolishing poetry Peacock elevated the claims of other aspects of "mind" to extraordinary heights, to heights indeed which he made fun of elsewhere; he could never bring himself to do without the hedging bet of mockery. But these were claims that others, the scientists, political economists, and even the politicians that he catalogues, were making perfectly seriously, and have continued to make and enlarge upon since: if nobody talks about "the march of mind" nowadays, that is only because most people have until very lately taken it for granted. At the time Peacock was writing, and in the revolutionary years leading up to it the supreme position accorded to "mind", "reason", or intellect—indeed during one brief but notorious episode the actual deification of it—had spread and increased its hold to an unprecedented extent. Other periods had perhaps paid as much respect to intellect, but never before so generally, or with so inclusive an application to every kind of active intellectual inquiry: for it was needless to say the active and not the contemplative powers of "mind" that were so venerated.

It was, as we suggested at the beginning, a Promethean age, one in which the story of Prometheus in its several variations seized hold of people's minds in many different places.

It is instructive to listen to the views of a modern historian on the intellectual driving force behind the huge transformations taking place in Western Europe at that time. Not so much that the views are new, but they are put with a peculiar appositeness to the present discussion. The writer, David Landes, maintains that what is known as the Industrial Revolution was indeed "a major turning point in man's history" without precedent in human affairs, whose effects are still acutely felt and continually accelerating. The ground for this explosive change (since even explosions must have powder-trains or fuses) he finds especially in the exceptionally high value placed in European culture on "the rational manipulation of the environment": "rationality", "the antithesis of superstition and magic", allied with "what we may call the Faustian sense of mastery over man and nature".

The alliance was cemented, or made operative by science: "Science indeed was the perfect bridge between rationality and mastery: it was the application of reason to the understanding of natural and, with time, human phenomena; and it made possible a more effective response to or manipulation of the natural and human environment." The means for imposing the "will to mastery" is knowledge, that is, scientific knowledge:

it is noteworthy that in his conclusion Professor Landes speaks of "the march of knowledge" exactly as might any political economist or other observer when Peacock was writing; indeed very much as (with no disrespect intended) does Mr MacQuedy in *Crotchet Castle*. But Professor Landes doesn't only talk like a character from a Peacock novel, or like Peacock himself in *The Four Ages of Poetry*: he also talks very like Shelley. Behind the rationality he is discussing, the accumulation of scientific knowledge and its application to the mastery of nature, he sees, as "one of the primary stimuli of modern technology", "the free-ranging imagination". Modern technology, he says, has now created things that "would scarcely have been conceived in the pre-industrial era"; but he relates even these to imaginative or mythological metaphors which clearly have not been idly chosen, the spirit of Faust, the legend of Daedalus. The title of the book from which these quotations are taken is *The Unbound Prometheus*.[5]

Professor Landes does not mention Shelley, but presumably he had him in mind. On the other hand the young Marx, writing his doctoral dissertation less than twenty years after the first publication of *Prometheus Unbound,* is unlikely to have heard of it; the Promethean exclamations and avowals he allowed himself derived rather from Goethe or directly from Aeschylus. Philosophy, he said, has or ought to make the same profession as the Aeschylean Prometheus, " 'I detest all the Gods' ", it is "her own profession against all the gods of heaven and earth who do not recognise man's self-consciousness as the highest divinity. There shall be none other beside it". Philosophy, he said again, foreshadowing one of his most famous slogans, must turn from the passive task of acquiring understanding to the active one of bringing about change : "like Prometheus who stole fire from heaven and began to build houses and settle on the earth, so philosophy, which has evolved so as to impinge on the world, turns itself against the world that it finds."

These are obvious enough allusions, perhaps, and certainly do not make Marx a follower of Shelley, conscious or unconscious. But it is curious to see the Young Hegelian not only taking Prometheus as the symbol of thought in revolt against things as they are, but describing the same process by which it comes from "within" to grapple with the world "without": "It is a psychological law that once the theoretical intellect has achieved freedom within itself it turns into practical energy and, emerging from the shadow kingdom of Amenthes as will, directs itself against the exterior reality of the world", and again "What was an inner light becomes a consuming flame that turns outwards. As a consequence, the world's becoming philosophical coincides with philosophy's becoming worldly, the realisation of philosophy coincides with its disappearance . . ."[6] We have only to identify the "inner light" with the "free-ranging imagination", both being names for the fire that was stolen from heaven, to see an unbroken continuity of ideas.

Thus Marx in his youth, a modern scientist and, still more recently, a modern economic historian do not find the sort of claims that Shelley made in the *Defence* negligible. Emboldened, we may look at these claims without taking even their largest assertions as being, in Peacock's sense merely "poetical", nothing but ornamentation or diversion. For Shelley poetry or the poetical meant above all expression of the imagination, the terms were almost synonymous; and the imagination for him was the highest function of the mind. It was not thereby simply superior to invention, calculation, and other aspects of rationality but antecedent to them, it begot them, nourished them, and guided them. It was in fact the Creator Spirit making the mental world out of chaos for itself; and if the mental world, so the actual or material world in turn. Indeed, he did not distinguish between them, since matter for him was animate, "infinitely active and subtile" and "light, electricity and magnetism are fluids not surpassed by thought itself in tenuity and activity".[7] But from the "necessitarian" consequence of such a view he moved, by the time of *Prometheus Unbound* and the *Defence of Poetry,* to the more complete Platonic, or neo-Platonic position that conceives of thought as the organiser and illuminator; the lightning-flash of creation could be regarded simultaneously as actual lightning and as thought itself.

Poetry is the mediator of this original creative illumination;

poetry in this sense, says Shelley, is the organiser of the arts and sciences, the maker as well as the user of language, the path-finder far ahead of the ordinary pioneers of technique : "The promoters of utility . . . follow the footsteps of the poets and copy the sketches of their creation into the book of common life."[8] Although, or rather because "The imagination is beyond temporal notions of right and wrong" it, or poetry, is the source of ethics : "Ethical science arranges the elements which poetry has created . . ." and "the invisible influence of great minds"—the same "cloud of mind" accumulating and discharging its collective lightning that we have met already—"at once connects, animates, and sustains the life of all. It is the faculty which contains within itself the seeds at once of its own and of social renovation." Without poetic "excitements" the "grosser sciences and application of analytical reasoning to the observations of society" would never have been awakened. Poets are therefore "legislators" and projectors, or even more strongly creators of the future; which is "contained within the present as the plant within the seed". As a poet by the use of his imagination "participates in the eternal, the infinite, and the one; as far as relates to his conceptions, time and place and number are not", so "the spirit of events" is foreknown to him. "All high poetry is infinite; it is as the first acorn, which contained all oaks potentially." We may add to this small anthology of quotations from the *Defence of Poetry* one from an earlier essay on *The Revival of Literature* (1815) in which "mind" as such performs the functions which later Shelley attributed more precisely to the imagination :

> Superstition, of whatever kind, whether earthly or divine, has hitherto been the weight which clogged man to earth, and prevented his genius from soaring aloft amid its native skies. The enterprises and the effect of the human mind are something more than stupendous; the works of nature are material and tangible; we have a half-insight into their kind, and in many instances we predict their efforts with certainty. But mind seems to govern the world without visible or substantial means. Its birth is unknown; its action and influence unperceived; and its being seems eternal.

The imagination is unlimited, eternally aspirant, and—the most significant point in this passage—unpredictable because apparently without law; it is a law unto itself, or its laws are born in the same place and in the same continually self-renovating way. What Shelley claimed for poetry and poets was that they were closer to this unknown birthplace than all the other practitioners of "intellect" listed by Peacock, from mathematician to politician economist (and we may add as many more to their numbers as we please, to take in all new branches of knowledge and technique); that therefore poets not only knew more, or more vitally, of the future works of "mind", but actually brought these about. It was not necessary for them to have detailed scientific knowledge, not even knowledge of their own intuitions, whose birthplace was unknowable : poetry "acts in a divine and unapprehended manner, beyond and above consciousness".[8] Through imagery and metaphor poets bring into consciousness the original forms, the "acorns" (it is indeed impossible to speak without imagery here) of whole departments of knowledge, analysis and inquiry. "Their language is vitally metaphorical : that is, it marks the before unapprehended relation of things and perpetuates their apprehension, until the words which represent them become, through time, signs for portions or classes of thought instead of pictures of integral thoughts." Language itself, which is both the instrument and the production of the poetic imagination, makes visible what before was unseen, and its self-organisation to this end is an act of making : "Every language near to its source is in itself the chaos of a cyclic poem."

Out of chaos, the universal disorganised potential, anything may arise that does arise—a tautology necessary to describe the feeling that, giving form to anything the imagination creates it *de novo*. We grope within the lucky-dip of unconsciousness; if we don't know who put the bran tub there we must assume that we make what we find. Imagination calls into primary being.

This was a fundamental belief of Godwin, a necessary consequence of his doctrine of the supremacy of "mind", and it was one that Shelley endorsed in every line that he wrote. Godwin's novel *St Leon* (a Faustian romance whose hero acquires both the Philosopher's Stone and the Elixir of Life, and is consequently alienated from his fellow men) opens with the apophthegm : "There is nothing that human imagination can figure brilliant and enviable, that human genius and skill do not aspire to realise", in itself a fairly moderate statement. Shelley characteristically took it further, though one can scarcely say (in view of the story the words introduce) that he distorted its spirit. We find him urging on others with the same reflection : for example, encouraging Mary to go on with her own writing, he admonished her to remember the "proud and true sentiment" in St Leon " 'There is nothing which the human mind can conceive, which it may not execute.' "[9] We may jump forward from this interesting misquotation (as will be noticed, Shelley greatly sharpened Godwin's thought) to Wittgenstein : "Whatever is imaginable, is possible."

That saying can be taken two ways, according, so to speak, to our view of the nature of the bran tub. We may suppose its contents to be limited, in which case we will be inclined to say that only those packages can be found in it by the lucky-dipping imagination as are already there. On the other hand, we may say that, since nothing whatever is known or can be known about the bran tub except the evidence of its contents, it is reasonable to assume that these are innumerable, or infinite; in which case, the possibilities being without limit, the act of finding, or choice, is also creation. The lucky-dipper is creator : in taking something from the bran tub he does not simply demonstrate its possibility, he *makes* it possible. The spectacle of mankind gathered round the infinite lucky-dip, genius withdrawing parcel after parcel to be unwrapped and displayed by technology, is in the strongest sense a fascinating one; significantly, it seems a much more appropriate metaphor nowadays than the older one of the cornucopia or even of Pandora's Box. The variety of gifts (which, of course, we no longer consider as gifts) taken out is appalling, and as they are unwrapped (our exclamations of astonishment and delight soon turning to cries of terror) it is upon their detail that attention is concentrated.

The detail is bewildering in the deed, seductively distracting even in the prior thought :—the astronautical visions in *Prome-*

theus Unbound and *Queen Mab* of a distanced earth, the huge, "long, long sound" of earth's emancipation splitting the welkin all round the world like a supersonic message-bearer; Mary's gleanings from her Sybilline leaves in *The Last Man,* the sombre projections of warfare and disaster; more copiously the expectation in the *Atlantis* of Shelley's revered Lord Bacon, the submarines and flying machines and weapons of Solomon's House, a favourite resort of those who like to watch how wishes may come true; or, with more sinister effect, the Menageries in which are found the effects of Bacon's "dissections and trials", to make creatures greater or lesser than their kind, or "continuing life in them, though divers parts, which you account vital, be perished and taken forth : resuscitating of some that seem dead in appearance, and the like".[10]

But Shelley's admiration for the "almost superhuman wisdom" of Bacon was certainly not on account of this prospective programme for technology, the projected raree-show of tricks and gadgets; in fact the minutiae of prediction and their more or less superstitious interpretation obscure the principles underlying them. That men, who have always wanted to fly and penetrate the depths of the sea and travel to the moon and resuscitate the dead and prolong life indefinitely, should have found the means to do these things is really not surprising or even particularly interesting. What fires the imagination is why men should want to do so. It is the Bacon speaking in the Preface to his *Interpretation of Nature* that must have seized Shelley's mind and filled him with the gratitude and awe that arise when one finds another person thinking in exactly the same way as oneself :

Now among all the benefits that could be conferred upon mankind I found none so great as the discovery of new arts, endowments, and commodities for the bettering of man's life . . . But if a man could succeed, not in striking out some particular invention, however useful, but in kindling a light in nature—a light that should in its very rising touch and illuminate all the border regions that confine upon the circle of our present knowledge; and so spreading further and further should presently disclose and bring into sight all that is most hidden and secret

in the world—that man (I thought) would be the b
indeed of the human race, the propagator of man's en
the universe, the champion of liberty, the conqu
subduer of necessities.

Superhuman wisdom indeed; and it is "that man" o
thought—or rather that Titan or angel, for it is
apparent who it is that will "kindle a light in nature"
the champion of mankind—who truly engages our a
and of whom poetry can tell us something. What things he finds
in the boundless bran tub—which he is himself inside, and
which is also inside himself—is of no more than slight secondary
interest, and may even be a hindrance to understanding. They
delude the searcher, for they are not what he is looking for, if
he is looking for anything and not groping at random. And
what that is can certainly not be named or described, but it does
show itself in images which, so long as they are allowed to
remain as images or metaphors and do not solidify into fact,
can teach something about his situation.

Shelley's *Prometheus Unbound* and Mary's *Frankenstein*
between them represent to an unsurpassed extent a comprehensive poetic statement of the future that mankind may envisage
for itself and increasingly and at an increasing pace strives to
realise, in fact. To put it another way, they combine to give a
full account of the present state and future prospects of the
metaphor they deal in. We have seen that both can be interpreted in personal terms : not so much in the individual details
of derivation and association, though these may offer useful
corroboration, as in the way that both works give expression to
something essential in their shared life : Mary's story of "the
modern Prometheus" as a commentary on the consequence of
being Shelley, of being wholly gripped by the Shelleyan Idea;
Shelley's great poem as his most successful attempt to free the
Idea from all trammels upon it.

We have seen how much of Shelley's life, and of the writings
he produced in its short and meteoric course, was a continuous
action, or description, of flight and pursuit, and we have been
able to conjecture, with the aid of *Frankenstein* especially, what

he was simultaneously flying from and towards. Because Shelley was an extreme case or, as it is alternatively expressed, a genius, and because Mary shared in, sympathised with, and reflected his genius to a very high degree, they were together conductors for the "uncommunicated lightning" of their time and ours. The lightning both reveals and sets in motion; though no more than instantaneously, it shows what is happening. That is to say, Shelley flying towards the light and the monstrous shadow behind him that Mary saw were aspects of their personal lives and of events within their souls which expressed what had been happening, was then happening, and is still happening in society at large. The Promethean visions of Shelley and Mary were more than mere mirrors of their time and social surroundings, the visible "march of mind"; they were, and are, an intense expression of its marching orders : as the words of the dumb-crambo which society crassly and blindly continues to act out.

Both *Prometheus Unbound* and *Frankenstein* end in a formula of liberation, only apparently of different sorts. The giant unchained and released from divine tyranny beautifully, marvellously, and compellingly points the way upwards and outwards, to nowhere. The Monster, his creator dead, also launches out into nothing. Both narratives show man re-made and freed from himself; each is a different way of telling how man can get outside and beyond himself. The work of exteriorisation takes it up from these prophetic utterances and makes it literal, realising or materialising the psychic programme by turning its actors into mechanisms freed from the restraints of flesh and blood. The process now seems to be perfected : men, who could not look at what lay within themselves, now find it staring them inescapably in the face, their own creation, apparently free from all control, and completely alien.

There is no need here to elaborate upon the monsters of men's making which they now feel are so far outside their nature as to have a life of their own, threatening human life. They are too familiar, from the processes which lead, by logical steps, to the devastation and pollution of the earth to the equal logic of preparing mutual military annihilation. But it is necessary to look more closely at the conviction that these forces, being now quite "inhuman", although all of human origin, are therefore out of control. For it is exactly the drive to obtain control that creates them in the first place.

If we look for the furthest origins of the Shelleyan Idea we doubtless have to go back to the Fall, and the search even in terms of personal biography is likely to lead back to beginnings. But there is a point in Shelley's life, recorded in his verse, which may conveniently be taken as the start of that race that ended among the flying shadows of *The Triumph of Life*. In the prologue to *The Revolt of Islam* he is able to recall it exactly :

> I do remember well the hour which burst
> My spirit's sleep : a fresh May-dawn it was,
> When I walked forth upon the glittering grass,
> And wept, I knew not why : until there rose
> From the near school-room, voices, that, alas !
> Were but one echo from a world of woes—
> The harsh and grating strife of tyrants and of foes.
>
> And then I clasped my hands and looked around,
> But none was near to mock my streaming eyes,
> Which poured their warm drops on the sunny ground—
> So, without shame, I spake :—"I will be wise,
> And just, and free, and mild, if in me lies
> Such power, for I grow weary to behold
> The selfish and the strong still tyrannise
> Without reproach or check." I then controlled
> My tears, my heart grew calm, and I was meek and bold.

The poem goes on to say how "from that hour did I with earnest thought/ Heap knowledge from forbidden mines of lore" and "from that secret store/ Wrought linked armour for my soul, before/ It might walk forth to war among mankind". The moment of revelation was perhaps the same as that recorded in the *Hymn to Intellectual Beauty,* when the spirit's "shadow" fell on him and "I shrieked, and clasped my hands in ecstasy" and dedicated himself to its service. (He was thus bound "To fear himself, and love all humankind".)

The spirit which the intellect resolves to serve is itself intellect, and its function is to command. In the agonising chaos of the world outside and within—between which consciousness does not at first make distinction—the intellectual powers promise order, arrangement, and control. Armed with them, whether or not meekly—the peculiar Shelleyan meekness, which is perhaps like the devastating humility of science, meek before facts and overpoweringly arrogant in relation to everything else—the individual can go forth to war among mankind and to subdue the forces of disorderly nature. The war is characteristically an outward one; though waged with mental weapons it is not like Blake's mental fight between internal forces but is a sallying forth.

We can see, indeed, that the first act of control preceded the Fall, when Adam in his solitude (Eve not yet having been taken out of him) named the beasts and established their exterior existence and his God-ordained dominion over them : for before that they had lived undifferentiated in his own mind. From that time forth, one may say, the business of extending control has gone on without interruption and at a steadily increasing rate, its scope only enlarged—and that to infinity—by expulsion from the Garden. It is carried on by means of knowledge, but knowledge is itself control; to know a thing previously unknown is to bring it into existence and at the same time to dominate it as creator does creature : science appears simultaneously to reveal, appropriate, and command the world it brings into being.

It is a form of begetting, just as to know is a synonym for sexual union; it is not beside the point to note that in the earliest derivations conjectured for the Prometheus myth the fire-stick with which he regenerates the spark from heaven is phallic, operating upon the passive, though inflammable material of the universe. Such activity is clearly as inseparable from man's existence as his sexuality, and perhaps more so, since it offers distinct advantages over sexual life. For in his sexual nature man confronts another individual who by virtue of her existence imposes limits; dream of it as he may, man will never altogether dominate woman, from whom he comes. But he can turn from her to the outer world which lies boundlessly and, so far as any opposition of soul goes, completely passively before him; and his knowledge of that inexhaustible object, his penetration of it, and laying of it open—all phrases used to describe scientific discovery and its exploitation—take more and more upon themselves the aspect of a rape.

In discovering the world, "penetrating the secrets of Nature", the intellect creates and takes possession of it : before discovery it may exist, but indescribably. Discovery starts with description. Man plants his flag upon new territory and it is now *his*—there is so close a connection between the actual voyages of discovery and territorial acquisition of the fifteenth and sixteenth centuries and the intellectual expansion that accompanied them that one can't say which makes a better simile for the other; and both put into action the same urge. But the great land-discoveries and empire-makings were commonly accompanied by extermination or enslavement of the inhabitants; in the same way, when any region of "nature" is brought within the empire of scientific knowledge it is de-natured, the life is taken from it.

The life of pre-scientific nature, the nature of animism, is free, as anything with a soul is free, a rock as much as a beast or another man, to be controlled if at all by magic, which is most uncertain. (For magic, even though it be the precursor of science, and even called "science" by its practitioners, operates in a quite different way, not simply in being ineffective, but in its assumptions. It is at bottom a work of the emotions, making an emotional appeal to the nature it seeks to command. The magician who puts a spell upon a stone, or the wind, or the sun, is really trying to *move* it to do as he wishes; and in the dealings of one feeling being with another there is always and necessarily choice. The sorcerer may have an extremely strong magic, he may be "reasonably" certain that autonomous nature will obey him, the sun be persuaded to rise or the rain to fall, but he cannot be sure as a scientist is. Not because he is "wrong", since he is not wrong from his own point of view, but because his attitude to the natural world as a series of beings, or persons, must allow for uncertainty. One can be sure of a thing, but a person can always refuse to be persuaded.)

But when subject to truly scientific "law" or (another name for the same thing) accurate prediction, nature is not only bound but made dead, and there is no difference between "living things" and "dead matter", both the organic and the inorganic are equally robbed of the soul-liberty which is the essence of life. It is a remarkable thing that just as scientific Cartesian man was confining the world within the system of rational knowledge, depriving it of liberty and independent life, his own liberty became more and more important to him. He knew in his own mind that he was free, and therefore alive, the conscious *cogito* being necessarily at once free and living. But he didn't know it of any other object, and the dead weight of imprisoned matter, which included before long the matter of himself, his too too solid flesh, pressed terribly upon him. The only escape from the burden of the "dead", or "unthinking", or "indifferent" universe seemed and must seem through more control (i.e., knowledge and its application) over everything else, and more freedom for himself, but in a beleaguered fortress, the steadily shrinking part of himself that he knew to be free. "Above all things, liberty!" was the passionate cry of the youthful Shelley, the "necessarian": was there indeed any of it left in a world of "dead" matter—and matter, to make matters worse, which could only be thought of as living if allowed to be made and ruled by a tyrant-God.

The Shelleyan way out of this impasse can be seen in *Prometheus Unbound*, which does indeed represent an heroic attempt to restore soul to the world. Shelley's universe, in this poem especially, is animist; everything (as Carl Grabo has pointed out) is endowed with soul, from the Earth itself, conceived in Platonic terms as a living being, to the "elemental genii", present as much in "man's high mind" as the "central stone of sullen lead", which may be identified as chemical elements. They are all alive, or brought to life, wakened from "oblivion" at the end of the poem; the implication here is that man's knowledge of the cosmos will have precisely the opposite effect to the one traced in the preceding argument. Science will bring the universe to conscious life, and in this sense it will be a "world set free". But it is set free to be at the disposal of man : thus Grabo, for instance, interprets the union of Prometheus and Asia as meaning that "the universe becomes man's to do with what he will".[11] We shall have occasion to consider this point later; in the meantime we may note only that the problem of freedom and necessity in the natural world, though it clearly emerges in the poem at the crucial point of Prometheus' unbinding, is too rapidly disposed of for any real grappling with it. Hercules unbinds Prometheus, remarking only,

> . . . thus doth strength
> To wisdom, courage, and long-suffering love,
> And thee, who art the form they animate,
> Minister like a slave.

In Aeschylus, it is Force and Might who bind Prometheus; Shelley unbinds him by force under control, in fact enslaved. Control is the fruit of knowledge, but it is also, as knowledge extends, a requirement of it; it seems indeed to be a corollary of liberty itself, now in the last hiding place of individual self-consciousness. For though Force and Might, the "forces of nature", have ceased to be endowed with will, being depersonalised—having lost their autonomy, that is to say, and become locked as objects in a system of "law"—they remain, even though predictable, not wholly obedient. Though dead, they go marching on in a manner that seems capricious and may be dangerously destructive.

They can, however, be commanded, or made to command themselves. For Bacon, the scientist or inventor who "masters" nature does so in obedience to her own laws; but his invention may also be thought of as a kind of trap for her. A machine is nothing more than one or more of the "forces of nature" tricked, so to speak, into driving itself. That is a marvellous thing (if we can put ourselves for a moment outside the state of mind in which it is taken for granted) : something that can perform marvels, but is wonderful in itself. It carries out actions exactly prescribed and under control, and yet works *of itself*, and will go on working until it is told to stop.[12] It is almost like a man, but in all ways but one it is much better : because it is *made* for obedience, it is a piece of nature which has become absolutely and unequivocally man's. And with it, once you have the knack, nature can endlessly and astonishingly be brought into line; and the more it is done the easier it becomes, until the prospect opens up of a transformation that will leave no uncertainties at all, for the whole of known nature will have become, not subject to the machine, but simply a machine itself.

There are flaws, however, in the forward view, not because machines are imperfect—that can and will be remedied; already we have the formula, if not the actual achievement, of "zero error"—but because they are so like men they become unchancy things for man to have around. Almost they seem to mock him; for if he—the individual solitary consciousness—knows within himself that he is not a machine, it is something he is not altogether sure of concerning his own nature, and not at all sure of concerning others. No sooner are machines invented, indeed, and brought into general use than the description of "machine" begins to be applied to other things, social institutions, other individuals; and if to others (so a principle of fairness suggests) why not also to oneself?

Shelley was, as we would expect, much interested in the wonders of the dawning machine age, and the comparisons suggested between man and machine were certainly not unknown to him. In a long speculative letter to Hogg while still at Oxford (moving on from the pains of rejected love to the "non-existence of a Deity") we find him ingeniously reversing the "argument from design": from the supposition that God is the original "actuating principle" of existence, or "soul of the universe" to the question "Why *too* is *not* gravitation the soul of a clock?"[13] Why not indeed? And why not—we can see the question pushing in—also of man, who is also in all visible respects subject to gravity? Because of Reason, which distinguishes him from beasts. But Reason is an unlucky fail-safe here, even if Shelley didn't know, or guess, that machines could be made to reason. The argument goes on, by impeccably rational stages, to reduction of soul to a tautology: "if the principle of life . . . be *soul*, then gravitation is as much the soul of a clock, as animation is that of an oyster. I think we may not inaptly define *Soul* as the most supreme, superior, and distinguished abstract appendage to the nature of anything." The concluding sentence appears to restore "soul" to a position of high regard; but at the cost, removing it from subjectivity to objective existence, of rendering it an attribute of absolute indifference.

It is interesting that on the occasion when Shelley had some direct practical dealings with machinery it was as the entrepreneur—the capitalist-god who sets the machines in motion—of a steamboat : the vessel which, financed by him and designed by George Reveley, the son of Maria Gisborne by her first husband, was to have plied between Genoa and Leghorn. The scheme fell through, and Shelley, who with great generosity had put up the funds, lost his money and got little from the business but vexation. He undertook it to help his friends; yet we cannot help suspecting that the plan, which took up much of his time and attention, also signified something for himself, if only because it represented the application of power to a boat, of all the works of man the one that held most symbolic meaning for him.

What took the popular imagination when steam-engines first became practical prime-movers was the regularity of their operation, their logic, but even more, perhaps, the fact that they moved themselves. It is difficult for us today, universally machine-riding and machine-ridden—no longer thinking why locomotives and automobiles are so-called—to remember how extraordinary that was : that nobody, no exterior force had to push or pull the cranks and wheels, that the machine, like a living creature, was apparently its own mover, refining and concentrating the "forces of nature" and able to circumvent them in a way absolutely unheard of. (Though not undreamt-of : that is another matter.)

A steamboat can move against the wind, it can actually ignore it : that is what makes it so very strange. (As strange, indeed, as a spectre-bark that "comes onward without wind or tide".[14]) We must remember Shelley's feelings about both wind and boats, endowed with even more significance for him than for most people. His imagination rode upon the wind, it seemed in the imagery of his poetry often enough that he *was* the wind, the wind that flies and chases itself for ever, and bloweth as it listeth. He also felt (in an image not of course his own, but of great antiquity and almost universal occurrence) that his essence was boat-borne, wind-driven on the face of the waters or, more tellingly for him, their bosom : his soul was "as a boat", and he was happiest, perhaps, when acting in body what his soul seemed, even to his body's destruction.

But he also feared the wind, at any rate the wind of chance and fate : when in another recurrent image he thought of himself as, or thought himself into a cloud, it was the cloud's complete obedience to, or actual identification with the wind, as well as its perpetually changing form, that he dwelt upon. "We are uncertain people . . . like clouds in the wind", he wrote[15] while discussing the steamboat project, and it was something both he and Mary must have thought of often enough. ("What wind! What changes!" she noted in her *Journal,* with more sombre foreboding on Shelley's birthday a year later; it was his last.[16])

To be carried by the wind is beautiful, but annihilating. But a steamboat, that can defy wind and master tide, and impose its will on all uncertainties, suggests other voyages for the soul. We can follow some of Shelley's thoughts on the subject in the long verse-letter to Maria Gisborne written when the steamboat "adventure", as he called it, was at full pressure. In this letter[17] he allowed his musings to run on unimpeded, with something of the effect of free association, and it is curious to see where they lead. He starts by speaking of a spider, and then of himself as silkworm (another recurrent self-image) spinning a more delicate kind of web "from the fine threads of rare and subtle thought" : thus, though the most helpless and innocuous creature, making for himself and round his "decaying form" the cocoon of immortality in the loving hearts of friends. Yet, he says, he presents a quite different aspect at the moment; anyone who saw him now, surrounded as he is by blueprints and bits and pieces of machinery connected with the steamboat design, would think him "a mighty mechanist,/ Bent with sublime Archimedean art/ To breathe a soul into the iron heart/ Of some machine portentous". He goes on to describe "such shapes of unintelligible brass", "Of tin and iron not to be understood;/ And forms of unimaginable wood" of which a silkworm-poet can, naturally, make nothing, but whose potential he can guess—

> Great screws, and cones, and wheels, and grooved blocks,
> The elements of what will stand the shocks
> Of wave and wind and time—

and it is a power (touching another of his common associations, between mountain and geologic forces and the work of creation) positively volcanic.

He sees the bowl of mercury on the table and thinks of it as the drink of gnomes or kobolds

> When at their subterranean toil they swink
> Pledging the demons of the earthquake, who,
> Reply to them in lava—cry, halloo !
> And call out to the cities o'er their head,
> Roofs, towers, and shrines, the dying and the dead,
> Crash through the chinks of earth—and then all quaff
> Another rouse, and hold their sides and laugh.

It is a not altogether coherent but very suggestive melange of images, combining construction and destruction; and it leads on to a further cluster of associations. Speaking again of himself, Shelley thinks of himself as a maker, reverting first to his boyhood games with paper boats and, yielding "to the impulse of an infancy/ Outlasting manhood", setting a piece of metal, the "rude idealism" of his early playthings, to float in the bowl of quicksilver on his table. He then moves on to his present function as a poet and preacher of liberty, described as a magical Faustian engineer, combining the imagery of mechanism with the wizardry of his boyhood fantasies :

> And here like some weird Archimage sit I,
> Plotting dark spells, and develish enginery,
> The self-impelling steam-wheels of the mind,

Which pump up oaths from clergymen, and grind
The gentle spirit of our meek reviews
Into a powdery foe of salt abuse . . .

Behind the bantering irony may be glimpsed a real power, conceived in very striking terms: a self-impelling intellectual machine which is an engine of revolution. No wonder that Shelley already thinks of the little steamboat as a "machine portentous".

It is worth looking again at the rather odd phrase Shelley used to describe the metal floating in the bowl of mercury—some working part or other, "a hollow screw with cogs"—which seemed to him the "rude idealism of a paper boat". It is not like Shelley to use such a term loosely, even in fun; but it is clear that here it is the paper boat of his boyhood sailing that is the "idealism", the poetic form of the power-boat, to be made of Vulcanic materials, of which the parts lie around him. The steamboat itself originates in his mind, a poetic image before it can become an actual piece of engineering. Perhaps it was at this time that he drew the sketch in one of his notebooks, a dashing representation of a black, sharp-prowed vessel, with a tall funnel spouting smoke; and it is tempting to think that he had this doodle in mind some months later when he was writing the *Defence of Poetry* and said that "the promoters of utility . . . follow the footsteps of poets and copy the sketches of their creations into the book of common life".

Shelley's sketch is already, of course, of a very different sort of boat from the delicate pinnaces that sail through his poems; though these, too, were sometimes self-propelled—the "rare device" which with its "web of texture fine and frail" catches "unknown winds" to bear the prophetess and the visionary "with steady speed" in *The Revolt of Islam*; or the very similar boat, too "feeble" to carry Venus, in which the Witch of Atlas voyaged, with Hermaphrodite as motive-force, on the surface of the waters or, being winged, in the air. (We may note in passing that the Hermaphrodite, although wholly a creature of fantasy, a relative of "the snowy Florimel" in Spenser's *Faery Queen*, cold, beautiful, sodomitical, is "moulded of fire and ice", and can be thought of, therefore, as an embodiment of steam.)

The boats are different, but the point is that they are related; the light and airy soul-skiffs of poetry, built by the imagination or naturally grown—half-vegetable, as in the case of the Witch's pinnace—which can transform themselves so readily from one element to another, as often flying as sailing, can also be transformed into actuality, constructed of a "horrid mass" of tin and iron and unintelligible brass. It is not that the boats of poetry are "poetical" representations of such solid constructions; they are metaphors for psychic entities, not to be described except in such metaphoric terms. It is rather that, as has been said before, the metaphor itself can be solidified, "copied"—though unintelligibly; it thereby becomes impossible to understand as metaphor—into the "book of common life". In its light and playful way, the *Letter to Maria Gisborne* describes the same process as does *Frankenstein*.

The place of all these transformations and re-emergencies is the tomb (or, if it is preferred, the unconscious). The *Letter to Maria Gisborne* begins with the image which Shelley found in Greek mythology and was so fond of, of the caterpillar or worm which, in its chrysalis-coffin, is changed into butterfly or moth, the winged soul. (Boats themselves can be so metamorphosed. Goethe saw in Venice that the gondolas were like coffins on top of cradles;[18] it was Shelley who thought they were to coffins as moths to their chrysalises.[19]) But he moves on, as we have seen, to envisage another death and resurrection : by way of images of torment and cruelty (the cogs and wheels reminding him of instruments of torture, and these in turn of the wreckage left by ships of the Armada, on which "the exulting elements in scorn,/ Satiated with destroy'd destruction, lay/ Sleeping in beauty on their mangled prey,/ As panthers sleep") to the assembly of these "strange and dread" forms into something he cannot understand or, perhaps, refuses to, leaving "This secret in the pregnant womb of time,/ Too vast a matter for so weak a rhyme".

What is presaged is indeed entirely rejected by the silkworm-poet, it is ugly and unpredictable, but powerful; it is even identified with power. ("Strong men obeying the master motion like the wheels of a perfect engine", was how Shelley saw the Imperial Austrian forces expected to crush the Italian insurgencies of 1820; though the "good spirit of the world" might be out against them.[20]) The machine is indeed opposed to living or animated nature, and "the very elements" may be expected to fight against it, but one cannot be sure they will prevail, since a perfect engine is precisely a device to turn the forces of nature upon themselves. It has the attributes of reason and logic, by which it has been made, and it has the power of a dead nature whose soul (the good spirit of the world) has been destroyed by reason. It rises from the grave not as a new living body or one restored to life, but truly a walking corpse.

The machine, as a piece of dead nature, has no feeling; yet is strongly prone (as may be any revenant in revenge for its own death) to exhibit malevolence. The transformations and reversals that take place here are bewildering. In the *Letter to Maria Gisborne* it is a spirit of liberty which cries " 'My name is Legion!' "; in *The Revolt of Islam* it is more canonically

> The Fiend, whose name was Legion; Death, Decay,
> Earthquake, and Blight, and Want, and madness pale,
> Winged and wan diseases, an array
> Numerous as leaves that strew the autumn gale.

This Fiend, moreover, is God, or is taken to be God by deluded men; and later in the poem, in the attempt to remove the delusion, a remarkable comparison is made. Cythna, the conscientious proselytiser of atheism, addresses the sailors who have rescued her (they are sailing to "the warm home of happier destiny") and attempts to disabuse them of belief in a power other than human that "builds for man in solitude":

> What is that Power? Ye mock yourselves, and give
> A human heart to what ye cannot know:
> As if the cause of life could think and live!
> 'Twere as if man's own works should feel, and show
> The hopes, and fears, and thoughts, from which they flow,
> And he be like to them. Lo! Plague is free

To waste, Blight, Poison, Earthquake, Hail, and Snow,
Disease, and Want, and worse necessity
Of hate and ill, and Pride, and Fear, and Tyranny.

As if man's own works should feel: the relation of creator to creature, and the possibility or otherwise of exchange of feeling between them, which is at the core of *Frankenstein*, is stated here with an appearance of clarity, in fact with an extreme ambiguity. For if man's works should feel then by analogy it is possible that man should be the work of a thinking and feeling deity; and if that is not to be admitted (since manifestly man's works do *not* feel) then perhaps man does not feel either, but is an automaton that has made other automatons, which now have as little, or as much freedom as he. Thus the clock with the soul of gravity and the portentous engine return to present him with his own likeness, which is also the likeness of a God whom reason has calmly abolished : incapable of feeling, and notionally therefore indifferent, but conceived in terms of active and "fiendish" malevolence, bearing with them all the multiplied plagues of the earth.

Despite his contempt for Paley's "proof" of the existence of God from mechanical analogy, Shelley was willing to use the analogy the opposite way, that is to show man, in his mechanical creations, as like to God. Returning briefly to the steamboat scheme, we find him writing—at an earlier stage in the project than the *Letter to Maria Gisborne*—in an exchange with the engineer himself, Henry Reveley, pointing to the parallel in striking terms. Reveley had already given him an account of the crucial operation of casting the cylinder of the steam-engine, himself using vivid and evocative language : the parts, he said, were "really perfect; they are massive and strong to bear any usage and sea-water, *in saecula saeculorum*".[21] Shelley was stimulated to prompt reply :

Your volcanic description of the birth of the cylinder is very characteristic of you, and of it. One might imagine God, when he made the earth, and saw the granite mountains and flinty promontories flow into their craggy forms, and the splendour of their fusion filling millions of miles of the void space, like the tail of a comet, so looking, so delighting in his work. God sees his machine spinning round the sun, and delights in its success, and has taken out patents to supply all the suns in space with the same manufacture. Your boat will be to the ocean of water, what the earth is to the ocean of ether—a prosperous and swift voyager.[22]

The links both with the humorous imagery of the *Letter to Maria Gisborne* and, beyond that, to *Prometheus Unbound*, will be apparent.

Shelley was deeply interested in the Book of Job, and planned, it seems, to make that work of "irresistible grandeur"[23] the subject of a poetic drama of his own. It is clearly at the back of his mind in the last years of his life; the *Letter to Maria Gisborne* itself is full of imagery that seems to have originated there. What he would have made of it is an open but irresistibly inviting question. It may be that his interest in Job was confined, as it seems to be in most of his passing references, to its bearing on what one may call the Shelleyan dossier on Lord God Almighty, the tyrant-god of power and mystery against whom he prosecuted his case elsewhere: certainly he could have used as evidence the quite a-moral and inexplicable way the debate is closed by Jehovah steam-rollering Job into the ground. The Almighty who answers Job from the whirlwind is superficially at least identical (even extending, it may be thought, to the slightly comic element in his boasting) with the Jupiter overthrown and cast into the pit in *Prometheus Unbound*; and Job, obstinately adhering to his integrity, is a paradigm of Shelley's Titan.

But what one would like to know is how far Shelley, seeing and applauding the way that Job morally displaces Jehovah, also saw what cannot help striking every reader of the Book nowadays, namely the fact that God's vaunted power and achievements, insofar as they are physical, have been taken over by man as well. It is certainly much more ominously apparent now than in 1820, but Shelley in his prescience could and did (especially in *Prometheus Unbound*) foresee the time which is now ours: in which in the crassest sense it is man who

knows all the breadth of the earth, who commands the
lightnings and divides the watercourses, who walks the deeps
of the sea and draws out Leviathan with an hook, who has
ready access to the treasures of snow and hail, and has in
reserve, indeed, far more potent weapons against the day of
battle and war; who knows all about the way the light is parted
and the wind scattered, who understands very well the ethology
of the wild goat, who speculates freely and cogently on the
foundation of the earth; who either can or expects soon to bind
the Pleiades and to loose Orion; who sets himself with promising medical and surgical ingenuity to open and close the gates
to death.

To every rhetorical question that the Lord asks Job, canst
thou do this or that, man can now reply, literally and in deadly
earnest, Yes, I *can*, or I shall soon be able to : and the only
difference is the manifest joy that God takes in his wonderful
works. Man's works indeed are precisely *not* wonderful, it is
just because he has replaced wonder by rational understanding
that he can perform them; and though, on the evidence of the
Book of Job, and most other parades of the physical power of
God, anything the Almighty can do man can do better,[24] what
he cannot do is look upon his work and see that it is good.

It scarcely needs saying, perhaps, that such a reading of Job
and assessment of the Lord's claims on a literal physical basis
are quite beside the point in a true evaluation of the poem. To
speak thus is entirely to miss the force of Job's expostulation as
suffering and indomitable self-consciousness, and the intimation
of overwhelming power, that the poet of 600 BC was talking
about and that Blake drew. Quite so : we don't begin to understand, indeed we effectually prevent understanding if we look
at it in such a way. But that is precisely the way that modern
man does look upon and act out the mysteries of his nature.
The Book of Job is a stage in the metaphorical history of which
Frankenstein and *Prometheus Unbound* are also stages; and
they have a stronger affinity with it, possibly—more than many
of all the stages in between—because they deal in the very
situation we have described, when man, taking God's speech
literally, seeks to answer him back by taking all the outward

power and knowledge for himself. And *Frankenstein* most of all
shows one aspect of the result : when man, much more helpless
in the grip of his own creation than was Job before the mighty
works of God, is now beside himself in the literal enactment of
the metaphor : almighty, omniscient (for what man does not
know is not yet knowledge) and vainglorious, but most bitterly
without either the righteousness of Job or the ineffable glory of
God.

TWELVE

THE REDEEMING IMAGINATION

OF THE MENACE as well as the promise of the scientific or machine age no one, except Blake, was more aware than Shelley himself. Its monstrous effects in the enslavement of men to industry, their transformation to machines themselves, and the natural appropriation of the machine's power by the hated powers that be, moved him to eloquent indignation. ("Wherefore, Bees of England, forge,/ Many a weapon, chain and scourge,/ That these stingless drones may spoil/ The forced produce of your toil?" he asked in the *Song to the Men of England* in the near-revolutionary year of 1819.)

The alliance of mechanisation with its own ideology of private gain—the "calculating principle", as Shelley called it, covering at once the calculations of power and output that machines can be subjected to, and the calculation of profit and domination—was seen quite clearly by him as a threat to human life. In the *Defence of Poetry* he not only claimed for the poetic imagination the origin of scientific advance, in the most fundamental sense ("the promoters of utility" following in the footsteps of poets and copying their creative sketches "into the book of common life", as we have seen), but also gave a forcible description of what happens when these "copies" are made, or the work of the imagination is literalised. By "poetic excitements" in the first place both the "grosser sciences" and the "application of analytical reasoning to the aberrations of society" were, he said, brought into being; but now,

We have more moral, political, and historical wisdom than we know how to reduce into practice; we have more scientific and economic knowledge than can be accommodated to the just distribution of the produce which it multiplies . . . We want

the creative faculty to imagine that which we know; we want the
generous impulse to act that which we imagine; we want
the poetry of life; our calculations have outrun our conception;
we have eaten more than we can digest. The cultivation of
those sciences which have enlarged the empire of man over the
external world has for want of the poetical faculty circumscribed those of the internal world; and man, having enslaved
the elements, remains himself a slave.

For want of "those first principles which belong to the imagination" the "extremes of luxury and want" are "exasperated" and
with them political situations are driven to extremity :

The rich have become richer and the poor have become poorer,
and the vessel of state is driven between the Scylla and
Charybdis of anarchy and despotism. Such are the effects which
must ever flow from an unmitigated exercise of the calculating
faculty.

Things have not changed much, we may say, since the times
of "Peterloo".

It is easy enough, and has commonly been taken as response
to these accusations, to treat them as "poetical" exaggerations,
overstatements of a case which may have something in it but
not very much more than may give one an agreeably high-
minded sensation in momentarily entertaining it; as expressions
of amiable but not real feeling, having little to do with "real
life", the voice indeed of the "ineffectual angel". Nowadays we
may be ready to take them, and the whole of the *Defence*, more
seriously. As a succinct description of the present condition of
industrial society, self-poisoned in a state of chronic economic
dyspepsia, and self-locked in a moral tangle which sociological
knowledge appears only to draw tighter, the passages just
quoted could hardly be improved upon. If the diagnosis is
accepted, it may be possible to pay more attention to the
remedy proposed; at least to try and understand what it is.

"We want the creative faculty to imagine that which we
know." What does that mean? In what sense is knowledge
understood here? If, as is assumed in the *Defence* and elsewhere

in Shelley, imagination is primary and knowledge the offspring of it, in what way other than in this originating process can knowledge be imagined? It seems clear enough, for a start, that the knowledge spoken of here is for use, or control, the possessive or rapacious kind we have been speaking of, and which applied science, if not scientific knowledge in itself, especially exemplifies. And the imagination which should both accompany and compensate for it is the great faculty which the Romantics called upon to supply all deficiencies, the remedy for all shortcomings and the centre of their universe. But what they meant by it, and what Shelley in particular meant is not so easily pinned down; as a faculty it can be described in action, but scarcely can be defined.

How closely Shelley followed the critical debate on the powers and nature of the poetic imagination set off by the *Lyrical Ballads* and, more particularly, how much the *Defence of Poetry* owed to Coleridge's much more searching discussion diffused through the *Biographia Literaria*, is impossible to tell. Shelley's admiration for Coleridge is known, and it is said that he eagerly read all his works as soon as they were published, but his intellectual relationship to him, his equal and opposite, whom he never met, can only be guessed at. The well-known description in the *Letter to Maria Gisborne*—"You will see Coleridge—he who sits obscure/ In the exceeding lustre, and the pure,/ Intense irradiation of a mind/ Which, with its own internal lightning blind,/ Flags wearily through darkness and despair"—suggests that he thought of him much as he thought of himself, but under restraint; he uses the same epithets that he applies to himself, but they are modified—"a *cloud-encircled* meteor", "a *hooded* eagle". Almost, one may say, a Prometheus Bound.

It is a fair enough assumption, perhaps, that what Coleridge said about imagination, in Shelley's view the true Promethean fire, he endorsed. Certainly the imagination that must qualify knowledge, or is a superior form of it, is much like Coleridge's "shaping spirit" or "esemplastic power". The claim for "the primary Imagination" in *Biographia Literaria* as "the living power and prime agent of all human perception, and as a repetition in the finite mind of the eternal act of creation in the infinite I AM" may be set beside that in the *Defence*, "A poem is the very image of life expressed in its eternal truth . . . [it] is the creation of actions according to the unchangeable forms of human nature, as existing in the mind of the Creator, which is itself the image of all other minds".

And imagination (or poetry, for both use the terms interchangeably) is, for Coleridge as much as for Shelley, an essential normative or regulative power : again (in *Biographia Literaria*), "The poet, described in ideal perfection, brings the whole soul of man into activity, with the subordination of its faculties to each other according to their relative worth and dignity. He diffuses a tone and spirit of unity that blends and (as it were) *fuses*, each into each, by that synthetic and magical power, to which I would exclusively appropriate the name of Imagination."

In the *Defence*, "Ethical science arranges the elements which poetry has created . . . nor is it for want of admirable doctrines that men hate and despise and censure and deceive and subjugate one another. But poetry acts in a diviner manner. It awakens and enlarges the mind itself by rendering it the receptacle of a thousand unapprehended combinations of thought." And the idea of the inward and outward motions of intelligence put forward by Coleridge, the "centrifugal and centripetal forces" ("The intelligence in the one tends to *objectize* itself, and in the other to *know* itself in the object") not only bears upon much that has already been said about the Shelleyan thought-process, but may be applied particularly, perhaps, to his own formula that poetry "is at once the centre and circumference of knowledge", and therefore "that which comprehends all science and that to which all science must be referred".

That is the crux, and the point where these parallels can no longer be maintained. For in truth, very close though they come to each other, Coleridge is speaking the language of speculative inquiry, Shelley the language of prophecy, and though they say nearly the same things and mean (we may suppose) very much the same by them, the consequences they envisage are different. It is not simply that the "passion for reforming the world", which had long since relaxed its rather light hold upon Coleridge, still had Shelley fiercely in its grip; rather it is something connected with that passion but underlying it and, it may be, prior to it. At Oxford, we find Shelley, according to Hogg, impatient of "polite letters" and indeed of the study of languages generally: these are only "the names of things" and "it is surely far better to investigate things themselves".

This youthful utterance by one endowed with extraordinary mastery of words, the celebrant of language which in a liberated world will be "a perpetual Orphic song,/ Which rules with Daedal harmony a throng/ Of thoughts and forms, which else senseless and shapeless were", has been taken merely as paradoxical, but it is not so contradictory as it seems. What gave the young Shelley a disgust with words and "literary pursuits" was the feeling that they were not real, and that only "things", to be investigated by chemistry and physics, were, though even then he owned himself most strongly interested in metaphysics, as capable of revealing "mind" and not "mere matter". What he was after then was the *real*, which we will not attempt to define further except by saying that it was the same that later he sought to touch in words; by the time of the *Defence* we can see that reality was for him an essence to be grasped, and even perhaps created by the imagination alone.

Reality, of course, is the only thing that really matters—we are forced to use tautology again; and just as words fail here, so we can see that Shelley's early impatience with words and his mastery of and (with one important exception, to which we will return) reliance upon them, and his indignant repudiation of the view that poetry, using words, had nothing to do with real life, were all of a piece. Poetry, or imagination, is not simply a reflective product of life, but an active force within it, changing it and even making it. Coleridge would not have disagreed, it was his perception of the positively creative or "plastic" power of imagination that led him to reject Hartley's theory of association. But the scope of imaginative creation and the urgency of its work, above all the feeling that its private and hidden operations had in the largest sense public and historic functions, were considerations that weighed upon him very differently, or not at all. It is a matter of temperament, rather than any real divergence of ideas (and nothing directly to do with the fact that the Coleridge of *Biographia Literaria* had arrived at a settled conservatism); but it is a long distance from the self-defensive position, "By what I *have* effected, am I to be judged by my fellow-men; what I *could* have done is a question for my own conscience" (in Chapter X of the *Biographia*) to the self-abandonment to the wild west wind of history which shall

> Scatter, as from an unextinguished hearth
> Ashes and sparks, my words among mankind!

That the "trumpet of a prophecy" may speak through a poet's lips to "unawakened earth" reminds us of the other poet, unknown to Shelley and only late in life to Coleridge, who stated the supreme claims of the imagination with even more assurance:

> Poetry Fetter'd Fetters the Human Race. Nations are Destroy'd or Flourish in proportion as Their Poetry, Painting and Music are Destroy'd or Flourish! The Primeval State of Man was Wisdom, Art and Science.

William Blake cannot be allowed more than a marginal place in the present inquiry; but we may go a little further with him, from the uncompromising declaration above, which ends the Prologue to *Jerusalem*, to the visions both of destruction and regeneration in the first chapter of the greatest of his Prophetic Books. The clouded banks of Thames, the mountains of Albion running with blood, the "horrible Shadow of Death among the Furnaces beneath/ The pillar of folding smoke", and the imprisoning Laws of Moral Virtue within which the proclamation is made, "Humanity shall be no more, but war and princedom and victory!"—all these have their close equivalents in Shelley, though not always with the same emotional tone. And in the *Defence of Poetry* we can see Shelley making an effort, though with something desperate about it, to deal with these overwhelming evils, and even with the "starry wheels" of scientific knowledge turning in the void, in the same terms.

The visionary of *Jerusalem* says :

> . . . I rest not from my great task !
> To open the Eternal Worlds, to open the Immortal Eyes
> Of Man inwards into the Worlds of Thought, into Eternity
> Ever expanding in the Bosom of God, the Human Imagination.

Shelley says :

> The functions of the poetical faculty are twofold : by one it creates new materials of knowledge and pleasure [the "circumference" of knowledge, or "centrifugal" movement already noted] : by the other it engenders in the mind a desire to reproduce and arrange them according to a certain rhythm and order which may be called the beautiful and the good. The cultivation of poetry is never more to be desired than at periods when from an excess of the selfish and calculating principle, the accumulation of the materials of external life exceed the quantity of the power of assimilating them to the internal laws of human nature. The body has then become too unwieldy for that which animates it.

It is for Shelley as for Blake the poetic imagination alone which can reanimate the world, or restore meaning to the mass of objects crushing the psyche by their literally dead weight. But first it must restore itself, because it is in itself that the process of mortification has begun, in the expansion of knowledge which has deprived the world of meaning and value :

> The end of social corruption is to destroy all sensibility to pleasure [i.e., to recognition of value in experience] and therefore it is corruption. It begins at the imagination and the intellect as at the core, and distributes itself thence as a paralysing venom, through the affections, into the very appetites, until all becomes a torpid mass in which hardly sense survives.

It is typical that Shelley should speak of "social corruption" as itself a malevolent force (like "the system"), capable of having an "end"; and, perceiving that the imagination is its first victim, he is placed in the usual quandary of those who, seeing man corrupted by society, or mankind by mankind, want to start afresh : for if in truth men's ways and even the source of their thoughts are the product of "the system", how is the system to be altered? When anyone, poet or not, begins to think of social man and the continuous process by which society moulds individuals, who in turn make society, it takes extraordinary daring, indeed what must always seem to society itself folly or madness, to name a point at which the process can be interrupted and a new beginning made. Shelley had daring, or faith enough to proclaim in the imagination, the seed ("The future is contained within the present as the plant within the seed"); it is necessary for all who make such a decisive declaration to forget that the seed is produced by the plant.

In the opening of the *Defence* Shelley is visibly struggling with the Hartleyan theory of association which Coleridge (having once espoused it) firmly repudiated, and which, as he pointed out in the *Biographia Literaria*, makes man no more than the unthinking mirror or echo of his environment. From this Coleridge freed himself by his insight into the autonomous existence and active power of the imagination, the shaper and maker; and Shelley, though by a process less deeply thought out, arrived at or leapt to the same belief in the potency and spontaneity of what he spoke of, to begin with only as the arranger or harmoniser of impressions. Having seized it, he put upon it much more than Coleridge could or would, the actual transformation of the external world.

The "chain" which elsewhere is the chain of flesh, the apparently unbreakable fetters of cause and effect, becomes, by a reversal of imagery, the means of liberation : the poetic imagination, says Shelley, has never been utterly destroyed even in the worst periods of "social corruption", but has survived as a prophecy and promise :

The sacred links of that chain have never been entirely disjoined, which descending through the minds of many men is attached to those great minds, whence as from a magnet the invisible effluence is sent forth, which at once corrects, animates, and sustains the life of all. It is the faculty which contains within itself the seeds at once of its own and of social renovation.

It is the same "chain of linked thought" with which in Act IV of *Prometheus Unbound* Man will control both himself and the elements; and we see with misgiving that it is at its old game of extending domination. For neither in the poem nor in the *Defence of Poetry* is the problem solved of continuity and new birth, the mutual influence of "inner" and "outer"[1] and the question which is to determine which. But a heroic effort is made, and we should look more closely at what it is, and what makes it possible.

The change brought about in *Prometheus Unbound* is an instantaneous one; possibly it symbolises a slow process of emancipation by the inevitability of gradualism, but it is not thought of or presented as such. The Titan is unloosed, the news of it is sounded about the earth and everything is regenerated with Pauline swiftness, as has already been pointed out; it may be intended to represent evolution, but it is conceived as revolution. It is this that gives it authenticity: not, needless to say, as a cryptogram of political revolution—Shelley by this time, though certainly not an enemy of violent insurrection, was very far from advocating it—but as a true picture of an internal, or psychic event. The change within the soul is felt as instantaneous, it might be argued that it must be so felt, since the soul cannot watch the process of its own change, or if it does it won't change; and though it may be unsatisfactory to those who want alteration to be spelled out syllable by syllable, there can be no other truthful way of describing what happens in Act III of *Prometheus Unbound* except as "in a moment, in the twinkling of an eye". In the experience of conversion the event itself is indescribable, but the effects are visible and well testified; the world is transformed.

What leads up to "conversion" (a word Shelley doesn't use, naturally, as being tainted with piety) can however be described and analysed; it may even to some extent be consciously chosen as a course of action. The action Shelley advocates and illustrates is a mental one before it is anything else, it is in fact a

turning back from "outer" to "inner", a recourse to the imagination. The remedy for the corruption of society is there alone,
or, as Shelley uses the word, in poetry, which can both change
outward things and change itself, so that chains of gold, the
symbol of man's self-fettering and enslavement to necessity, can
become an image of shared liberation. What is needed, says
Shelley in the *Defence of Poetry,* is a reference back of undigested knowledge and consequently perverted custom to poetry
itself, "that to which all science must be referred". He even
promised to perform the task in an analytic as well as a poetic
way himself, in the projected second part of the *Defence* in
which he was to deal with the poetry of his own time and show
the significance of its "new birth".

That this second part was never written is certainly to be
regretted, but surely is not surprising : for already Shelley had
demonstrated how difficult it was for him to make any such
returning movement with steadfast and open eyes. In the final
passage of the *Defence* as it stands he spoke of the poets of his
time as performing both of poetry's functions to an extent
beyond themselves: "They measure the circumference and
sound the depths of human nature with a comprehensive and
all-penetrating spirit, and they are themselves perhaps the most
sincerely astonished at its manifestations; for it is less their spirit
than the spirit of the age." The "electric life which burns
within their works" is more, indeed, than the "collected
lightning" of their own time; in the noble and celebrated peroration of the *Defence* poets become prophets, "the hierophants
of an unapprehended inspiration; the mirrors of the gigantic
shadows which futurity casts upon the present". As "the
unacknowledged legislators of the world" they are, moreover,
not see-ers merely but doers; they are mirrors of the future, but
more than passive reflectors of what will come to pass, for by
reflection they bring it into being; the act of imagination is a
deed.

And what the gigantic shadows of the future might be,
though reflected and even born within the imagination of the
present, Shelley still found it difficult to face.

The magnificent and headlong assault upon reason and

emotions of the *Defence of Poetry* does indeed carry all before it. Together with *A Philosophical View of Reform*, the pamphlet (unpublished in Shelley's lifetime) which he wrote a year earlier, and which overlaps it at several points, it represents an attempt to do what it itself prescribes—"to imagine that which we know"—which has not been surpassed in eloquence and persuasiveness in the 150 years of political and social argument since. Indeed a great deal of subsequent thought and expression of all "the Left" (a term which here can be understood as stretching from anarchism to Marxism, and from the *Communist Manifesto* to the pamphlets of the Fabian Society) is to be found here concentrated, as it were, in germinal form : truly the acorn of the oak. The *Defence* does moreover succeed in relating political aspirations to fundamental moral principles; or rather perhaps it sweeps up with it in its impetuous onrush the beautiful and the good, the necessary centre of Shelley's Platonic system. Poetry, Shelley says at an early stage in the argument, contains the "eternal proportions" of beauty within whatever temporal disguise of form and fashion successive ages may impose; it serves the good as it serves, not the transient pleasure produced by "the promoters of utility" but that which is "durable, universal and permanent".

A poet is not concerned with direct moral precepts, since "his own conceptions of right and wrong . . . are usually those of his place and time", while his poetry, being eternal, belongs to neither. Even in a sense it may *contain* both right and wrong, or good and evil, as "it subdues to union, under its light yoke, all irreconcilable things". Here, it may well be thought, is the most profound thing said in the whole essay; and it is here, combining the echo of the Gospel with an adapted Platonism (poetry "lays bare the naked and sleeping beauty which is the spirit of its [the world's] forms") that the enduring core of the *Defence* as a defence, or justification, of art may be found. But Shelley does not rest there; immediately thereafter the anxiety to locate and even to possess the beautiful and good, the source to which all misshapen thought must be referred for healing, betrays him into claims of the most grotesque kind.

Already poets have been given proprietary rights, so to speak, in the beautiful and good: "Poetry is the reward of the best and happiest moments of the best and happiest minds". At this point, it is true, these best moments are thought off as "visitations", the "interpenetration of a diviner nature than our own", and even as being "at war with every base desire". But Shelley is so far from facing the reality of this war in the members (to which indeed he gives no further attention, passing rapidly on to the effects of poetry as able to make "immortal all that is best and most beautiful in the world" and to the all-important passage examined above) that a little later he is saying not only that a poet in the abstract, "as he is the author to others of the highest wisdom, pleasure, virtue, and glory so he *ought* personally to be the happiest, the best, the wisest, and the most illustrious of men", but that poets actually are so: "the greatest poets have been men of the most spotless virtue, of the most consummate prudence, and, if we could look into the interior of their lives, the most fortunate of men."

This preposterous assertion is doubtless to be understood in a Pickwickian sense: that poets are outstanding examples, not of what is commonly reckoned virtue, but of the true virtue to which they have access by their poetic or imaginative faculties. Virtue is itself poetic, and poets are virtuous because they are poets; they are happy in the same way because happiness is itself a quality of poetry. Self-defining and self-defending, Shelley's position can therefore be upheld: a poet participates personally in the good, the beautiful, and the true, is "wisest, happiest, and best", "inasmuch as he is a poet"; and if any are found to be wanting then it can only be because they have "possessed the imaginative faculty in a high yet inferior degree". Shelley thus makes his argument "incontrovertible" but unreal: the perfect poet, he whose life is a complete reflection of the perfection of his art, is an abstraction no less than the poetic ideal itself, and cannot be taken as an actual example of human conduct.

It cannot indeed contribute anything further to the *Defence* than has been urged already; in particular it cannot, and Shelley evidently feels it cannot, defend individuals against the provocative jibes of Peacock. That Shelley took these personally, on his own and others' behalf, presently appears; for though saying that he will not cite living poets as examples and will speak only of the established great, from Homer to Spenser, to whom "posterity has done ample justice", he immediately concludes that it will also justify the poets of his own day, the victims of "contemporary calumnies". "Look to your own motives," he says, "and judge not, lest ye be judged."

Nothing can be said against that. But one cannot help noting a slight shift in implication of the command of Jesus, whereby now those whom others should not judge have already a special position claimed for them; poets have *already* been judged, by Shelley, and found to be virtuous. More importantly one must note the way in which he was drawn, by a justifiable indignation at the accusations of Peacock, into the same confusion of the personal character of poets as men with the ideal nature of poetry. And therefore he was trapped into making a quite insupportable, one may even say a monstrous claim on their behalf; and, most important of all, into losing sight of any real source of the beautiful and the good by which poetry, which does not possess it but can point to it, may strive to redeem the corrupt world.

(It is interesting to see, and should not be forgotten, that when Shelley was not stung by hostile mockery but on the contrary moved by the approval of friends, he reacted very differently: in a letter to the Gisbornes of slightly later date than the composition of the *Defence*, he said in reply to their "high praise" of a poem and himself: "The poet and the man are two different natures; though they exist together, they may be unconscious of each other and incapable of deciding on each other's powers by any reflex act. The decision of the cause, whether or no *I* am a poet, is removed from the present time to the hour when our posterity shall assemble; but the court is a very severe one, and I fear that the verdict will be 'Guilty— death!' "[2] But in the superb counter-attack of the *Defence* such an insight is lost and the most telling, though also the hardest part of what he claimed for the poetic imagination, lost with it.)

Poetry, Shelley says in the *Defence*, is the means by which, in the midst of ever-increasing outward activity and acquisition, "the accumulation of the materials of external life", man may be recalled to himself, to the "internal laws of human nature". It is the call—at once the call and the inducement—to repent. Shelley, of course, specifically includes among his historic examples the sayings of Jesus, "this extraordinary person", whose words "are all instinct with the most vivid poetry"; the whole of the *Defence* is full of imagery and phrase echoing the Gospels. To repent, however, is not a term Shelley uses (except, in the final lines of *Prometheus Unbound*, explicitly to abjure it). As an exhortation in the language of pious orthodoxy, to acknowledge and renounce sin, it must have been repugnant to him; and even as a morally neutral demand, if one may so speak of it—no more than a call to stop and *think again*—it was one which in his centrifugal career he could scarcely hear.

When one is going faster and faster a stop or a sharp turn, i.e., conversion, seems impossible. The metaphor works within the mind (we can see it in dreams), urging to still faster motion just as obstacles, threatening alteration of course or even catastrophic halt, loom up; fear calls for speed and yet more speed to pass or surpass them, to break through and leave them behind. ("I always go on until I am stopped, and I never am stopped.") But in such mental flight other forces than the subject can see may act upon him. There is a powerful, indeed a tragic irony in the way Shelley, his eyes wide open, fled to meet his fate, even saying out loud what he was doing but, like a somnambulist, unable to understand his own words. (Writing to Peacock a year before he was provoked to the *Defence of Poetry*, and using the same image that recurs in it, he mentions in passing "a theory I once imagined, that in everything a man ever wrote, spoke, acted, or imagined, is contained, as it were, an allegorical idea of his own future life, as the acorn contains the oak".[3] The poet shows the man an allegory of himself, but the man cannot see it. Acorns grow willy-nilly into oaks, and have no control over the process.

A letter to John Gisborne dated 18 June, 1822, less than a month before his death, makes several personal revelations, more easy perhaps for Shelley when writing to someone with whom he was not closely intimate (and didn't, in John

Gisborne's case, even much like). Indeed the letters to both the Gisbornes show a detached insight hardly to be equalled elsewhere, as though in his usual intense sympathy with his correspondents Shelley was seeing himself from their point of view. It is in the letter in question that he spoke of his *Epipsychidion* and made the much-quoted admission, "I think one is always in love with something or other; the error, and I confess it is not easy for spirits encased in flesh and blood to avoid it, consists in seeking in a mortal image the likeness of what is perhaps eternal". In the same letter he expresses the deep disquiet about the future, the "precipice" on which he stands, which has already been noted.

But in between these confessions is another, apparently quite lightly made, the implications of which he scarcely seemed to recognise. He described the pleasure he took in the company of the Williamses (Jane Williams having at this time joined other likenesses "of what is perhaps eternal" in his mind, and her husband, his boating comrade, being "the most amiable of companions") and their sailing together in the Ariel: "Williams is captain, and we drive along this delightful bay in the evening wind under the summer moon until earth appears another world. Jane brings her guitar, and if past and future could be obliterated, the present would content me so well that I could say with Faust to the passing moment, 'Remain thou, thou art so beautiful'."

Shelley was deeply impressed by Goethe's *Faust*, of which at this time he had only recently read the whole of Part I; the "Fragment" of his translation (of the opening Prologue in Heaven, and the Walpurgisnacht scene) was produced in the early months of 1822. To John Gisborne again he wrote in the spring of 1822, describing his enthusiasm as he read *Faust* "over and over again", and "always with sensations which no other composition excites. It deepens the gloom and augments the rapidity of ideas, and would therefore seem to me an unfit study for any person who is a prey to the reproaches of memory, and the delusions of an imagination not to be restrained". It is clear that he was referring to himself. Despite such painful stimulation, he read on: "the pleasure of sympathising with emotions known only to few, although they derive their sole charm from despair, and the scorn of the narrow good we can attain in our present state, seems more than to ease the pain which belongs to them. Perhaps all discontent with the *less* (to use a Platonic sophism) supposes the sense of a just claim to the greater, and that we admirers of 'Faust' are on the right road to Paradise."[4] He went on to say that such an idea was "not more absurd, and is certainly less demoniacal" than that (quoting Wordsworth) the earth is the place where "We find our happiness, or not at all" : an interesting reversal of his earlier declaration that earth is the "reality of Heaven".

Such a properly Faustian response to *Faust*, echoing the drive onwards and upwards and the determination never to rest, was only to be expected of Shelley. What he said in the later letter to Gisborne expresses something he was much less ready to admit; yet it is scarcely to be believed that, knowing the play as well as he did, he missed its significance. In Part I of *Faust*, it will be recalled, the contract between Faust and Mephistopheles hinges on precisely the exclamation Shelley quoted in the letter from Lerici; it is when Faust shall say to the passing moment, Stay, that the Devil will have him. It is made, like all bargains or wagers with Mephistopheles, when fulfilment of the conditions seems impossible, and Shelley did not live to see what, in Part II of *Faust*, happens when Faust eventually thus gives himself away. But he can hardly have forgotten what the bargain was; he must have known that, surrendering to the moment, or even thinking that he might do so—for he only admitted to John Gisborne that he *could* utter the fatal formula, he did not actually say it—he was inviting the Devil with fetters, doom, bondage, in a word with mortality.

It was an admission of crucial importance, the more so because it confronts the problem round which so much of Shelley's poetry circles but which it scarcely ever tackles, the mysterious relation between beauty and mortality. The Shelleyan flight was urged on by awareness of mutability and the pathos of beauty's decay, but just for that reason, pursuing permanence and trying to lay hold of it, it rarely touched the moment or could be touched by it. Of the two poetic meditations explicitly concerned with impermanence, the earlier is unable to get closer than the conventional paradox that "Naught may endure but Mutability"; the later speaks of the present as a dream :

> Whilst yet the calm hours creep,
> Dream thou—and from thy sleep
> Then wake to weep.

Compare the burning directness of Blake :

> He who bends to himself a joy
> Does the winged life destroy :
> But he who kisses the joy as it flies
> Lives in eternity's sun rise.

Shelley seems to escape inclusion in that formula, since what he aspired to in imagination, was actually to be the winged life himself; but such elevation and acceleration are not achieved without penalties. The Spirit of Delight, the same as Blake's flying joy, eludes or deserts him, although he identifies himself with it—what difference, he asks, is there between them except that the Spirit actually grasps the mutable and ungraspable : "thou dost possess/ The things I seek, not love them less." Longing to possess them too, he even allows himself the cruel fantasy, though disguised as an act of "pity" for himself, of cutting away the wings of joy, so that it will stay with him.

In this particular poem ("Rarely, rarely, comest Thou", dated 1821) it may be seen, moreover, how the flying joy, concrete and real in Blake though instantaneous, becomes by the very act of trying to possess it, abstract and general :

> I love snow, and all the forms
>   Of the radiant forest;
> I love waves, and winds, and storms,
>   Every thing almost
> Which is Nature's and may be
> Untainted by man's misery.

The marked weakness of "Every thing almost" is, one may say, typical of the worst vice in Shelley's poetry, its vagueness. The word "some", nearly always a sign of failure in imagination, occurs with discouraging frequency in his verse—some many-winding vale, some eyed flower, some artist, some weird arch-image, some bright spirit, some inquiring child, some fierce Maenad, some half-idiot, some slave of power, some tyrant, some mood of wordless thought, examples chosen at random—diffusing imagery and reducing the impact of simile to generalisation. The poet, hurrying on, has no time to particularise : indeed he has not seen his own images with the instantaneous vision which alone makes both inner and outer worlds real.

To say as much is at once to remember exceptions. Immediate, and therefore vivid imagery does occur; in particular, there is one example, to be found in more than one place, which is itself both an instance of direct *seeing* and an image of the way the instant *can* be seen, like a reflection in the flowing river :

> Within the surface of the fleeting river
> The wrinkled image of the city lay,
> Immovably unquiet, and for ever
> It trembles, but it never fades away[5]

This short, unfinished lyric is remarkable in several ways, especially as introducing a whole series of objects or creatures—swallows, bats, toads, dew, wind, cloud, star—which are among the common components of Shelley's symbolic language but which here appear (without losing the echo of their symbolic meaning) not as hieroglyphs but as themselves. But its most important statement is in the verse quoted, which concludes,

> Go to the [the end of the line is missing]
> You, being changed, will find it then as now.

The moment is indeed the moment, ungraspable, but capable of being seen, as the mind reflects, in the continuity of memory. The poems of these last years return frequently to the theme of memory; and memory for Shelley is ordinarily something to be fled. "The curse of this life is, that whatever is once known, can never be unknown",[6] he wrote to Peacock; memory constantly pursues and accumulates by the act of moving through time, and it belongs to the past, it brings it into the present, while the future, the goal of Prometheus, moves on out of reach. Thus Shelley addresses the future in another poem of the same time:

> Where art thou, beloved To-morrow?
> When young and old, and strong and weak
> Rich and poor, through joy and sorrow,
> Thy sweet smiles we ever seek,
> In thy place—ah! well-a-day!
> We find the thing we fled—To-day.

And in "to-day", that is, now, recollection overtakes and seizes the fugitive. The only presentiment of evil that Shelley knew to be "infallible" was (so he said a little before his death, according to Mary) "when he felt peculiarly joyous". Such a foreboding is not only a sop to Cerberus, a notion that joy must bring retribution because one doesn't really deserve it (though Shelley may well have felt that too) but also the direct fruit of joy, since joy *is* mortal, and cannot be entirely felt without acknowledgement of its mortality. In his last months Shelley came back again and again (especially with reference to Jane Williams) to the subject of present and precarious joy and memory in pursuit. In the *Lines Written in the Bay of Lerici*, among his last, he was thinking of Jane, of past and present, and aspirations which had become almost despairingly vague, watching boats "like spirit-winged chariots" gliding "o'er *some* serenest element", to "*some* Elysian star"; and, more definitely, of his own personal memory:

> Her presence had made weak and tame
> All passions, and I lived alone
> In the time which is our own;
> The past and future were forgot,
> As they had been, and would be, not.
> But soon, the guardian angel gone,
> The daemon reassumed his throne
> In my faint heart . . .

The daemon catches up, and no one can escape, not even Prometheus, immortal and sublimely in control of himself on his rock. Prometheus, it is true, "firm, not proud", immovably virtuous, triumphs over evil and all memory of evil; but the memory is actual, and much more real than the blown up—indeed exploded—bogy of the Almighty. As we have noticed, Prometheus, in this crucial scene of the drama, is too absolutely pure of motive even to recall directly the original curse he levelled at God. Being wholly without hatred, he can only summon the "phantasm" of the accursed being himself to repeat the terms of the curse: an instance of self-separation and projection so ingenious and extreme that only Shelley, perhaps, could have devised it. Prometheus utterly disowns his hatred, but memory is disturbed, and from its underworld, which is the same in which "The Magus Zoroaster . . . Met his own image walking in the garden", there are summoned forces which are in fact beyond Prometheus' control: the Furies.

The Furies, who arrive immediately afterwards, are potent and actual. They lust after the satisfaction of torturing their victim with openly sexual appetite, crying "joy, joy", and saying "The beauty of delight makes lovers glad,/ Gazing on one another: so are we"; and Prometheus is already drawn towards them with a like sympathy, the symbiosis of sado-masochism. A few lines earlier he has attempted an isolation of evil which makes it, it is interesting to see, as "incorruptible" as himself or even more so: "Evil minds/ Change good to their own nature", and "He who is evil can receive no good". There is to be no reconciliation or forgiveness: yet despite this he, absolutely good, is attracted to the Furies, emissaries of the absolutely evil. He is both puzzled and fascinated by them:

> What and who are ye? Never yet there came
> Phantasms so foul through monster-teeming Hell
> From the all-miscreative brain of Jove;
> While I behold such execrable shapes,
> Methinks I grow like what I contemplate,
> And laugh and stare in loathsome sympathy.

So close a rapport is established between them that it is the

Furies who tell Prometheus what he is thinking about themselves :

> Thou thinkst we will live through thee, one by one,
> Like animal life, and though we can obscure not
> The soul which burns within, that we will dwell
> Beside it . . .
> That we will be dread thought beneath thy brain,
> And foul desire round thine astonished heart,
> And blood within thy labyrinthine veins
> Crawling like agony.

It is clear that the Furies are within Prometheus, are indeed
a part of him, brought to life out of the past; but they are not
under his command. His reply is only the assertion that he is
yet

> . . . king over myself, and rule
> The torturing and conflicting throngs within,
> As Jove rules you when Hell grows mutinous—

which is itself a remarkable admission on the part of the Titan
that he and his enemy, Jupiter, are actually equals and in some
sense identical. And there is even a hint in the lines that follow,
a dialogue between Prometheus and a single Fury, of the reconciling that a little earlier was declared impossible. The Fury
describes the present state of affairs on earth as a confusion of
good and evil :

> The good want power, but to weep barren tears.
> The powerful goodness want : worse need for them.
> The wise want love; and those who love want wisdom;
> And all best things are thus confused to ill.[7]

—to which Prometheus replies that although such an account
of humanity is torment, the words of torment are welcome, "I
pity those they torture not". At the word pity the Fury vanishes.

As many commentaries have pointed out, the word "pity"
marks a crisis, it is at this point that Prometheus regains control,
purges himself of the last vestige of evil and, indeed, unbinds

himself. But though pity can thus exorcise the forces of evil it is essentially a superior virtue ("Pity would be no more/ If we did not make somebody Poor", said Blake) and is a long way from forgiveness or what is allied to it, the kind of acknowledgment of the Furies that was possible for Aeschylus. They are given no underground home, nor is their guardian status allowed for: after this interview they are heard of no more, and Prometheus, increasingly Apollonian, turns his back on them and points the way only upwards. But they are, of course, dogged. Their function, as they say in the *Eumenides*, is to follow, and they are not easily left behind. In the moment, as we have seen, when, beguiled by beauty, man halts his flight to to-morrow, they are on him. There may be a sanctuary for both fugitive and pursuer (the Areopagus is at once refuge, court of judgment, and fore-ordained home of the Eumenides themselves), but there is no hiding-place; it is rather a place of meeting.

The Promethean spirit aspires (like Phaeton, or the passengers in an artificial satellite) to ride with the sun, which seems to be an actual way of cheating time: if night never overtakes one surely one has got away? But it is a flight of this sort, of course, which is spoken of in the 139th Psalm: he who takes the wings of the morning and goes with sun across the heavens and into the western sea. He is also a fugitive, but knows that he will not escape even so, since he is already possessed by God; he remembers his origins in the unconscious past and, in the reality of the conscious present, "when I awake", finds that his pursuer, to whom darkness and light are both alike, is there before him. The Furies are also divine, daughters of a god, for Shelley the Almighty's emissaries: in conflict with Apollo, with whom the fugitive hopes to outdistance them, they speak in the same terms as the psalmist:

> Though underneath the ground
> He hide my prey, there, too, he shall be found.[8]

THIRTEEN

ROBOTS AND RESURRECTION

THE *Eumenides* OF Aeschylus ends in a general meeting of opposed powers, chthonic and apollonian. It is a court of law, also a council or soviet; the "decision-making body" is a jury, the basic unit of democracy, preceding any formal political democracy and also (at any rate in Godwin's view of an egalitarian future) likely to succeed to it, the collective expression of the mutual respect of persons. Within the court of men, the Athenians assembled to judge between Orestes and the Furies, Clytemnestra and Apollo, the forces of light and darkness are held in balance; the votes are equal, and by the casting vote of Athena, divine wisdom, Orestes, or man, is given a new lease of life. The Furies, though their destructive rage is thwarted, are not themselves destroyed or banished, but given their own sanctuary underground.

No such renewal or resolution is achieved for Prometheus. The classical *Prometheus Unbound* is (we may be tempted to say symbolically, or providentially) lost; the Aeschylean drama remains suspended at an interim stage. The conclusions attempted since have not, as we have seen, resolved or reconciled anything. In the continuations of the myth we have been examining, Prometheus himself disappears from the scene. On the one hand Shelley's Titan, released by Hercules, retires to recuperate his "exhausted spirits" in seclusion, inhabiting with Asia a cave which seems rather an Eden-refuge than a place of meeting and struggle. Mary Shelley's "modern Prometheus", on the other, is dead. Those left behind are Shelley's collective man, casting off the clogs of gravity and heading towards his goal of "the intense inane"; and Mary's Monster, severed finally, it seems, from his origins and raging off alone into "darkness and distance". Though described in such different terms there is not so much difference between them; though Mary's inconclusive conclusion may seem to be more closely related to our actual situation. For in her vision man is already in the background, either perished or, like Walton, a spectator only; it is the Monster to whom the last act of the drama, as yet unwritten, is left. In him the "Promethean work" is to be fulfilled, its consummation awaited with helpless dread: what began with fire is expected to end with fire.

But it has not yet happened. The profundity of Mary's insight, in leaving the Monster alive at the end of her tale, is not simply that the Monster as the external creation of Promethean man continues to exist and to extend his power over human life with the fatal marvels of technology. That is obvious, a continuation and extension of monstrousness in the circumstances of life which has its due reflection in the continuing life of the Frankenstein fable. The much more potent intuition of Mary, as we have seen, was to show the Monster as the projection of Frankenstein's (and Shelley's) own shadow, an internal being or psychic creation given visible shape; and thus we can see further that in leaving her story without an end she was obeying an impulse of profound mercy. For while the Monster has not yet carried out his intended self-immolation, which will be ours as well, not merely are we respited again and again from physical destruction, though drawing nearer all the time, but we still have the chance to meet him as he truly is, a part of ourselves. He has not yet completed his task of destruction; for our part we have not even started ours, of reconciliation, but are given a continually extended stay of execution in which to come to ourselves and begin.

It is not easy. The Monster is lost in a world as desolate and trackless as the Arctic waste; it seems impossible to get in touch with him again. If he leads we can follow, but only towards nothingness and despair. Nor can any meeting be *arranged*.

All arrangements for the Monster, as attempts to manipulate what is itself a metaphor of the breakdown of manipulation, render an actual meeting more difficult. What makes the Monster so terrifying is his unpredictability and independence of human will: he is an instrument disobedient to his maker.

But as an image of scientific creation in general he cannot be brought back under control by scientific means; that is only to multiply monsters or to render the Monster more monstrous. And this effect is typically to be seen in the growth of science fiction, where imagination (or more accurately, fancy) attempts to deal with the present works and future possibilities of science within scientific terms. Some reference has already been made to the limitations of SF in treating what seems pre-eminently to be its subject. If the story of *Frankenstein* is to be taken further, and if fiction, which in this area is notoriously only the forerunner of fact, can help to tame the Monster, surely it will be science fiction? But in truth we see the opposite : when SF tries to tackle the anxieties engendered by the situation, it only makes them worse, since its means are those which produced the anxiety in the first place. If SF is indeed to be reckoned a separate category of imaginative writing, it is because it concerns itself not with man as such but with "scientific man"; and it is the very idea of man in those terms that has become monstrous. SF may try to tackle the monstrosity, but while it remains true to its frame of reference, it is inescapably trapped in seeking to cast Satan out with Satan.

We may now make a brief excursion to look at these efforts somewhat more closely : for a great deal more of SF than the direct progeny of the story in the *Frankenstein* films can be seen as related to it. We may even say that the whole of SF represents an attempt to solve the problem with which Mary's novel leaves us.

For typically, SF can be described as seeking ways of directing the Monster, of imagining new scientific situations and exploring their implications. Multiplying as rapidly as the practical applications science which it both apes and anticipates, its fantasies show an increasing moral concern, but with moral questions—all of which can be expressed as the question of meeting the Monster, of re-establishing relationship between Monster and man—dealt with as an area taken over by science and subject to scientific calculation. Innumerable new inventions and discoveries are offered, of great ingenuity and variety, but, insofar as they are shown as having moral effects, all based on the same assumption, that moral decisions are calculable and their "correctness" or otherwise capable of being scientifically demonstrated and established. Again, the division between fantasy and fact becomes ever harder to see : the idea of "invented futures" has gripped the writers of avowed fiction and those who pour their calculations into "think-tanks" in the same way, and with the same failure to illuminate the choice between one future and another.

Everything is possible; that is just the trouble. It shows itself in the feverish proliferation of SF not so much because fancy has no limits as in direct reflection of what is felt about science itself. The origin of SF as a genre lies precisely in the notion of scientific knowledge and its application as infinitely expanding. But it brings its own penalties in fantasy as in fact, each taking turns to caricature the other. Anxiety fastens upon the problem of "scientific responsibility", and automatically exacerbates itself, since it arises, at bottom, not from perceiving that "wrong choices" have been made, but from the situation of choice itself, infinitely extended. Insofar as it remains fiction, SF merely explores some of the choices not yet made; it doesn't thereby make choice either avoidable or any more clear. Everything, it is assumed, is literally possible; but, literally again, man cannot do everything at once. Selection, or a "choice of priorities" still confronts scientific man, in fiction or in fact; but on what principle is it to be made?

The evolution of machines, as Samuel Butler divined in *Erewhon*, apes that of living forms, filling up every space in the universe of possibility. But it is no longer guided by "natural selection", that is, by obedience to necessity. Man, in the terms in which he is conceived by modern science fiction and the scientific-technological thinking of Butler's day, has conquered necessity : "That old philosophic enemy, matter, the inherently and essentially evil, still hangs about the neck of the poor and strangles him; but to the rich [i.e., to those who have machines at their disposal] matter is immaterial; the elaborate organisation of his extra-corporal system has freed his soul." His soul is free; he has the free choice of doing, through the machine, what he wills.

But what he wills he no longer knows. Everything is possible; but it is not even conceivable to will everything. Baffled by his unlimited power just because it is unlimited, he is reduced again to the state of the infant, all-powerful in wish, who can only say, "I want . . .". He wants now, before all other desires, to be told what he wants, to have choices made for him; since he looks to the machine to supply all wants, choice is, in fiction and in fact, to be a mechanical product. Science fiction, quick to follow the lead, has seized on the possibilities offered by cybernetics to provide instances of futures thus machine-made and machine-chosen; great inventiveness has been used in showing man relieved even of his powers of invention as well as of his responsibility. But these devices do not still the authors' anxieties, they evidently increase them; the typical mode of SF seems to be that kind of obsessional fantasy which at once partially quietens and feeds an underlying fear, and which becomes, in the absence of insight, progressively more acute. The mechanical futures envisaged in these fantasies are nearly always terrible; the very act of imagining them leads logically to the attempt to imagine a world without men.

When machines have taken over choice there are two consequences for man—or rather two aspects of the same consequence. Both have been amply explored in scientific fantasy, from H. G. Wells onwards. One assumes that when the machine takes over control and guidance of affairs, it will, rather because of than despite its infallibility, run counter to the residual wishes of man. Man may no longer have any idea *what* he wants, but he does still *want*, and wants, as an irreducible minimum, to be, to continue to exist; but the mere desire for life without function, quite irrational in itself, is something the machine may very well ignore. There is no *reason* why the machine, which is a reasonable device, should not—having thoroughly subdued man and assumed control over his life—in due course abolish him : a logical extension of the machine's present operations worked out in detail by Butler and repeated by many other writers since. A notable recent example occurs in the satire-fantasy of a Swedish writer, himself a scientist of distinction, who, taking up Butler's suggestion that man might be permitted to survive as servant of the machine, rather as our domestic animals are kept, imagines a debate in which the machines discuss among themselves whether or not it is worth the trouble to keep man, even as a pet; the conclusion being left ominously in doubt.[1]

The other result foreseen in these fantasies is an effect akin to entropy; with choice, responsibility and accompanying risk removed, the world becomes emotionally flattened; even scientific discovery itself, which (when machine-planned) is not any longer a matter of will but an inevitable and predictable process, is robbed of all zest. The intolerable boredom of life in which all action is calculable and has in fact been calculated in advance pervades a good deal of current SF; the attempt is even made to convert boredom itself into a stimulus to action. An increasing number of stories envisage man's enterprises, and especially the characteristic SF enterprise of space exploration, as being inspired not by any positive urge to discovery, but merely by the hope of finding something more interesting than the perfectly and automatically controlled life on earth.

An early and famous example of SF, Wells's *Time Machine*, shows both these effects at once. The Time Traveller exploring futurity—he never thinks of going *back* in time—arrives eventually on a cold earth almost wholly devoid of life, but before that, in the main episode of the tale, visits a time in which the effects of mechanical perfection are found to have produced two separate races of mankind, those of the "Upper-world", childish and reduced to "feeble prettiness", and those below, the Morlocks, servants of the machine and closely identified with it, who have become cannibals and prey on the first. The obvious expression of unconscious fears and wishes is not the present point, nor the rather remarkable allegory, which crops up elsewhere in Wells's fiction, of a sub-human but powerful industrial proletariat, terrorising an effete bourgeoisie.

The point is rather to see the way that Wells, supreme popular exponent in his day of the mechanical powers of "intellect", filling his guesses of the future with elaborate gadgetry, and setting the fashion in this kind of fantasy for innumerable imitators and successors, also foresaw a time when "the human intellect" should have "committed suicide" through mechanical perfection. The energy and inventiveness of Wells at the end of the nineteenth century seem to caricature the flights of the imagination at the beginning of it. But Wells's vulgar optimism, just because it was "vulgar", i.e., expressed in terms of mechanical efficiency and a proliferation of devices to "do" everything for mankind, was visited by doubt. He could see quite well how even the gadgetry in which he revelled might become a surfeit; and as enthusiastic participant in and by profession leader of the March of Mind, was liable to think of the result as *Mind at the End of its Tether*.[2]

In *The Time Machine*, as in many subsequent imitations, the withering of all the driving force of human life precedes the cooling of the sun and the run-down of the universe. For us physical entropy remains a theoretical threat scarcely credible and too far distant to be a real cause of anxiety. But its psychic equivalent is vividly imagined : and, once more, fact appears to reflect and even to overtake fiction. The sense that the world is a rubbish dump from which man cannot escape except by leaving it altogether does not have to be projected into the future. It takes the present form of anxieties about "pollution", which seem to be amply justified by physical fact; but even while observing these outward effects of civilisation, from the sterilised land to the oil-fouled sea, one may suspect that the primary pollution, the reason why the earth looks like an ashpit, or cesspool, or waste land, is within. To a child in whom the boredom of control and predictability has not destroyed all appetite for discovery, even a rubbish-tip may be intensely interesting.

The machine is expected therefore either to carry out a direct physical extermination of man, or more subtly to destroy him by leaving him with what appears only the most rudimentary reason for living, to exist in order to exist. Each complex of fears and obsessions is closely allied to the other, and indeed both commonly intermingle and even change places. The fantasy-reaction to both is usually the same, to destroy the machine before, one way or another, it destroys us.

Thus the Erewhonians have their civil wars which result in

the abolition of all complex machinery, examples only being preserved in museums along with other extinct forms of life. In E. M. Forster's short story *The Machine Stops* a world of men characteristically deprived of all motive except an obsessional search for "ideas" to overcome boredom is saved by the apparently spontaneous breakdown of the Machine itself; there is an interesting hidden suggestion here, indicative of the way external and internal objects are confused and the machine is interchangeable with the mechanised psyche, that the Machine stops because it too is bored, has no purpose left and no point in existing. The degenerate Wellsian men and women (Forster wrote the story, it will be remembered, as a riposte to Wells's predictions) perish with the Machine, but are vouchsafed a saving glimpse, from the wreckage of their subterranean civilisation, of "scraps of untainted sky"; and there are others, though unsuspected, leading primitive Eden lives on the surface, who, we are left to assume, will continue human life in a more promising direction.

Samuel Butler's "Book of the Machines" in *Erewhon* makes play with the notion (which is, like much else in the book, only half-satirical) of evolution as a process continued by machinery in which, even possibly after the abolition of man, the different species of machines will go on developing, differentiating, and struggling among themselves. In Forster's story the Machine has become singular, one all-pervasive, all-providing, and (very nearly, and assumed by all civiilsed men to be so) all-powerful entity, in fact a mechanical caricature of God; it looks forward to the Party-machine which in Orwell's 1984 is also a parody of God.

But what may be called the classic mode of imagining man's subordination to or replacement by the mechanism is the robot, the imitation man, man-made, intended to be the servant of men, which is the exact equivalent in modern terms of Prometheus's creation. Mechanical men abounded in romantic literature and were well known, of course, in actual fact : the clockwork dancing-partner of Hoffmann's horror-story had plenty of exemplars in the practical ingenuity of toy-makers and illusionists, who had been making "working models" of men and women since ancient times. The essentials of the robot, as a model, of human manufacture, which will mimic human action at human command, were already given. But these machine-men were still toys, even if toys which were liable to get out of hand.

The idea of factory-made men who would themselves work in factories, performing all the tasks of what has long been called mechanical labour, acquired its typical form, as well as the name now universally attached to it, only in the early nineteen-twenties, in the work of Capek. The word robot, derived in Karel Capek's play *R.U.R.* from the Czech *robota,* servitude—and occurring in Slav languages generally to signify work at its most laborious—has passed into international usage; its range of meaning extends from the traffic lights which in the North of England are called "robots" to an endless multiplication of robot-creatures in science fiction. One SF writer in particular, Isaac Asimov, has attempted to reduce robot-fantasies to order by propounding a code of "laws of robotics" which shall govern the design and manufacture of all robots and consequently their functioning.

The first of these laws, it is interesting to see, tries to pre-empt the whole problem of conflict between creature and creator by laying it down that "no robot shall be capable of doing anything to harm man". Even as a starting point of fantasy, such a formula well illustrates the inadequacy of SF to deal with the moral problems it raises : what is "harmful" or beneficial to man is here presupposed to be calculable by a machine, or not at all; and to imagine a robot thus rendered innocuous is to miss the whole point at the outset of what it represents. Indeed it would not be worth discussing if it weren't again visibly the case that fact here echoes fiction. Mechanical systems sufficiently elaborate and autonomous to be called robot-like have already been made with any number of such "fail-safe" devices built into them. But it should not be necessary to point out that the most elaborate system of such safeguards merely underlines the fact that men are trying to resign moral choice to a machine.

Capek's play makes no such assumptions; as a morality, indeed, it deals precisely, not simply with the unexpected but the incalculable. It is thus untypical of science fiction in general and perhaps should not be considered as such; in many ways it is the true heir of *Frankenstein,* the only work in which Mary Shelley's imaginative creation is continued with something like similar freedom. That it represents a conscious intention to take the story further seems doubtful, but doesn't matter; the living metaphor establishes its own connections. The resemblance is rather that in Capek's work it is at least partially restored to life. The problem, we have said, is to meet the Monster and renew the dialogue broken off at the end of the novel. The attempts of SF to *engineer* a meeting are necessarily self-defeating; but in *R.U.R.* there is, we may suppose, a real attempt to discover some other way of coming to terms with him.

The starting point of the play, antedating the action and explained in the "comedy prologue", is almost exactly a sequel to *Frankenstein,* taking up the dying hero's last words to Walton, "yet another may succeed". Old Rossum, who doesn't appear in the play (having been "found dead in the laboratory" long before the action begins) follows directly in Frankenstein's footsteps, and is in every way his intellectual successor, a scientist driven by thirst for knowledge and the specific desire to be "a sort of scientific substitute for God", to "supply proof that Providence was no longer necessary". His name is derived from the Slav *rozum,* reason.[3] He retires to a "distant island" to conduct experiments, in the course of which, like Franken-stein, he discovers "the principle of life", a "second process by which life can be developed". He is imagined "sitting over a test-tube and thinking how the whole tree of life would grow from it, how all animals would proceed from it, beginning with some sort of beetle and ending with man himself".

He is able consequently to construct a man, not a mechanical imitation, but a living, though artificial being. Like Franken-stein again he has no thought of practical purpose beyond demonstrating the power of the intellect, but his nephew, Young Rossum, takes possession of his discovery as technology appro-priates the work of pure science, and turns the manufacture of men—or rather, not men, but simplified man-like creatures, modified for use—to a large-scale industry.

It is at this point, with the factory in full production and robots being supplied to all parts of the world, that the play begins. The cosmopolitan milieu of the firm, Rossum's Universal Robots (the name is given in English in the original), is clearly intended to convey the international character of applied and capitalised technology—pre-eminently the technological empire of international monopoly capitalism, but not confined to that: science-based industrialism as such is the target. That the factory is located on the same "remote island" where Old Rossum, like Wells's Dr Moreau, conducted his experiments, not only makes the internationalism of the firm more plausible, but refers at a deeper level to the alienation at the back of the whole process. The tendency for Prometheus Plasticator to go to work in isolation has already been noted.

The robots turned out in Young Rossum's factory and rapidly distributed to every country as a universal force are therefore at once the proletarian masses created and exploited by industrial capitalism, and its mechanical products, the machines themselves; above all, their condition, deprived of all emotion, incapable of pleasure, with no reason for existence except the purpose of work, "rational employment", is that of industrialised mankind as a whole. This general enslavement is, of course, thought of as liberation: it is the dream and pretext of Domain, the managing director ("Dominion") that the robots, taking on all labour, will free mankind—

> Everything will be done by living machines . . . There'll be no employment, but everybody will be free from worry, and liberated from the degradation of labour. Everybody will live only to perfect himself . . . the servitude of man to man and the enslavement of man to matter will cease. The Robots will wash the feet of the beggar and prepare a bed for him in his own house. Nobody will get bread at the price of life and hatred.

The visionary ring is familiar; we are back, even to the echoes of Scripture, in Act IV of *Prometheus Unbound*. Yet it is clear that the "perfection" of man has not been realised, or if it has, in an intolerable sense: the Robots are superior to men in that they are simpler, more efficiently designed for specific work-purposes, and unhampered by emotion; and men are coming to resemble robots. The point is made explicit in the play when the heroine, Helena, comes from outside to the robot works and mistakes robots for people and the board of directors for robots. The same interchange of moral charactertistics that we have noticed between Frankenstein and the Monster can be seen between Domain and the robot leader, Radius; who, rebelling against servitude, takes on the arrogance of Dominion and says, "I don't want any master. I know everything for myself".

Elsewhere we are given to understand that men have ceased to breed : no children are being born, artificial reproduction has replaced procreation, and men have thus lost the one significant difference between the Robots (who, lacking the formula, cannot yet turn out replacements) and themselves. The Robots are a reflection of mankind, men are reflections of the Robots : it can be seen either way, or both ways at once. Needless to say by the persons of the play it is not seen at all, for they are already in the position in which the metaphor becomes opaque. Truly, as the old engineer, Alquist, says later, "nothing is more strange to man than his own image".

Into this situation a disturbing factor arrives in Helena, whose name, like those of all the characters in the play, has a part in the symbolic scheme. She is the stirrer up of strife, a representative of sexuality not as reproductive force but as a source of unease and disequilibrium. She is herself not over-rational, rather is she foolishly rash; at the same time she has a reality— the reality, one may say, of the present, as distinct from the dreams of the future elaborated by Domain—more than most of the others. She is repelled by the "coldness" of the robots and at the same time pities them; she induces one of the directors of the robot-factory to increase the component of "nervous irritability" in their make-up, and also endeavours herself, like a well-intentioned bourgeois "bringer of culture" to the masses, to introduce them to the pleasures of the arts.

The result is disastrous, though whether the disaster would not have happened anyway is open to doubt. The robots revolt in a co-ordinated rising all over the world, with the slogans and ideological trappings of international proletarian revolution. The only emotion they have learnt is hatred of their creators and exploiters, and they set to work to abolish mankind. Work remains their sole object, and the only man spared in the general massacre is Alquist, the engineer and builder, because he "works with his hands". Helena dies with the rest, but not before, in her terror of the robots, she has destroyed the formula which would enable them to manufacture and replace themselves. Thus the machine-made men and the mechanised humans are apparently doomed to equal extinction : the situation is the same as that at the end of *Frankenstein,* when Victor Frankenstein is lying dead and the Monster departs with the declared intention of ending himself.

From this state of despair Capek endeavours to find a way out in the third act of the play, which is indeed a genuine development of the metaphor. The robots now rule the world and men and women have all perished, except for the aged Alquist, reserved by the robots in the hope that he will be able to rediscover the secret of their manufacture. He does his best, but fails; as he says, he is no scientist but merely an engineer, without either the knowledge and skill or the *hubris* of a Rossum. Urged by the robot leader, he even agrees to dissect living robots in order to discover "the principle of life", but unlike Frankenstein, who did not scruple to use vivisection in the course of his monster-making, he cannot bring himself to do it. He is a man who lives in charity with all his fellow-beings, and is moved in his relations with the robots chiefly by pity, the pity neither Frankenstein nor the Rossums could feel. His charity enables him to see (or, one may say, itself helps to engender) a new emotion in the robots themselves : his two attendants, male and female robots, have fallen in love, and the play ends with the hopeful prospect that the pair, having regained humanity even out of their artificial substance, will go forth as a new Adam and Eve to repeople the earth.

Through Capek's robots, therefore, there is a resurrection; and the idea of resurrection in and through scientific discovery, or "the machine" itself, emerges in more than one place as alternative to the downright reaction of a Butler or a Forster. E. M. Forster's dream of salvation was simply primitivism, a regression to Eden *before* the Fall, when humanity, having "learnt its lesson", would no longer be tempted by the fruit of knowledge. Butler's Erewhonian anti-mechanist is consciously obscurantist: in "The Book of the Machines" he foresees the possible replacement of men by machines as "higher beings", but utterly rejects it:

"I shrink with as much horror from believing that my race can ever be superseded or surpassed, as I should do from believing that even at the remotest period my ancestors were other than human beings. Could I believe that ten hundred thousand years ago a single one of my ancestors was another kind of being from myself, I should lose all self-respect, and take no further pleasure or interest in life."

With the customary ambiguity of Butler's satire this opinion (which, in prevailing, is said to have been responsible for the precautionary policy of destroying the machines) is not only an attack on a mechanised culture but explicitly a denial of evolution: the Erewhonian sage refuses to believe in the descent of man from other beings or the possibility that such modification or transformation will occur in the future. He is arguing, and Butler satirically shows him arguing, for a completely static view of man, to be imposed if necessary by force. Elsewhere in "The Book of the Machine" however—and arising no doubt from the extreme ambivalence of Butler's own views—evolution by mechanical means is welcomed: man is a "machinate mammal", mechanical inventions of all kinds are "the mode of development by which the human organism is now especially advancing", and, as we have noted, it is by mechanical means that the human soul may be freed from "that old philosophic enemy, matter". Such a conquest of matter implies also a conquest of death; though here the speaker—illustrating again Butler's inextricably mixed feelings—has doubts about the result:

He feared that the removal of the present pressure [i.e. of "matter"] might cause a degeneracy of the human race, and indeed that the whole body might become purely rudimentary, the man himself being nothing but soul and mechanism, an intelligent but passionless principle of mechanical action.

The hints embodied in this sentence have been extensively taken up in later fantasies, approving or rejecting the prospect according to taste or temperament. A recent dramatic satire, *Who'll Do It Next Time?*, by the Scottish playwright Jack Ronder, is an interesting example of the two directions—both implied in *Erewhon,* and both by now translated into actual practice—in which this projection may lead. In this play the perpetual postponement, if not absolute abolition, of death is shown, on the one hand, through the triumph of "spare-part" surgery by which one character attains the age of Methuselah and more, ending up as no more than a brain attached to a box of tricks. On the other, the same failure of natural reproduction imagined by Capek is seen to overtake mankind and the rest of organic creation, and life is only saved by the machines themselves. The computers, supposed by this time to be capable of superhuman calculation and invention, rediscover "the principle of life" and thus, though man is dying, make him, or something better, anew.

Both these notions—the perpetuation of existing life, and the creation of new forms—are present embryonically in Frankenstein's initial dream that "if I could bestow animation on lifeless matter, I might in process of time . . . renew life where death had apparently devoted the body to corruption". The phrase itself echoes the Scriptural promise, no doubt unconsciously; and the hint is powerfully followed, again one may assume without conscious intent, in the frontispiece to the 1831 edition of the novel, showing the first stirring into life of the Monster.[4] The engraving is distinctly ecclesiastical in feeling, showing the workshop of Frankenstein rather as Gothic chapel than scientific laboratory, though with chemical retorts and electrical apparatus, together with a cabbalistic pentagram, in place of an altar. It is dim and tomb-like, filled indeed with the bones and skulls of a charnel-house; something like a complete human skeleton lies on the floor, and on top of it, almost as though rising from it, the Monster is coming to life.

In the first pictorial representation he is far from the blank-faced zombie with electrodes in his neck familiar from the movies : he is a large, muscular, naked man, perfect except for hands and feet, which still appear slightly "unfinished"; otherwise he is more like the then current notion of the classical ideal, or possibly of the noble savage, than anything specially monstrous. He gazes on himself with amazement; Frankenstein, visible at the door, looks on with much the same expression. The whole scene suggests a wakening from the dead: the naked figure, the discarded cloth, the shaft of light striking down through darkness, are all elements familiar from the Resurrections of Christian iconography.[5]

The picture may be taken as parody, just as the story itself, and some of its successors more grossly, parody the Gospel. That they do so for the most part quite unintentionally only reinforces the effect: the idea of resurrection has its own inextinguishable life, which cannot be wholly suppressed by rationalism but finds for itself increasingly grotesque disguises. The most impenetrable of these—impenetrable, that is, by those who use it—is the attempt to make resurrection literal, tangible, and controllable: the word, that is to say, made not flesh but mechanism. For eternal life such a shift to literalism offers the possibility of a human being surviving indefinitely with new bits and pieces, or of being deep-frozen to survive geological ages; for the metaphor of rebirth out of death it offers the manufacture of an automaton.

To their metaphorical or mythological originals such prospects—quite seriously canvassed—are in the same relation, to sum up the whole process, as is "faith in science" to faith as defined by Paul. Indeed to speak of "faith in science", though popular, has always been self-contradictory, since such faith rests precisely on the evidence of things *seen*. And it is curious to observe how, when men thus repose faith in something that does not demand it, but is properly to be served with scepticism, the faith turns to fear. Science made into an idol betrays those who "have faith" in it like a capricious and, worse, an actively malevolent deity; for whom in turn metaphors must be found in the revengeful robots and computers of science fiction.

To this faith which is no faith, and which brings with it the growing fear of destruction, Capek in *R.U.R.* opposed the real faith of the engineer Alquist: real in the sense that he persists in it without reason but on the evidence of things not seen, having their roots in his humility and love. He loves and pities the robots condemned, like man, to die; his love allows love to grow in them, and so the miracle is accomplished and the resurrection takes place. That it is miraculous, that is, spontaneous, is quite clear : love is not planned or provided for by the robot-makers, nor any emotion whatever; even the "irritability" of the robots is only added to the blue-print at the instigation of Helena. She wishes, quite irrationally, that they should be more like human beings, and the result is her own death together with the rest of mankind. But from her impulse and through the female robot who bears her name—for the "robotess" in whom love is reborn is also called Helena—the possibility of life is recovered.

And yet, moving and illuminating though the third act of *R.U.R.* is, it is scarcely satisfying. Various critical reasons have been adduced for that, including the just but unhelpful observation that the work as a whole "lacks eloquence". Capek, who himself disliked the play, may have meant the same when he said it was one "anyone might have written" : not only or chiefly that "anyone" might see the warnings contained in *R.U.R.*, except that everyone is blind, but rather that it lacks the force of inward personal conviction which is the foundation of true "eloquence". Love, says Capek, is the only answer and the only hope, and he is right. But something so easy to say cannot be so easy to believe or, if it be true, so easy to act, or our problems would be non-existent. Such simple formulas seem indeed to mock us; we suspect that they are only another way of pointing to what is impossible.

And in truth we must ask whether it is possible to love a robot, or seriously to imagine that robots might come to love one another. Technology, with its instruments and products, may be the object of wonder and a source of vast satisfaction, most typically the satisfaction of pride : men—those at least who haven't become fearful of the results, and even they in some degree—are intensely proud of what technique has enabled them to do. But technique, which is from its beginnings a means of dominion and control, precludes the love which rejoices, without controlling it, in the being of another, which *allows another to be*.

A person or a thing brought under control is to the same extent—it may be no more than partial—excluded from love. The machine, though it may mediate an active benevolence, does so in a way which necessarily widens the area of control and diminishes that of freedom in the object of love. Such an effect is often not apparent in individual cases, and may be hidden by the fact, which is the motive of benevolent or loving intervention in the lives of others, that some degree of control may produce a greater degree of freedom. But the machine, whatever it may be—political, social, or literally mechanical— that is employed to this end, has an apparently logical mechanical tendency to extend control further and further : the less left to chance the more efficient the machine, the more efficient the machine the better an instrument of goodwill. It becomes more and more difficult therefore to *let be* the object of benevolence, and at the same time the means, which is the machine, progressively attracts to itself the regard due to the end.

But this regard is not love. The affection that men commonly feel for their devices, their often passionate attachment to a particular unit of machinery, is not the love which allows life to another, but a form of self-love, of pleasure in one's own ingenuity and the extension of one's powers, "the cleverness of me". Such at any rate was the view of Butler's Erewhonian who urged the retention and development of machines as enormously elaborate artificial limbs : the love that a rich man might have for all the machinery at his disposal was simply the love of himself. Nor—though Butler's example was of course a capitalist—is the principle affected if we suppose the machine to be socialised, at the disposal of a group of men or of mankind as a whole : the change is then only from an individual to a collective narcissism, and this is likely to be intensified as personal attachment to the machine is less, for it can masquerade as benevolence. It is in such a state of mind that men will willingly immolate themselves to mechanism of their own devising, and the machine becomes a juggernaut.

Again, a machine can certainly be beautiful, and a detached aesthetic appreciation of it may be uncontaminated by personal possession. But the beauty of machines lies wholly in function, in the efficiency and economy, or elegance, of their working; which working, again, is an extension of control. The machine, whose only reason for existence is in its function, is in itself "dead matter", in a way which a natural object, organic or inorganic, is not; and it is not possible to love a dead thing.

It is true that machines, once obsolete, may acquire the status of natural objects and thus also become the objects of a real non-controlling love. Ancient mechanisms, no longer useful, can evidently inspire an animistic love which is quite genuine, if rather ridiculous; and the growth of what may be called the antiquarian affections in a wealthy industrial society is an obvious consequence of what that society itself does to the world. For "natural objects"—things neither directly the instruments nor objects of human control—become scarce; and the human affections, which yearn towards a loving attachment to the surrounding world, endeavour to find such objects even among the things which, when they were newly in use, were an expression of precisely the opposite aim. By the besotted antiquarian in us an old engine of war or an instrument of torture may be loved "for itself". But the engineer who makes new instruments for the conquest of his fellows and of the universe knows better. He may feel an inordinate pride in his engines, he may actually worship them; but it is himself, his own power, that he is adoring.

And the robot, as robot, is an engine : that is the whole point of it. Whether conceived as a mechanical imitation of man or as actual man reduced to pure mechanism, it is wholly under domination, which makes love impossible. Robots get out of control, as we know, in fantasy and in the fact it reflects, but that does not make them loving or possible to be loved : for the robot on the rampage is not an independent being but an idea, the idea of dominion on its own, in concrete form and separated now completely from its origins. It is pure will, expressed in cogs and wheels; and will, though it can serve love, cannot command it or show the way to it.

FOURTEEN

THE DEEP TRUTH : CONCLUSION

MEN HAVE MADE a world which they believe they can
manipulate at will, but which they are unable to love. Love, as
we are often enough told, is the answer to our problems; but
love is also the problem. I cannot love what I manipulate and
either control or seek to control. I can imagine a robot, which
is a mechanical symbol of myself; if I can imagine it, sooner or
later I shall make it. But I do so in order to control it, or to
make myself controllable, and the more control I achieve, and
the more fail-safe devices I build into it, as insurance against
myself, the more alien and terrifying it appears. It becomes, not
an extension of my power but a substitute for myself. As I extend my power and the whole external world is absorbed into
my robot-self, so it is estranged from me and becomes, through
control, uncontrollable.

Frankenstein's Monster, though man-made and the product
of scientific knowledge, is not, or *not yet* a robot; it is just the
intermediate stage of Mary Shelley's vision in the evolution of
the myth that makes it so potent. The Monster is Frankenstein's
"other self", his denied and repudiated part; no less as such is
he a living being who can love and be loved; the strongest moral
implication of the story is that he should be loved. From the
moment of his awakening this rough beast who has slouched
toward Bethlehem to be born is looking for love and is ready to
return it. As Mary repeatedly points out, and as Shelley himself
could see and say, it is because the Monster is not loved, but
rejected by Frankenstein and everyone else, that he becomes
wicked. Love, he feels, is his due as it is the due of every living
creature; the denial of it is an "injustice" which from beginning
to end he passionately resents, and which drives him frantic.

But love, however much owed, is not for that reason

311

forthcoming; no more than belief (as Shelley was fond of pointing out) is it subject to force. "Love", he said, "withers under
constraint; its very essence is liberty".[1] Though it has its own
laws of growth and development, these appear to be of a kind
only to be expressed by begging the question : "Love is inevitably consequent upon the perception of loveliness". And hate, by
the same token, follows upon perception of hatefulness : therefore
(so in his comments Shelley tortuously admitted) "It was impossible that he [the Monster] should not have received among men
that treatment which led to the consequences of his being a
social nature. He was an abortion and an anomaly". The Monster, it is repeated over and over again, is unlovely in the extreme, he is "hideous", "loathsome", "deformed", all the
adjectives of ugliness are heaped upon him. Frankenstein cannot help himself; he may feel for a moment the compassion
that the Monster asks, but pity for what one loathes because it
is so loathsome is a flimsy and unstable emotion. One look at
"the filthy mass that walked and talked" is enough to change
his feelings back to "horror and disgust". He ought to love the
Monster; but how can he when the Monster is so unlovable?

Thus *Frankenstein* states the question, but gives no answer.
Love is pointed to in the novel by negatives, as something that
is absent; and that is the only way, perhaps, that it can be
spoken of to-day. Shouldn't we therefore look where it is positively spoken of, and especially in Shelley? "The great secret of
morals is love" : the world knows that, and it is in incalculable
degree owing to Shelley, whose formulation it is, that it does
so. In the *Defence of Poetry,* the *Philosophical View of Reform,* and most of all in *Prometheus Unbound* the message of
love as the source of all good and as saving power is urgent and
apparently unequivocal. Love in *Prometheus Unbound* is the
universal law, and more than law, since it transcends cause and
effect and transforms force, ruling by other means; it animates
dull matter, it will renew life in the dead.

The poem, more than any other of its time or since (except
Blake's *Prophetic Books,* which go to work another way) makes
an heroic effort not only to lift the world and propel it hope-
fully into the future, but to redeem the past and restore what

has been lost. If it fails, what can succeed? It is foolish, rather, to think of success or failure, such as might be looked for in a system of ethics or political philosophy: as the *Defence* says, "poetry acts in another and diviner manner. It awakens and enlarges the mind itself by rendering it the receptacle of a thousand unapprehended combinations of thought. . . . The great instrument of moral good is the imagination, and poetry administers to the effect by acting upon the cause". After the awakening of *Prometheus Unbound* the world cannot be the same, however obdurately it seems that the voice is unheard.

Furthermore, we can see, jumping the century and a half between Shelley's age and our own, and looking for signs of the times, that it *is* heard, and newly. Even more strikingly, it is being repeated as though it were indeed new, by those who have scarcely heard of him. It is a remarkable thing, and hard not to find hopeful, to see and hear so many young men and women to-day not only reading and quoting Shelley but, even when they don't, talking like Shelley, evidently thinking like Shelley, in many curious ways looking like Shelley. With natural ease and apparently without prompting they share his beliefs and jump to his conclusions and if indeed they do read *Queen Mab* and *Prometheus Unbound* they may well think themselves the true audience he was addressing, the posterity he looked to. A modern populariser of the Shelleyan Idea asserts: "He would have loved the hippies: their philosophy of sharing, their willingness to let a man do his own thing, their communes, their style of dress, by which they mark rejection of the world of the stockbroker",[2] and we must agree: they seem to be doing only what he imagined.

Several years before the *Defence of Poetry* and *Prometheus Unbound* Shelley produced a complete description of a hippy community in his fragmentary prose romance *The Assassins,* begun in 1814, when Mary and he were on their first flight to the Continent, and never finished. There we read of a "community of good and happy men" who combined the name of the Assassins, or hashish-eaters, followers of the Old Man of the Mountains, with the mode of life and common possessions of primitive Christianity and the opinions of Gnosticism: "They esteemed the human understanding to be the paramount rule of human conduct; they maintained that the obscurest religious truth required for its complete elucidation no more than the strenuous application of the energies of the mind". Especially they "could not be persuaded to acknowledge that there was apparent in the divine code any prescribed rule whereby, for its own sake, one action rather than another, as fulfilling the will of their great Master, should be preferred". These rational situationists become in consequence "peculiarly obnoxious to the hostility of the rich and powerful", and, "attached from principle to peace, despising and hating the customs of the degenerate mass of mankind", they retire to a distant, lost valley where they live in perfect seclusion, sharing goods and labour according to the demands only of "love, friendship, and philanthropy".

In their retreat they live in a state of "epidemic transport":

Thus securely excluded from an abhorred world, all thought of its judgment was cancelled by the rapidity of their fervid imaginations. . . . A new and sacred fire was kindled in their hearts and sparkled in their eyes. Every gesture, every feature, the minutest action was modelled to beneficence and beauty by the holy inspiration that had descended on their searching spirits . . . They were already disembodied spirits; they were already the inhabitants of paradise. To live, to breathe, to move was itself a sensation of immeasurable transport. Every new contemplation of the condition of his nature brought to the happy enthusiast an added measure of delight and impelled to every organ where mind is united with external things a keener and more exquisite perception of all that they contain of lovely and divine. To love, suddenly became an insatiable famine of his nature, which the wide circle of the universe, comprehending beings of such inexhaustible variety and stupendous magnitude of excellence, appeared too narrow and confined to satiate.

To such an ecstatic vision the hashish-eaters of to-day lay claim, and in much the same terms, with no more than superficial changes of expression. If there is a difference it is rather the difference of exaggeration, of multiplication and caricature;

which applies to every part of the picture. For if the spread of Shelleyan ideas and acts, in unconscious discipleship, is a sign of the times, it is manifestly not the only one that seems to repeat the situation of the eighteen-twenties; any more than everything to be said about Shelley can be embraced by the usual image of Ariel.

What has been said hitherto is an attempt to show that Ariel, the Shelleyan Idea, is not alone, but draws its shadow after it as it flies. So to-day, in conditions as critical, as "revolutionary" as prevailed in the first quarter of the nineteenth century—but exacerbated and magnified to grotesque and gargantuan pro- portions—the presence of Shelley, also multiplied and sub- divided, as it were, among the most hopeful and amiable groups of people, is matched by as gross a growth of everything mon- strous. The modern Shelleys are as much aware of the external features of the Monster—the monster of industrialism, of op- pressive institutions, of mechanised violence—as was Shelley, or Frankenstein. Their answer is the same as Shelley's, it is love. It is the right and only answer, as we know : why is it not effec- tive? Why with every repetition does its content seem to be more diluted?

Against the monsters of the time there is nothing more to be said, apparently, than Make Love, Not War, and were it heard the world might indeed be transformed. But it is not heard, the words return to the speakers, and perhaps they are bound to, being addressed rather to themselves than to actual others. They are messengers, as angels are; but an angel who speaks only to angels is certainly ineffectual. Can we say that Shelley, whose words have gone round the earth, deserves the jibe? Can it justly be cast at his heirs who now repeat his words or find out their equivalents for themselves? Is it not because those who should hear are wilfully deaf? Or is it because the message is not in truth spoken to them at all? The dialogue of angels, seraphically telling each other that they are angelic, is beautiful to hear, but not informative. And it is very clear that though these angels speak angelically to one another, what they say to others is quite different; or it is the mutual love-message of lovely and transported spirits turned inside out.

315

Once again, images and attitudes repeat themselves. We have already seen how quickly in Shelley's poetry scenes of loveliness and love can change into their opposites, the garden of flowers into a wilderness of poisonous weeds and decay. There is a similar transformation in *The Assassins*. In their paradisal valley-commune they are content, enjoying a different mode of being altogether from that of mankind in general, "the corrupt and slavish multitude", between whom and "the happy nation of the Assassins there was no analogy nor comparison". But they are not indifferent to the sad state of the multitude they have rejected, or perhaps they are unable to prevent thoughts of it pressing upon them; and if once more mixed among the wretched majority would be bound to respond with violence. Against the mode of life of the many "an Assassin, accidentally the inhabitant of a civilised community, would wage unremitting hostility from principle".

Immediately the scene is changed; or rather everything in it, though in form the same, looks entirely different. The Assassin, who has declared the universal scope of his love and the divine nature of his experience, puts his enemy in another category altogether, not human at all but an abstract evil disguised as man; therefore outside the considerations of philanthropy and unfit to live :

> Who hesitates to destroy a venomous serpent that has crept near his sleeping friend . . .? And if the poisoner has assumed a human shape, if the bane be distinguished only from the viper's venom by the excess and extent of its devastation will the saviour and avenger here retract and pause behind the superstition of the indefeasible divinity of man?

The question is answered in a mounting outburst of hatred; the enemy, who is whatever the Assassins reject, is to be wiped out without compunction :

> The perverse, and vile, and vicious—what were they? Shapes of some unholy vision, moulded by the spirit of Evil, which the sword of the merciful destroyer should sweep from this beautiful world. Dreamy nothings; phantasms of misery and mischief, that hold their death-like states on glittering thrones and in the

loathsome dens of poverty. No Assassin would submissively temporise with vice, and in cold charity become a pander to falsehood and desolation. His path through the wilderness of civilised society would be marked with the blood of the oppressor and ruiner . . .

Everything now is turned upside down, the saviour is the destroyer, charity itself has become "cold", not in its absence but in its practice. In his crescendo of hysteria the Assassin is drawn, as Prometheus is drawn in contemplation of the Furies, progressively to abandon himself to fantasies of evil, destruction and corruption :

How many liars and parasites, in solemn guise, would his saviour arm drag from their luxurious couches and plunge in cold charnel, that the green and many-legged monsters of the slimy grave might eat off at their leisure the lineaments of rooted malignity and detested cunning. The respectable man— the smooth, smiling, polished villain whom all the city honours; whose very trade is murder; who buys his daily bread with the blood and tears of men—would feed the ravens with his limbs. The Assassin would cater nobly for the eyeless worms of earth and the carrion fowls of heaven.

There is no need, perhaps, to enumerate resemblances between what is expressed here and what can be found among the fantasies, and sometimes the acts, of bearers of the Shelleyan Idea to-day. With more dismay than surprise we recognise the picture : not accidentally, we may think, does the modern Shelleyan already quoted choose so very incongruous a figure of speech to describe the inheritance of Shelley's advocacy of non-violence—"he gave birth to the idea of non-violent political action which has *ticked away ever since and exploded in our own time*"[3] (my italics). An explosion of non-violence is so very strange a notion that, however much we may desire and would welcome it, we can hardly feel it is real.

What has happened to the all-persuasive and omnipresent power of love? In *Prometheus Unbound* the claims made for it are even larger and the voice of the angel is certainly more sure; when threatened by an overflow of the hate embodied in the Furies the power of love is rescued by pity, extended even to evil and indifference, just as Frankenstein momentarily pities the Monster. Yet beautiful and winsome though it is, there and elsewhere—and most in that poem, where most is said—Shelley's continual evocation of love and loveliness lacks substance; marvellously extolling and reaching out for the reality of love but grasping air. Or, if that seems too harsh, we may say it is too airy for anyone to grasp but another angel.

Let us complete the definition and prescription from the *Defence of Poetry,* with its striking but partial insight into the springs of human conduct :

> The great secret of morals is love, or a going out of our own nature and an identification of ourselves with the beautiful which exists in thought, action, or persons, not our own.

At once we are brought up short; for love, we will say, is not thus adequately defined. Love, we want to protest, is exact and particular, not diffuse, itself an abstraction but always manifest in concreteness or (if we dare say it) in the flesh; and though "common as light", a universal inheritance "like the wide heaven, the all-sustaining air", it is costly. Its costliness is its essence, and also its proof. If we love them that love us—by "an identification of ourselves with the beautiful", or by loving loveliness—what reward have we? Do not even the publicans so? For it costs them nothing. It is only the other kind of love, not an identification with likeness but a recognition of difference, which is, as the saying goes, its own reward, and therefore truly and certainly rewarded. To speak of such a reward is both ironical and literally true. For such love, which is given to an opposite and rejoices in it, is tested to the full : it must be its own reward, for nothing else will reward it. Yet it alone, the regard for another as another, is the love which, like labour, creates value; and therefore its reward is real. But also, being the reward of a free act, it is incalculable, not to be known or even guessed at or hoped for in advance, in no way to be anticipated.

How, then? How is it possible genuinely to love our opposites and enemies, for their sake and not our own? How is Frankenstein to love the Monster, or Ariel Caliban? Love is owed to them : Mary Shelley's own life-long fear of loneliness and rejection allowed her to see and state with great force where it is owed. For, since love is the inheritance of every living creature under the sun, the shadow of its deprivation is felt as black injustice; but how is light to be cast into the shade? Once again, love is due to the unlovely; from which impasse there appears to be no way out. What can be said of the command, that we be impartial in love even as the light of heaven is impartial, except that it is preposterous? But also that, though unreasonable, it has occurred.

Reason, or at any rate the faculty which detects and depends upon verbal distinctions, is no longer any help. But the processes of which formal reason and verbalisation are a part are larger than these parts and therefore, though ungraspable, still effective when reason comes to a full stop, and still capable of changing the situation. No one can say who or what is the Great Boyg, where it sits on the path blocking the traveller's way; much worse than Apollyon, it is simply and horribly negative, and there seems to be no getting away from it, "forward or back, the way's as narrow". But, rescued from his terrifying encounter with it, Peer Gynt learns and moves on. And though the Boyg, a troll, says nothing but "Go round about", there is more to be gained than that compromising advice from such an encounter; or rather from more profound encounters of which it seems to be the reflection. There is a similarly shapeless, invisible, and invincible being to be met in *Prometheus Unbound,* which has something to say when the position seems hopeless, and the contradictions between omnipotence and defiance, irresistible force and immovable resolution, the double bind that holds Prometheus in adamantine bonds, looks absolute and insoluble.

At this point in the poem Asia and Panthea, still free to search though Prometheus is bound—sharing between them the affective powers, the qualities of his soul—descend from the Shelleyan mountain-top, where they are dizzied by cloud and mist, "to the deep". The movement, "down, down", away from the usual airy heights, is "through the shade of sleep" and below it, into darkness and unknowing : through the void, drawn by a force like gravity, to "the remotest throne". Demogorgon, the being dwelling in these nethermost depths, has a potency far beyond that of the Boyg, sitting shapelessly on its mountain-top; but no more than the Boyg can it, or he or she—in truth, and necessarily, Demogorgon is impersonal—be defined by the light of reason. Its shape is only expressible in paradox. "I see a mighty darkness," says Panthea, some thing emitting "rays of gloom", reminding us of the flames of Hell in *Paradise Lost,* which give "No light, but rather darkness visible"; Demogorgon's dwelling place is not Hell, but Hell may be one of the aspects of it. The invisible being, unveiled, is still not visible, it is "Ungazed upon and shapeless; neither limb,/ Nor form, nor outline; yet we feel it is/ A living spirit".

Demogorgon, though indefinable, is accessible as the reposi-tory of knowledge not to be gained by reason; especially know-ledge of the apparently irreconcilable. The answer is there of "all things thou dar'st demand", it is only needful to have the courage first to make the descent and then to ask. Asia's first question is about creation, asking in effect who or what is God? —and Demogorgon's replies do indeed attempt to embrace the reasonably insoluble contradictions presented by definitions of absolute goodness and absolute power with which Shelley, as others, wrestled so long. God, Demogorgon says, made "the liv-ing world"; not, it should be noted, the objective universe of "dead matter", but the world which, having a soul, can be loved. God is also, therefore, the author of joy in the world, the joy which for Shelley belonged to feelings connected with spring and young love, "the voice/ Of one beloved heard in youth alone", but which really means all joy of the moment, kissed as it flies.

But Asia then asks,

> . . . who made terror, madness, crime, remorse,
> Which from the links of the great chain of things,
> To every thought within the mind of man
> Sway and drag heavily, and each one reels
> Under the load towards the pit of death—

who, that is, is the origin of evil and necessity, death, hell, and sin? Demogorgon answers ambiguously, "He reigns"; and Asia's further attempts to get a definition or formula are answered only by repetition. Not even the hinder parts of God are to be seen. When she persists, running through a history and hierarchy of deities and immortals and still wanting to know which is original and supreme, whether Jove himself is "a slave", Demogorgon tells her, not that there is no answer, but that it cannot be spoken: "a voice/ Is wanting, the deep truth is imageless."

Love is eternal, alone not subject to "Fate, Time, Occasion, Chance and Change", the attributes of mutability and the forms of necessity; in love the infinite distance between the necessary and the good is overcome. But the nature of this love cannot be seen or put into words; even the paradoxes used to describe the indescribable, "a deep and dazzling darkness", are now silent. Nevertheless Asia recognises the truth of what, without words, she is told; here and indeed throughout the interview, Demogorgon is telling her not new truths but those in her own heart. The answers to her questions are given, and she acknowledges it, "As my own soul would answer": the "deep truth" underlying them is real to the soul but literally ineffable.

The reply of Demogorgon is, though undramatic, the crux of the whole poem, the centre round which the whole whirling and otherwise centrifugal apparatus turns. It is more important than anything that happens on the mountain-top; and it is incidentally a sufficient witness in itself upon a point much argued about, the development of Shelley's "atheism": which clearly by this stage is an inappropriate term. "Faith", meaning formal orthodoxies, he continued to denounce. But that "the deep truth is imageless" is an assertion that can only be made in faith, indeed it is a paraphrase of the definition in Hebrews XI. It is the antithesis of the "faith in science" which demands that everything true must be held so only on the evidence of things seen. The deep and imageless truth convinces in another way, not by reference to anything else (i.e., to "facts") but by itself, it is "its own evidence" or as Asia says, "of such truths/ Each to itself must be the oracle". There is here a confession (as it may well be called) of vital significance in Shelley's thinking about the "mind of man" and in his whole idealist outlook; not inconsistent with his Platonism, in fact essential to it, but with implications for the Promethean scheme, the limitless explosion of art and science, that were not, perhaps, fully recognised.

For if the deep truth is imageless it is not only a permanent corrective to the idolatry of science, but also the limit set to every kind of artistic expression. The last act of art is to stand at this limit and define what is beyond in the only way possible, as that which cannot be expressed. In such a way it may bear witness to the deep truth—though it is always possible to avoid the position altogether and say in effect that what can't be expressed isn't worth expressing, does not in fact exist. ("Whereof we canot speak, thereof we must be silent" can be taken in two ways, in awe or indifference.) Shelley, just because he placed so high a value on the poetic imagination, the image-creating powers, was never really in danger of the second attitude. Although he seldom remained long enough on the edge of the abyss to contemplate it steadily, he was far from a positivist denial of it. Nor, as a dealer in images, did he shrug off concern with what is beyond imagery. On the contrary, his compulsion to flight, to visit the "recesses" of his own mind only as a rapid bird of passage, shows him continually circling about the place of "the deep truth".

And if in the main he ventured there only to flee again, the charge that he never stayed long enough in these regions to learn anything cannot be sustained after the descent to the cave of Demogorgon. What the poet's soul, as Asia, encounters and learns there lends strong authority to the *Defence of Poetry* and the extraordinary claims made in it for the potentialities of art. For the poetic imagination is limited (as mere fancy is not) just because it bears a relation to a reality beyond it but of which it, and it alone, can speak. "There is no portal of expression from the caverns of the spirit . . . into the universe of things"; but there is a point where creative power is transmitted. In such a sense the deep truth, though imageless, is the source of the images themselves, to be expressed in the "vitally metaphorical" language of poetry.

In this language certain perennial questions—the questions
Asia puts to Demogorgon—are not, therefore, answered, but
they are themselves revealed. They are revealed as metaphors,
marking "the before unapprehended relations of things" and
their oppositions and contradictions. For Shelley the metaphors
of poetry are the makers and users of language, it is through
language that they are communicated and in them are to be
found the origins of language and its modification. But a metaphor as an expression of "integral thought" (a term, again,
borrowed from the *Defence*) has a life pre-existing language as
a dream pre-exists the words in which it may later be recalled
and described. Language, the "perpetual Orphic song" of
Act IV of *Prometheus Unbound,* rules the "thoughts and forms
which else senseless and shapeless were", but does not originally
make them or absolutely govern their growth. It discloses the
questions already inherent in them.

But language and the other materials of art are not the only
means by which a metaphor can take shape : here we return to
the main theme. It can, as has been suggested, be translated
into action or, being in origin an expression of the unapprehended relation of things, be itself turned into a thing. Only
then the thought embodied in it cannot be communicated; language, now trying to deal with the metaphor-turned-thing, can
only describe the object itself. To see what an automaton or a
"space-probing" rocket may mean, to understand the questions
it asks, is almost beyond us, and grows more and more difficult
as time goes on and these solidified metaphors multiply. It is
difficult even to see them as questions : on the contrary, they
look like answers. Thus they become idols : that is, things which
seem to provide the answers that the soul seeks, but give false
ones.

The creations of art are not so deceptive. They can never
satisfy us, and (being mere imitations) don't pretend to : they
remind us that we are unsatisfied. Thus art is like play, which,
being make-believe, is also prevented from offering false satis-
factions as true ones; or rather, again, we may say that in play
the metaphors of act, not being "real", are not obscuring, but
capable of revealing through themselves the questions behind

them. Both art and science have their origins in the play of childhood, where the question How, which technology can answer, is asked together with the unanswerable question Why; which the scientist learns to eschew, but the artist will continue to ask. It is there, where the opaque metaphors of techniques and the translucent metaphors of art are side by side and still merge with each other, that the process starts; it is a long way back, but something may be learnt there even now of where it is tending.

Look back for a moment to Shelley's youthful game-playing, of which Hogg has given us a vivid description; especially of his fondness for playing with or on water, the most living of materials. Shelley was always drawn to water "whenever he found a pool, or even a small puddle, he would loiter near it, and it was no easy task to get him to quit it". He would throw stones and break the calm and enigmatic surface, pointing to the circling ripples as demonstration of sound-waves; he would play ducks and drakes; most of all, he liked to make paper boats and sail them, keeping at it to the point of obsession. On one occasion, says Hogg, he refused to leave off, though the weather was freezing, "busily constructing more, with blue and swollen hands", till Hogg, a man whose questionings were more easily satisfied and who liked comfort, reproached him : " 'Shelley, there is no use talking to you : you are the Demiurge of Plato.' "

Plato's Demiurge is certainly related to Demogorgon, one may have grown out of the other; both are primordial powers, sources of original creation. The child, or child-like youth by the edge of the water, making his ripple-rings and sailing his toy boats on the boundless sea of possibility, is a demiurge in his freedom; in his irresponsibility, which is part of the gaiety of childhood.

And when we come to think of it we can see how like he is to the mythological fathers of the arts and sciences, at any rate when they were young. They also were playful, filled with the same delightful and delighting spirit of irresponsibility. Prometheus, when his story begins, is not the grave suffering being of Aeschylus, chained and loaded with the cares of the world, but a cunning thief who steals the fire of heaven for sport; Loki, his brother, is a trickster; the Devil himself, before he comes to take his wickedness too seriously, is chiefly a maker of mischief. Ariel, that tricksy spirit, is no better and no worse. He is, it is true, answerable to authority, but uncertainly, for authority is never sure of his obedience, and in any case leaves the actual work of creation—the improvisation of a storm, a feast, a whole world out of nothing—entirely to him. Ariel is not wicked, but neither is he virtuous; what he does works for good, but that is, in a manner of speaking, no more than accident. It is because he exists within a comedy, a play with a happy issue, and a comedy is so only by faith.[4]

Ariel's chief task, in his relations with ordinary mortals, is to lead them by the nose; to perform marvels and produce bewilderment. Thus he brings them back to themselves, ducked in the horsepond and stinking or confronted, in the midst of murderous designs and illusory dreams, with the accusing shape of a harpy. And here too, we can say, Ariel is performing the functions of both science and art : or rather, as in play, he embraces science within the forms of art. The question How?—how comes it all about, how is the tempest raised and stilled, how is the island filled with noises, how do banquets appear and disappear out of and into thin air—presents itself as Why?—the much more powerful and fundamental question that small children ask, and that their parents cannot answer. In Ariel's acts the How of technique, the nature of the quaint device, is swallowed up in Why, a question of emotion, or what moves : if the three men of sin, Alonso, Sebastian, Antonio, expect an answer they must look within themselves. They have nowhere else to look, for they, "whom Destiny,/ That hath to instrument this lower world/ And what is in't, the never-surfeited sea,/ Hath caused to belch up", are isolated from everything else. They are alone, traitors to one another, their murderous weapons useless in their hands :

> . . . the elements,
> Of whom your swords are temper'd, may as well
> Wound the loud winds, or with bemock'd at stabs

Kill the still-closing waters, as diminish
One dowle that's in my plume—

the instruments of natural science cannot reach or touch the
hidden Why of nature, either within or without.

Nature, in fact, against which their swords have seemed to
be so potent, returns to mock them. Now we are near the end of
the play; but first let us take a turn about to look at the way we
have come. "Yet another may succeed", said Frankenstein,
dying : on the shores of possibility his scientific heirs continue
to pick up their grains of Newtonian "truth" and to play ducks
and drakes with whole worlds. As they play they transform; the
curiosity from which they start turns with technique into control, conferring extraordinary and increasing external powers
and simultaneous loss of contact with internal sources, "the
actions and passions of our internal being". But although the
separation of external act and internal motive, the How and the
Why, becomes always wider, and man, acting on the explo-
sively expanding circumference of the technically feasible and
understood, removes himself every moment from the meaning of
what he acts, the process contains its own tendency to restoration, even if the restoration be catastrophic.

Just because there seem to be no limits to expansion, technology continually overreaches itself, for the world on which it
seeks to project internal imagery is larger and stranger than any
technique can contain. There is always room for further action,
and there is always certainty that the action will fall short of
perfection. The aim of technique is to subdue to human will
everything external to it, to bring about by force what in poetry
is the pathetic fallacy, so that Nature in literal fact shall sympathise with man. But the fallacy, literally, remains a fallacy;
Nature is too much to grasp, enlarging even as technology
advances. The sterility of perfection is always out of reach.[5]

And scientific inquiry itself, going before technique and de-
animating as it goes—so that the scientist progressively removes
from the universe all but his own intellect—also contains a contrary principle in its impartial curiosity, which brings more of
the universe into being as object of inquiry than inquiry can

encompass. A scientist such as Whitehead found it possible to reject "subjectivism", or solipsism in scientific knowledge because he recognised an "instinct for action" in science which is itself "an instrument of self-transcendence".[6] Scientific inquiry and technical resource, aiding and abetting each other, seek to re-make and rule the world in the image and the name of human reason. But even as their activity enlarges the area on which the image may be imposed, so its limits move further on. The work of science, said Whitehead, is "actively directed to determinate ends in the known world; and yet it is activity transcending itself and it is activity within the known world. It follows, therefore, that the world, as known, transcends the subject which is cognisant of it".

To this process there would appear to be no end. Every widening of possibility invites further trial with what evidently has the force of moral obligation. If a thing can be known, it must be; if, what for science is the same thing, it can be done (for knowing is doing), again it must be. The principle which the Athenians invoked in their dialogue with the citizens of . Melos, that in the relations of men with men power will always be exercised to the limit, may be modified by convention; but transposed to men's relations with things, including men considered as things, it appears to be absolutely limitless, and imperative. The Pelagian assurance within a bounded universe, that what was right was also possible, is now parodied by the belief, acted upon if not explicit, that what is possible is right : no longer, If ought; can; but If can, ought. Nothing will interpose itself on the journey to the intense inane; the catastrophes on the way will only be counted as setbacks and obstacles to be overcome—unless one should happen to be complete, in which case nothingness will be achieved. And the risk of such a catastrophe, though foreseen, will hold back nothing.

Nevertheless, the boundlessness into which we move, which always defeats the desire to put Nature within bounds of analytical knowledge, and which always draws us on, does itself have something to say which, though increasingly deaf, we may never be quite unable to hear. It laughs at us; it mocks at the weapons in our hands; it may even suggest that there is no difference between the most advanced state of knowledge and application and that of a child sailing toy boats upon a duck-pond. It is the consequences of childish acts that bring their nature home. "Strange", said Mary Shelley after Shelley's death, "that no fear of danger crossed our minds! Living on the seashore, the ocean became a plaything; as a child may sport with a lighted stick, till a spark inflames a forest and spreads destruction over all, so did we fearlessly and blindly tamper with danger and made a game of the terror of the ocean".[7] With the same figure of speech Walton rebukes the remorseful Monster at the end of the story: "You throw a torch into a pile of buildings, and when they are consumed you sit among the ruins and lament their fall."

But in truth there is no point, though his claims to foresight are most cruelly mocked by the results of his act, in reproaching fire-stealing Prometheus for moral irresponsibility. The irresponsibility of science is inherent, there is nothing to be said about it, before or after the event. The peril arises rather when science puts on a moral disguise and proposes for itself a moral goal, no less indeed than perfection. *How* is now given the moral force of *Why,* and every fresh answer to the first is believed to be an answer to the second, so that its real meaning is forgotten. The winged man soars towards the idea of perfection; the danger is not that the wax will melt and he'll fall, but that, techniques having improved since Icarus's day and dream having changed into actuality, he won't, but will be able to continue on and up into endless space and moral nothingness. Then the game which began in an innocent spirit of mischief, a child stealing fire to play with, becomes monstrous, a chase in which fear replaces curiosity and cannot stop, though what lies before is more terrible than what's behind. The winged spirits have all been brought together, put in armour, and given a common object: faith—in nothing; hope—of nothing; love—for nothing, for there is nothing left that seems worthy to be loved. The known universe itself, re-animated back to front, turns into a monster of evil, waiting to revenge itself for its violation.

But when in the derision of catastrophe these dreadful playthings, tin men and robots, are found to be only toys, the moral life imprisoned in them may be released. It may then flow back again to myth and the creatures of myth, the inhabitants of the inner world which has for long lain desolate, may once more walk abroad. The Monster, restored to flesh and blood, will return to look his creator in the eye : and what then?

How can we imagine such a meeting, or its effects? What possibility is there of reconciliation? The point at which Shelley broke off *The Assassins* was where, by the verge of a lake, two divine children, a boy and girl, were playing with a "favourite snake", to which they spoke and sang, and which the girl fondled in her bosom. It is, we may say, a beginning; but can we go back to it? The snake, when grown, can still with courage and the correct formula be turned into a man, as Tam Lin was restored. When Beauty pities the Beast and embraces him, he turns at once into the handsome Prince. That is the solution to the question, how to love the unlovable; but it hardly seems possible for us. Even if we take it as the behaviourist prescription that it seems to be—an assurance that if you go through the motions you'll feel the effects—it asks more strength than, we suspect, is now available. Frankenstein, who had so little himself, has left us less. It is just because he threw it away or excised it ("something, God knows, wants to be cut out of us all", said Shelley)[8] that the Monster has such terrible strength. And the Monster for his part cannot take the initiative; even the Beast in the fairy-tale couldn't make the step which would change him, for as a beast he wanted to remain beastly still.

If the Monster returns now, and if we can bear to look at him, he will not touch us or speak—we are long past that. All he can do is to show his ingenious maker the end of his ingenuity, his present helplessness. The Monster, allowed to be a living creature, brings back with him from darkness and distance some of the Arctic desolation into which he vanished. He exhibits in himself a void as dark and complete as any that his outward flight was directed towards. But now, if he returns, it may be recognised as a void within and below, to be reached "down, down", and not even by effort, rather by cessation of effort; drawn only by longing to "the deepest abyss" :

Resist not the weakness,
Such strength is in meekness
That the Eternal, the Immortal,
Must unloose through Life's portal
The snake-like Doom coiled underneath his throne
By that alone.

The snake promises a new birth; but what it will be can in no way be foreseen.

At the end of the play Prospero, releasing Ariel, leaving Caliban, abandons the cloak, staff and book of his power, steps back and down. He will return to Milan, no longer in control of events, nor pressing on to the edge of things. That is left to Ferdinand and Miranda, young and hopeful, in whose mutual delight there is a real promise of making love, not war : a chance that the brave new world of actual experience is not in itself a wasteland but may be entered upon in the spirit of discovery and joy. Prospero is finished with all that, not denying it, but detaching himself. He is indeed finished with the whole game of metaphor, and his farewell reminds us that metaphorical crea-tion, whether in the language of poetry or (for we now see the cloud-capp'd towers, the gorgeous palaces, solidly standing around) in crass concrete fact, is limited. Without these spells, no longer artist creator, he has none but his own strength, "which is most faint". He is reduced to nothing, and prayer— the pure cry of longing, the unadulterated and unanswered question, Why?—is his only resource.

Prayer, its discourse couched in metaphors, is not in essence metaphorical as art is. It is, as perhaps no other kind of speech can be, direct. The need of Prospero to make his meaning plain, to himself and to us, by the help of Caliban and Ariel, is over. As a man he is speaking, with every third thought his grave, where interpretation is unnecessary because he is fully known. But also, of course, he is still speaking to his audience and thus necessarily in metaphors—his actors, and the fantastic imagery of the great globe itself, through which he addresses his prayers for understanding to us. But they will all dissolve into thin air in the end.

The Monster could only pray to Frankenstein, who rejected him; but in the last situation, when metaphor vanishes, it is not possible to reject him, for he is no longer separate, he is quite simply ourselves. When by his agency, which is ours, we are bereft of everything, we will forgive him for being us as he will forgive us for trying to deny it; by which, merged with each other, we may ask to be forgiven.

NOTES

Chapter One

INTRODUCTORY : METAPHOR AND MYTH

1. The editions listed in the British Museum Catalogue are as follows: 1818, 1823, 1831 (revised) reprinted 1839 and 1849; 1856 ("Parlour Library"), 1886 (Routledge's "World Library"), 1888 (Routledge's "Pocket Library"), 1912 ("Everyman"), 1932 ("Readers' Library"), 1969 ("Oxford English Novelists"). American editions listed in the Catalogue are 1845, 1882, 1910, 1932, 1934 (twice), 1949.
2. *The Letters of Mary Shelley*, ed. F. L. Jones : to Leigh Hunt, 9 September, 1823.
3. *Edinburgh Magazine*, March 1818.
4. *Blackwood's Edinburgh Magazine*, March 1818.
5. *Gentlemen's Magazine*, April 1818.
6. *Quarterly Review*, January 1818.
7. *Quarterly Review*, March 1818.
8. R. Glynn Grylls, *Mary Shelley: A Biography*, London 1938.
9. *Blackwood's Edinburgh Magazine*, March 1823.
10. P. B. Shelley, *A Treatise on Morals* (1812–15?).

Chapter Two

BIRTH OF THE STORY

1. Autobiography of Sir Henry Taylor (1885), quoting a letter from his mother to his father. Quoted by R. Glynn Grylls, op. cit.
2. Quoted by R. Glynn Grylls, op. cit.
3. Mary Shelley, Introduction to *Frankenstein* in edition of 1831, reproduced in Oxford Novels edition, ed. M. K. Joseph, London, 1969. All subsequent references to and quotations from *Frankenstein* use this text.
4. Mary Shelley, letter to an unknown addressee, 17 May, 1816.

5. Mary Shelley, letter to an unknown addressee, 1 June, 1816.
6. Mary Shelley, *Journal*, 18 August, 1816. Mary noted, "talk with Shelley and write . . . I read a novel in the evening. Shelley goes up to Diodati, and Monk Lewis." An entry follows in Shelley's hand, adding that he "sees Apollo's Sexton [Lewis] who tells us many secrets of his trade. We talk of ghosts; neither Lord Byron nor Monk G. Lewis seem to believe in them; and they both agree, in the very face of reason, that none could believe in ghosts without also believing in God. I do not think that all the persons who profess to discredit these visitations really discredit them, or if they do in the daylight, are not admonished by the approach of loneliness and midnight to think more respectably of the world of shadows." Shelley then went on to summarise the stories told by Lewis, "all grim". He made the same comment in a letter to Thomas Love Peacock of the same date.
7. The Diary of John William Polidori, ed. W. M. Rossetti, London 1911.
8. Polidori's *Diary*, entry for 15 June, 1816.
9. One of the most remarkable instances of such "re-animation" of a corpse was the "resurrection" of a condemned and executed criminal, Matthew Clydesdale, at Glasgow University in 1818, some months after the publication of *Frankenstein*. It is an interesting speculation whether those concerned, the Professor of Anatomy, Jeffrey and the chemist Andrew Ure, who operated the "galvanic battery", knew of the novel. In this case, having apparently revived the corpse, Professor Jeffrey "killed" it again by cutting the jugular vein. The experiment was performed in public, and caused considerable furore at the time.
10. Shelley, letter to T. L. Peacock, 22–28 July, 1816.
11. "O happy Earth! reality of Heaven!" : *Queen Mab*.

Chapter Three
"THE MODERN PROMETHEUS"

1. Tertullian, *Apologeticus* XVIII; quoted by Olga Raggio in "The Myth of Prometheus, its Survival and Metamorphoses up to the Eighteenth Century" : *Journal of the Warburg and Courtauld Institutes*, 1958.
2. It is remarkable that in the creation story in Genesis I the

decrees of the Lord calling the earth, heavens, and sea into being, with their appropriate living creatures, are pronounced in the singular, but when it comes to the creation of man the mode and person change from "Let there be" to "Let *us* make man in our own image". This adoption of the plural, which is present in the Hebrew, suggests that more than one agent was involved, or more than one aspect of the One God.

3. Marsilio Ficino, *Quaestiones Quinque de Mente*, quoted by Olga Raggio, op. cit.

4. Mary Shelley, letter to Leigh Hunt, 8 April, 1825.

5. Shelley, letter to Charles and James Ollier, 15 October, 1819. He argued the same point at length in his Preface to *Prometheus Unbound*.

6. It is curious that Shelley's first discoverable reference to Prometheus, in *A Vindication of Natural Diet* (1812) treats him not as teacher and champion of mankind, but as seducer. Following the partisan of vegetarianism John Newton, he there interpreted the legend of Prometheus as it appears in Hesiod as allegorising the use of fire for "culinary purposes— thus inventing an expedient for screening from his disgust the horrors of the shambles", and "From this moment his vitals were consumed by the vulture of disease". By 1816, however, other and more heroic aspects of Prometheus had doubtless become more important for him.

7. Byron, letters to John Murray, 15 February, 1817 and 9 March, 1817. From vol. IV of Byron's *Works* (Letters and Journals), ed. R. E. Paterson, London, 1900.

8. Mary Shelley, *Journal*, 2 August, 1816.

9. Shelley, *Essay on the Devil and Devils*, 1819.

10. Shelley, "review" of *Frankenstein*; written presumably at the time of the novel's publication; not printed until after Shelley's death.

Chapter Four

GODWIN AND GODWINISM

1. William Godwin, letter to Mrs Cotton, 24 October, 1797; quoted by C. Kegan Paul in *William Godwin: His Friends and Contemporaries*, London 1876.

2. William Godwin, letter to William Baxter, 8 June, 1812; quoted by R. Glynn Grylls, op. cit.

3. William Godwin, quoted by C. Kegan Paul, op. cit.
4. William Godwin, *Enquiry Concerning Political Justice,* appendix to Book VIII, Chap. VIII, "of co-operation, cohabitation, and marriage". From facsimile of the third edition (1798), ed. F. E. L. Priestley, Toronto 1946. All subsequent quotations from *Political Justice* are from this text.
5. Mary Shelley, letter to Maria Gisborne, 30 October, 1834.
6. William Godwin, letter to Mary, 27 October, 1818 : quoted by R. Glynn Grylls, op. cit.
7. Mary Shelley, *Journal,* 8 March, 1831.
8. *Political Justice.*
9. William Godwin, Preface to 1832 edition of his novel *Fleetwood,* given as appendix to Oxford edition of *Caleb Williams,* London 1970.
10. Thomas Ogle, letter to Ralph Griffiths, 1792, quoted by Peter Faulkner in introduction to Oxford edition of *Anna St Ives,* London 1970.
11. Introduction to *Edgar Huntly,* Bentley's Standard Novels, London 1842.
12. In the *Journal* reading list for 1815 Mary simply enters the title, *Ormond*; F. L. Jones, editor of the *Journal,* supplies the conjectural author as "Maria Edgeworth", but this is obviously a mistake, since her novel of that name was not published until 1817.

Chapter Five

SHELLEY AND FRANKENSTEIN

1. Shelley, letter to Lackington Allen and Company (the eventual publishers of *Frankenstein,* after Ollier had turned it down) 22 August, 1817.
2. Shelley, letter to Mary, 20 August, 1818.
3. T. J. Hogg, *Life of Shelley,* London 1858.
4. Shelley, letter to W. Godwin, 10 January, 1812.
5. Mary Shelley, *Journal,* 1 August, 1816.
6. Shelley, letter to Charles Ollier, 11 June, 1821.
7. E. J. Trelawny, *Recollections of the Last Days of Shelley and Byron,* London 1858.
8. Mary Shelley, *Journal,* 11 November, 1822.
9. Mary Shelley, *Journal,* 31 December, 1822.

10. Mary Shelley, Preface to edition of Shelley's *Essays and Letters*, 1849.
11. Shelley, letter to T. L. Peacock, 20 June, 1819.
12. R. Glynn Grylls, op. cit.

Chapter Six

ARIEL AND CALIBAN

1. Jean Overton Fuller, *Shelley*, London 1968.
2. Mary Shelley, letter to Maria Gisborne, 2 June, 1822.
3. Shelley, letter to Trelawny, 16 May, 1822.
4. Shelley, letter to Horace Smith, May 1822.
5. E. J. Trelawny, op. cit.
6. Shelley, letter to T. J. Hogg, 8 May, 1811.
7. Mary Shelley, Preface to Shelley's *Essays and Letters*.
8. Shelley, *Essay on Love*, 1814–15.
9. Shelley, letter to W. Godwin, 10 January, 1812.
10. Shelley, letter to Mary, 16 August, 1821.
11. Shelley, letter to Claire Clairmont, 11 December, 1821.
12. Shelley, letter to Leigh Hunt, 19 June, 1822.
13. Shelley, letter to T. J. Hogg, August 1815.
14. Shelley's feelings about snakes were on the whole more of affection than revulsion; according to Trelawny he seems to have been content to be likened to a snake himself. Byron's nickname for Shelley in Italy was "the Snake", supposedly referring to Goethe's *Faust*, and Mephistopheles' remark about "my aunt, the learned snake". Trelawny says: "his bright eyes, slim figure, and noiseless movements strengthened, if it did not suggest the comparison". It seems probable, however, that Shelley himself explicitly suggested the source of "a snake walking on its tail". In his *Essay on the Devil and Devils* (1820) he speaks of the Greek regard for the serpent "as an auspicious and favourable being", and jocularly refers to the curse in Genesis that it should go upon its belly. "We are given to suppose that, before this misconduct, it hopped along upon its tail, a mode of progression which, if I was a serpent, I should think the severer punishment of the two. The Christians have turned this Serpent into their Devil and accommodated the whole story to their new scheme of sin and propitiation." The origin of this fancy for Shelley was no doubt the Serpent in *Paradise Lost* who "Addressed his way,

not with indented wave,/Prone on the ground, as since, but on his reare."

15. Shelley, letter to T. L. Peacock, 17 July, 1816.
16. Shelley, *Una Favola*, translated by Richard Garnett.
17. Shelley, letter to T. J. Hogg, 16 March, 1814.
18. T. L. Peacock, *Memories of Percy Bysshe Shelley*.
19. *With a Guitar* (to Jane Williams), 1822.
20. Lloyd N. Jeffrey, "The Birds Within the Wind, a study in Shelley's use of Natural History", *Keats-Shelley Journal* XVIII, 1969.
21. Shelley, letter to Elizabeth Hitchener, 20 January, 1812.
22. Shelley, letter to Fanny Imlay, 10 December, 1812. In *A Vindication of Natural Diet* Shelley claimed that by nature "man resembles frugivorous animals in everything and carnivorous in nothing : he has neither claws wherewith to seize his prey, nor distinct and pointed teeth to tear the living fibre."
23. The Moon, in *Epipsychidion* and elsewhere, is identified with Mary.
24. J. O. Fuller, op. cit.

Chapter Seven
THE PURSUING SHADOW

1. Shelley, letter to E. J. Trelawny, 18 June, 1822.
2. Shelley, letter to John Gisborne, 18 June, 1822.
3. Mary Shelley, *Journal*, 25 February, 1822.
4. *Political Justice*.
5. Mary Shelley, letter to Maria Gisborne, 15 August, 1822.

Chapter Eight
INNOCENCE AND GUILT

1. Mary Shelley, letter to Mrs. R. B. Hoppner, 10 August, 1821.
2. Shelley, letter to Elizabeth Hitchener, 26 November, 1811.
3. Shelley, letter to T. J. Hogg, 3 December, 1812.
4. Shelley, letter to Mary, 7 August, 1821.
5. Shelley, letter to Leigh Hunt, 8 December, 1816.
6. Shelley, letter to Mary, 15 December, 1816.
7. Shelley, letter to T. L. Peacock, 20 April, 1818.
8. Shelley, letter to Robert Southey, 17 August, 1820.

9. Mary Shelley, *Journal*, 12 February, 1839.

10. Mary Wollstonecraft Shelley : *Mathilda*, edited by Elizabeth Nitchie, *Studies in Philology* Extra Series, No. 3, 1959.

11. Godwin, when he read *Mathilda* in 1820, was against its publication, describing the subject as "disgusting and detestable", and saying that a preface would be necessary to prevent readers "from being tormented by the apprehension . . . of the fall of the heroine". (From the *Journals and Letters* of Maria Gisborne and Edward E. Williams, ed. F. L. Jones.) Godwin was anxious only to safeguard his own reputation.

12. The name of the heroine is supposed to be derived from the Matilda in Dante's *Purgatorio*; it may also have been suggested, along with some of the apparatus of the novel, by the grandfather of the Gothic genre, Horace Walpole's *Castle of Otranto;* one of the heroines of which, Matilda, is in a disguised incestuous relationship with her father, Manfred, who finally kills her "by accident".

13. Mary Shelley, letter to Maria Gisborne, 6 May, 1823.

14. ". . . so my hate/ Became the only worship I could lift/ To our great Father . . ." (*The Cenci*).

15. Editorial comment by E. Nitchie, op. cit.

16. Goethe : *Selected Verse*, with English prose translations by David Luke, Penguin Books, London 1964.

17. T. L. Peacock, *Memories of Percy Bysshe Shelley*.

Chapter Nine

PROPHECY AND PROJECTION

1. Shelley, letter to Hogg, 3 October, 1814. (From *New Shelley Letters*, ed. W. S. Scott, London 1948.)

2. Shelley, letter to Mary, 28 October, 1814.

3. Mrs Julian Marshall, *The Life and Letters of Mary Wollstonecraft Shelley*, London 1889.

4. *Valperga*, by the Author of *Frankenstein*, London 1823.

5. *The Last Man, a Romance of the Twentieth Century*, by the Author of *Frankenstein*, London 1826.

6. Shelley, letter to T. L. Peacock, 8 June, 1819.

7. S. T. Coleridge, *Anima Poetae* (1803), ed. E. H. Coleridge, London 1895. Compare the withered flowers brought back from the future by the Time Traveller in H. G. Wells's *Time*

Machine; here as in other ways a mechanised account of the journeys of the imagination.

8. Shelley, letter to Mary, 8 October, 1817.
9. Shelley, letter to T. L. Peacock, 8 June, 1819.
10. E. J. Trelawny, op. cit.
11. S. T. Coleridge, review of *The Mysteries of Udolpho*, 1794 : from *Miscellaneous Criticism,* ed. T. M. Raysor, London 1936.
12. S. T. Coleridge, review of *The Monk*, op. cit.

Chapter Ten
PROMETHEUS UNBOUND

1. The phrase, "a passion for reforming the world", which Shelley took to himself, has been identified as a chapter-heading in *Principles of Moral Science* by the Scottish radical writer Robert Forsyth (1805).
2. Shelley, letter to John Gisborne, 22 October, 1821.
3. In Shelley's *Essay on the Devil and Devils,* he makes the speculation that the Devil "occupies the centre and God the circumference of existence, and that one urges inward with the centripetal, while the other is perpetually struggling outwards from the narrow focus with the centrifugal force . . ." It is left as no more than a question, but it casts an interesting light on the "theology" of *Prometheus Unbound*.
4. T. J. Hogg, op. cit.
5. Simone Weil, *Intimations of Christianity among the Ancient Greeks,* ed. and trans. E. C. Geissbuhler, London 1957.
6. S. Weil, *Gravity and Grace*, extracts from her Notebooks, ed. Gustave Thibon, trans. Emma Crauford, London 1952.
7. Ibid.
8. Shelley, letter to Leigh Hunt, 23 December, 1819.
9. S. Weil, *Gravity and Grace*.

Chapter Eleven
SCIENCE AND POETRY

1. Carl Garbo, *Prometheus Unbound, An Interpretation,* North Carolina, 1935.
2. A. N. Whitehead, *Science and the Modern World,* New York, 1925.
3. Shelley, *A Defence of Poetry*.

4. T. L. Peacock, *Works*. Vol. 8.

5. David S. Landes, *The Unbound Prometheus,* London and New York, 1969.

6. Karl Marx, "Dissertation and Preliminary Notes on the Difference between Democritus' and Epicurus' Philosophy of Nature" (1839-1841); from *Karl Marx: Early Texts,* ed. David McLellan, Oxford, 1971.

7. Shelley, *A Refutation of Deism,* 1812-13.

8. Shelley, *Defence of Poetry.*

9. Shelley, letter to Mary, 22 September, 1818. This letter, it is interesting to see, was written during the illness of the infant Clara and makes passing reference to it. She died two days later.

10. Francis Bacon, *New Atlantis.*

11. C. Grabo, op. cit.

12. The machine will stop if one can remember the word of command : *The Sorcerer's Apprentice* is another poem of Goethe's one would much like to know if Shelley had read.

13. Shelley, letter to T. J. Hogg, 6 January, 1811.

14. S. T. Coleridge, *The Rime of the Ancient Mariner,* gloss to Part III.

15. Shelley, letter to John and Maria Gisborne, summer 1820.

16. Mary Shelley, *Journal,* 4 August, 1821.

17. Shelley, *Letter to Maria Gisborne,* 1 July, 1820.

18. Goethe, *Venetian Epigrams,* trans. David Luke : "I would compare this gondola to the cradle that gently rocks one to sleep; and the box on top of it is like a spacious coffin."

19. Shelley, letter to T. L. Peacock, 8 October, 1818.

20. Shelley, letter to Claire Clairmont, 18 February, 1821.

21. Henry Reveley, letter to Shelley, 13 November, 1819.

22. Shelley, letter to Henry Reveley, 17 November, 1819.

23. Shelley, *Essay on the Devil and Devils.*

24. Compare the phrase "the man almighty" in Southey's *Curse of Kehama,* which shocked contemporaries simply by being an unexpected echo of pious usage.

Chapter Twelve

THE REDEEMING IMAGINATION

1. The difficulty of deciding between "inner" and "outer" causes of regeneration shows in the description, in Act IV of

Prometheus Unbound, of man renewed and healed by being left "even as a leprous child is left,/ Who follows a sick beast to some warm cleft/ Of rocks, through which the might of healing springs is poured" : which seems to make the cause of moral restoration the sort of exterior physical magic that is found in science fiction.

2. Shelley, letter to John and Maria Gisborne, 19 July, 1821.
3. Shelley, letter to T. L. Peacock, 16 May, 1820.
4. Shelley, letter to John Gisborne, 10 April, 1822.
5. *Evening, Ponte a Mare, Pisa* (1821). Compare the *Ode to Liberty* (1820) : "Within the surface of Time's fleeting river/ Its wrinkled image lies, as then it lay/ Immovably unquiet, and for ever/ It trembles, but it cannot pass away !"
6. Shelley, letter to T. L. Peacock, 20 April, 1819.
7. A remarkable anticipation of Yeats's *Second Coming,* which seems likely in fact to contain a memory of *Prometheus Unbound,* but with very different implications : "Things fall apart; the centre cannot hold . . ./ The best lack all conviction, while the worst/ Are full of passionate intensity."
8. Aeschylus, *Eumenides,* trans. J. S. Blackie.

Chapter Thirteen
ROBOTS AND RESURRECTION

1. "Olaf Johannsen" (pseudonym), *The Great Computer,* 1967. The author is a distinguished physicist and Nobel Prize winner.
2. *Mind at the End of its Tether* is the title of H. G. Wells's last work, published in 1945, deeply pessimistic in outlook.
3. In a letter to the *Saturday Review* following public discussion of *R.U.R.* in June, 1923, Capek supplied his own gloss on the name of Rossum, saying that "his name in English signified Mr Intellect or Mr Brain".
4. The engraving, after a drawing by T. Holst, appears above the following lines from the beginning of Chapter V of *Frankenstein:* ". . . by the glimmer of the half-extinguished light, I saw the dull yellow eye of the creature open; it breathed hard, and a convulsive motion agitated its limbs . . . I rushed out of the room."
5. There is a very curious reflection, or echo of the *Frankenstein* frontispiece in the late nineteenth century *Resurrection* of the

341

ARIEL LIKE A HARPY

German Romantic painter Hans Thoma (1839-1924), in which the risen Christ is seen ascending from an entombed skeleton.

Chapter Fourteen

THE DEEP TRUTH : CONCLUSION

1. Shelley, note from *Queen Mab.*
2. Ann Jellicoe, "Shelley", article in *New Society,* 20 August, 1970.
3. Ibid.
4. The irresponsible spirit of Ariel, delighting in trickery, appears vividly in one of the inventions of Charles Brockden Brown, *Carwin the Biloquist,* an unfinished sequel to *Wieland* published in Brown's *New Literary Magazine,* 1803. Even in the novel, in which his ventriloquial tricks precipitate the catastrophe, Carwin is not wicked or malicious, but merely mischievous; in the sequel, in which he describes his earlier life, he is above all an artist. His motives are neither good nor bad : "I was incapable of knowingly contributing to another's misery, but the sole or principal end of my endeavours was not the happiness of others." What drives him on is simply the wish to use his talent, the "superior powers" represented by ventriloquy, or the gift of tongues : "I was prone to manifest that superiority, and was satisfied if this were done, without much solicitude concerning consequence." In conversation with his acquaintance the discussion turns upon "invisible beings" and thus, "by no violent transition", to Shakespeare's Ariel; whereupon, on the impulse of the moment, Carwin projects his voice, which can move "an heart of stone", to become Ariel, invisibly singing "Full fathom five". Carwin's art consists of such deceptions and tricks, but it is also his integrity, the one thing he will not give up. Later in the story he comes under the domination of an ambiguous and Luciferian philanthropist, Ludloe—a member of the Illuminati who, like God, "seek not the misery or death of any one", but who nevertheless employ murder and deception to further their ends. Ludloe sets Carwin, as his disciple, to write a *curriculum vitae,* which he gives with complete candour except for one thing : his "bivocal" adventures he cannot bring himself to reveal. At this point the

story breaks off, and the fascinating question whether the artist's skills in deception will be placed at the disposal of political manipulation is never answered. There is no record of Shelley having read the story, but as an enthusiast for the works of Brown, he very well may have done, and it adds a possible further source of his conception of himself as Ariel.

5. C. G. Jung, *Answer to Job:* "For, just as completeness is always imperfect, so perfection is always incomplete, and therefore represents a final state which is hopelessly sterile."
6. A. N. Whitehead, op. cit.
7. Mary Shelley, letter to Maria Gisborne.
8. Shelley, letter to Leigh Hunt, 26 August, 1821.

BIBLIOGRAPHY

The main works quoted or referred to are listed below. It has not been thought necessary to give references in the Notes to the most well-known and readily available works; letters and entries in journals are however identified.

Bacon, Francis : *Essays* and *Advancement of Learning* (Library of English Classics), London 1900.

Brown, Charles Brockden : *Wieland, or The Transformation,* and *Carwin the Biloquist,* ed. F. L. Pattee (Hafner Library of Classics), New York 1958; *Ormond, or The Secret Witness,* ed. E. Marchand (Hafner Library of Classics), New York 1962; *Edgar Huntly, or The Sleep Walker* (Bentley's Standard Novels), London 1842.

Butler, Samuel : *Erewhon, or Over the Range,* ed. P. Mudford (Penguin), London 1970.

Byron : *Poems and Letters,* from *Works,* ed. R. E. Paterson, London 1900.

Capek, Karel : *R.U.R.,* trans. P. Selver, London 1923.

Coleridge, S. T. : *Poetical Works,* ed. E. H. Coleridge, 1877 (Oxford Standard Authors edition, 1967); *Biographia Literaria,* 1817; *Anima Poetae,* ed. E. H. Coleridge, London 1895; *Miscellaneous Criticism,* ed. T. M. Raysor, London 1936.

Dowden, Edward : *Life of Shelley,* London 1886.

Fuller, Jean Overton : *Shelley,* London 1968.

Gisborne, Maria and Edward E. Williams : *Journals and Letters,* ed. F. L. Jones, Oklahoma 1951.

Grabo, Carl : *Prometheus Unbound, an Interpretation,* North Carolina 1935.

Grylls, R. Glynn : *Mary Shelley, a Biography,* London 1938.

Godwin, William : *Enquiry concerning Political Justice and its Influence on Morals and Happiness,* facsimile of third edition, 1798, ed. F. E. L. Priestley, Toronto 1946; *Caleb Williams,* 1794, ed. D. McCracken (Oxford English Novels) London 1970; *St Leon,* 1799; *Mandeville,* 1817.

344

Hogg, Thomas Jefferson : *The Life of Percy Bysshe Shelley,* London 1858. (London Library edition, ed. E. Dowden, 1906.)

Landes, David S. : *The Unbound Prometheus,* London and New York 1969.

Marx, Karl : *Early Texts,* trans. and ed. David McLellan, Oxford 1971.

Marshall, Mrs Julian : *The Life and Letters of Mary Wollstonecraft Shelley,* London 1889.

Milton, John : *Poetical Works,* ed. Helen Darbishire, London 1952 and 1955.

Peacock, Thomas Love : *Works,* ed. Henry Cole, London 1875.

Shaftesbury (Edward Ashley Cooper, 3rd Earl) : *Characteristicks,* ed. J. M. Robertson, London 1900.

Shelley, Mary Wollstonecraft : *Frankenstein,* ed. M. K. Joseph (Oxford English Novels, London 1969); *Valperga,* by the Author of *Frankenstein,* London 1823; *The Last Man, a Romance of the Twentieth Century* by the Author of *Frankenstein,* London 1826; *Mathilda,* ed. E. Nitchie, Chapel Hill, North Carolina 1959; *Journal,* ed. F. L. Jones, Oklahoma 1947; *Letters,* ed. F. L. Jones, Oklahoma 1944.

Shelley, Percy Bysshe : *Poems,* ed. E. Dowden, London 1891; *The Esdaile Notebook,* a book of early poems, ed. N. K. Cameron, London 1964; *Prose Works,* ed. H. B. Forman, London 1880; *Shelley's Prose or The Trumpet of a Prophecy,* ed. D. L. Clark, New Mexico 1954; *Letters,* ed. R. Ingpen, London 1909; *New Shelley Letters,* ed. W. S. Scott, London 1948.

Spark, Muriel : *Child of Light, a reassessment of Mary Wollstonecraft Shelley,* London 1951.

Trelawny, Edward John : *Recollections of the Last Days of Shelley and Byron,* London 1858.

Weil, Simone : *Gravity and Grace,* ed. G. Thibon, trans. Emma Crauford, London 1952; *Intimations of Christianity among the Ancient Greeks,* trans. E. C. Geissbuhler, London 1957.

Whitehead, A. N. : *Science and the Modern World,* New York 1925.

INDEX